# The Enemies of Progress

## The Dangers of Sustainability

Austin Williams

**SOCIETAS**

essays in political
& cultural criticism

**imprint-academic.com**

Published in the UK by Societas
Imprint Academic, PO Box 200, Exeter EX5 5YX, UK

Published in the USA by Societas
Imprint Academic, Philosophy Documentation Center
PO Box 7147, Charlottesville, VA 22906-7147, USA

ISBN 9781845400989

A CIP catalogue record for this book is available from the
British Library and US Library of Congress

For Martha

for whom the future should be a world of possibilities.

Thanks to Claire in particular, who has been a continual source of ideas, support, criticism and inspiration.

I am indebted to the Future Cities Project members and supporters including Martin Earnshaw, Alastair Donald, Karl Sharro, Dave Clements, Jane Sanderman, Pete Smith, Niall Crowley, Elisabetta Gasparoni-Abraham and Martyn Perks. Also, Shirley Lawes, Dennis Hayes, Daniel Ben-Ami, Jim Butcher, Alex Standish, Alan Farlie, Richard J Williams and Debby Kuypers. Also thanks to the team at spiked.

I owe a real debt of gratitude too to other friends, colleagues and associates for their challenging and illuminating political ideas over the years.

# *Contents*

# INTRODUCTION

In 1933, Chicago celebrated its centenary with an International Exposition entitled 'A Century of Progress'. It was held to commend the 'progress of civilisation'[1] that had turned a town of 350 people on the banks of Lake Michigan into one of the leading industrial power-houses of the world. As an expression of the city's futuristic ambitions, at the opening ceremony on 2 May 1933 rays of light from the third brightest star, Arcturus were converted into electricity in order to power the Exposition's illuminations (the organisers calculating that the light from Arcturus would have begun its journey at the time of Chicago's previous World's Fair in 1893).

The 1933 Exposition's inaugural statement explained that it would 'attempt to demonstrate to an international audience the nature and significance of scientific discoveries, the methods of achieving them, and the changes which their application has wrought in industry and in living conditions.'[2] Even in the depths of the Great Depression, forty million people visited (six times the number that visited the UK's Millennium Dome in 2000) with one visitor reporting 'how much fun it is just to be alive today.'[3] Aspects of the 1933 Exposition were undoubtedly guided by a politically motivated drive for social unity, but regardless of the political contrivances, primarily it proclaimed the future as a good, positive place to be. A few months earlier, Roosevelt had announced: 'when

[1]   University of Illinois at Chicago, 'A Century of Progress: An inventory of the collection at the University of Illinois at Chicago', A Century of Progress Records, 1927-1952.

[2]   'A Century of Progress. Chicago International Exposition of 1933 Statement of its Plan and Purposes and of the Relation of States and Foreign Governments to Them', Chicago, 1933. Program(me)

[3]   Quoted in, 'A dizzy young woman reviews the Hall of Science, Official World's Fair Weekly, 17 June 1933

there is no vision, the people perish'.[4] Even at a time of great political uncertainty, such was the confident vision of progress that 'bold, persistent experimentation'[5] was proposed alongside a New Deal.

That was then. Whereas once we looked to the future with anticipation, today we can only tremble with trepidation. The future, today, is regularly viewed with foreboding; experimentation is frequently discouraged as unnecessarily risky, and progress itself is presented as a fallacy.[6] Man has gone from being a solution, to becoming seen as the problem. By definition this has completely undermined the concept of human progress. In recent years, 'progress' has been reduced, at best, to a relativistic 'paradigm';[7] at worst, it is seen as a contradiction in terms, where social problems are deemed to be 'resistant to knowledge and its answers'.[8]

And so it came to pass that ever since the 1992 UN Conference on Environment and Development (the Rio Summit) promoted '"sustainable development" as a new name for progress'[9] it has became acceptable to regularly use the prefix 'so-called' when describing social advancement, development and progress. In effect, the very benefits of progress have been called into question. This book seeks to redress the balance.

I argue that sustainability is an insidiously dangerous concept at odds with progress and I hope to present a critical exploration of its all-pervasive influence on society. My proposition is that sustainability, manifested in several guises, represents a pernicious and corrosive doctrine that has survived primarily because there seems to be no alternative to its canon: in effect, its bi-partisan appeal has depressed critical engagement and neutered politics.

Unfortunately, sustainable development, masquerading as progress, is everywhere accepted. Taking just one example, the Royal Commission on Environment and Pollution in London want to

[4]   Franklin D. Roosevelt, The First Inaugural Address', 4 March 1933, Franklin and Eleanor Roosevelt Institute, www.feri.org
[5]   Franklin D. Roosevelt, 'Commencement Address', 23 May 1932, Oglethorpe University, Atlanta, quoted in William E. Leuchtenburg, 'Franklin D Roosevelt And The New Deal', Harper Perennial, 1963, p5
[6]   Tom Wessels, 'The Myth of Progress: Toward a Sustainable Future', Vermont, 2006, pxix
[7]   Dr. Indur M. Goklany, book review: 'The myth of progress: toward a sustainable future', Electronic Journal of Sustainable Development, 24 July 2007
[8]   George Myerson, Yvonne Rydin The Language of Environment: A New Rhetoric', Routledge, 1996, p211
[9]   Wolfgang Sachs et al, 'The Jo'Burg Memo: Fairness in a Fragile World — Memorandum for the World Summit on Sustainable Development', Heinrich Böll Foundation, 2002

make it incumbent on local authorities that they have a central 'duty to protect and enhance the environment'[10] identifying four priority themes: 'sustainable urban transport; sustainable urban management… ; sustainable urban construction… ; and sustainable urban design'.[11] This book will argue that sustainable development is the enemy of development; that environmentalism is the enemy of humanism; ergo sustainability is the enemy of progress.

***

In his final book, *On God: An Uncommon Conversation*, Norman Mailer reveals his troubled relationship with progress and a despondency with development. He writes:

> If, for example, the flush toilet is an improvement in existence, if the automobile is an improvement, if technological progress is an improvement, then look hard at the price that was paid. It's not too hard to argue that the gulags, the concentration camps, the atom bomb came out of technological improvement. For the average person in the average developed country, life, if seen in terms of comfort, is better than it was in the middle of the 19th century, but by the measure of our human development as ethical, spiritual, responsible and creative human beings, it may be worse.[12]

Linking modernism and barbarism sounds, initially, reminiscent of the post-war Frankfurt School writers like Theodor Adorno and Max Horkheimer. They too said that 'the fallen nature of man cannot be separated from social progress.'[13] However, their circumstances were very different to today. Adorno et al were coming to terms with the savagery of the Second World War and the concentration camps, and, as such, might be excused a certain emotional attachment that may have clouded their critical judgement. But Mailer's only excuse — aside from his own imminent mortality — for such a pathetic extrapolation between Thomas Crapper's flushing mechanism and Auschwitz; between Henry Ford and Hiroshima, is the inescapable anti-progressive zeitgeist of sustainability. Nowadays,

[10]  Professor Michael Herbert, 'Looking beyond environmental signposting', Town & Country Planning Journal, May 2007, p154

[11]  Royal Commission on Environmental Pollution, 'Twenty sixth report: The Urban Environment', RCEP, 6 March 2007

[12]  Norman Mailer in Norman Mailer and Michael Lennon, 'On God: An Uncommon Conversation', Continuum, 2008. The Estate of Norman Mailer

[13]  Theodor Adorno and Max Horkheimer, (1997), 'Dialectic of Enlightenment', (J. Cumming, Trans.), Verso (original work published 1944) quoted in Robert M. Burns, 'Philosophies of History: From Enlightenment to Post-Modernity', Blackwell Publishing, 2000, p251

everything — even the desire for better personal hygiene, it seems — is seen as potentially harmful rather than patently beneficial. It echoes the precautionary approach of sustainability, which says that where man's interference in nature is concerned, things are likely to turn out to have negative consequences.

Such is the misanthropic undercurrent in mainstream sustainability that even some radical environmentalists balk at the relentless calls for restraint. In their book *Break Through*, in which they simply attempt to rebrand miserablism in a more positive light, Ted Nordhaus and Michael Shellenberger are moved to claim that 'few things today are more offensive to liberal and environmental leaders than the notion of humans creating new realities, political or otherwise. But a certain hubris is always required of people, be they environmentalists or neoconservatives, who wish to change the world.'[14] But actually in the eyes of mainstream sustainability advocates, hubris is the problem; they think that economic and social development needs to learn a bit of humility. We need, so the tired old story goes, to take care of the environment lest the other pillars of sustainability — the economic and social — fall around our ears.

This sort of melodramatic tragedy is exemplified by Thomas Homer-Dixon's book *The Upside of Down*, in which he suggests that modern societies crumble when they over-extend themselves. For those in politics and policy, cautious sustainability is the last hope for a social glue to hold fragmenting, collapsing societies together. Today, with no hot or cold war to guide governmental actions, states are happy to fall back on the tried and tested unifying rhetoric of nations under attack and the war economy, albeit with a green spin.

So it is now common to hear phrases like 'environmental genocide',[15] or condemnations of global warming 'denial' and perverse demands for rationing. Others allege that even the forests are becoming 'victims of war'.[16] Always one to exaggerate, UK government minister David Miliband claims that an inability to get to grips with environmental matters 'could cause more human and financial suffering than the two world wars and the great depression put

[14] Ted Nordhaus and Michael Shellenberger, 'Break Through: From the Death of Environmentalism to the Politics of Possibility', Houghton Mifflin Company, 2007, p242

[15] Rik J. Deitsch and Stewart Lonky, 'Invisible Killers: The Truth About Environmental Genocide', Sound Concepts, 2007

[16] Derrick Jensen, George Draffan, 'Strangely Like War: The Global Assault on Forests', Chelsea Green Publishing, 2006, pix

together.'[17] Author Jared Diamond is cavalier with the phrase 'environmental holocaust' musing about bird species that 'humans (have) driven into extinction.'[18] Friends of the Earth are against the war in Iraq, primarily, it seems, because it creates 'vicious cycles of unsustainability.'[19] The idiom remains clear: war economics makes us tighten our belts and become more pliant for the common good. The serious tenor of such a moral high-ground is enough to silence debate.

Regardless of the linguistic hyperbole, the mere fact that governments and non-governmental agencies alike are trying to unify society through a common experience of wartime suffering and vulnerability, is not particularly healthy. Relying on fear to motivate people actually destroys the very thing — trust — that it is trying to create and engenders a 'fatalistic attitude towards the future.'[20] Rather than opening up society to the unfettered flow of ideas and human ingenuity, sustainability feeds the insular, cowed and aspiration-lite times in which we live. It nourishes only restraint. It encourages a world made up of individuals connected only by their common lack of trust and fear of the future.

To some, the war economy motif is simply a way of getting us to accept austerity ... for the common good, of course. Andrew Simms of the New Economics Foundation has actually written a pamphlet entitled 'An Environmental War Economy' in which he suggests that 'faced with a crisis in which individuals are to subordinate personal goals to a common good, they can, and do, respond'.[21] Demographics expert and proponent of a one-child policy for Africa, Dr Maurice King spells out the sort of sacrifices that Simms is referring to:

> for those in the industrial North, with its unsustainable economy, a sustainable lifestyle means consumption control — intensive energy conservation, fewer unnecessary journeys, more public transport — fewer, smaller, slower cars, warmer clothes,

[17] David Miliband, 'Oral statement by David Miliband on climate change', Defra, 30 October 2006, www.defra.gov.uk

[18] Jared Diamond, 'The Rise and Fall of the Third Chimpanzee', Radius, 1991, p313-314

[19] Friends of the Earth Media Briefing, 'War In Iraq: Why Friends Of The Earth Is Opposed', Friends of the Earth, England, Wales and Northern Ireland, 13 February 2003

[20] Frank Furedi, 'Invitation to Terror: The Expanding Empire of the Unknown', Continuum UK, p108

[21] Andrew Simms, 'An Environmental War Economy: The lessons of ecological debt and global warming', New Economics Foundation, 2001, p32

and colder rooms. It also means much more recycling and a more environmentally friendly diet with more joules to the hectare. The deliberate quest of poverty (for the privileged North the reduction of luxurious resource consumption) has an honoured history.[22]

To campaigners like Senior Fellow Emeritus at the Policy Studies Institute, Mayer Hillman, sustainability is more than a military campaign; it's a permanent state of siege:

> We should think back to the late summer of 1939. Against the reneging of the promises made by Hitler in Munich, 18 months previously and the possible need to go to war with fascist Germany, no one proposed a referendum … Neville Chamberlain, the Prime Minister of the time, did not simply invite the population to eat less owing to the inevitable curtailment of food imports, he imposed food rationing; nor did he issue a call to arms, he imposed military conscription. So it is today. The time for debate is past. We need to confront the emergency.[23]

Hillman forgets that rationing was proposed with a view to it being lifted in the near future—in a post-war world where there would be more goods available. As an aside, the Second World War was also seen to be a fight for freedom, not a fight for personal restrictions. In fact that was what many thought they were fighting against!

The rhetorical link between the traditional concept of war, and a war against un-sustainability, which is intended to provide a moral framework of right and wrong, means that pro-sustainability is now the default condition. Mention of sustainability brooks no challenge. Critics are berated. Even longstanding and sympathetic environmental commentators like journalist Roger Harrabin, founder presenter of Radio 4's environment series Costing the Earth, can be branded a 'climate-sceptic traitor'[24] for asking Al Gore an awkward question.

US political commentator Alex Gourevitch suggests that contemporary environmental ideology is built on a false premise: 'a collective threat that makes security the basic principle of politics and makes the struggle for survival the basic and central aim of our social and political life.' He reasons correctly that, in fact, this 'is not a pro-

[22] Maurice King, 'Health is a sustainable state,' Lancet 1990, 336, pp665-667.
[23] Mayer Hillman, 'Your Planet: The Case For Rationing', The Independent, 19 September 2005
[24] Roger Harrabin, 'The heat and light in global warming', BBC NewsOnline, 11 October 2007

gressive politics at all.'[25] But sustainable development, masquerading as progress, is everywhere. In practically every conversation it is the underlying code. Nowhere is the word 'development' printed without its adjectival corrective. But there is very little to recommend it. In its broad embrace it accepts the rubric of global warming, climate chaos, localism, personal blame, collective guilt, behavioural change, reduced consumption, minimal impact, ethical intervention, intrusiveness, public conformity and much more besides. There is nothing progressive in that list. The starting point of this book, then, is to begin to recognise that progress is under sustained attack by the environmentalist and sustainability lobby.

***

When I told colleagues that I was writing a book about sustainability, they all assumed that it would deal primarily with the issue of climate change. As it happens, this book has nothing to do with it. But just to get it out of the way, a few brief thoughts about global warming.

UN Secretary-General Ban Ki-moon has said that how we deal with global warming 'will define us, our era, and ultimately, our global legacy.'[26] Former chief executive of the UK's Meteorological Office, professor John Houghton adds fuel to the fire by describing global warming as 'a weapon of mass destruction.'[27] New Zealand's Marsden Medal winner, Professor Peter Barrett, says that 'if we continue (on) our present growth path, we are facing extinction ... by the end of this century'[28]. Everyone, it seems, wants to outdo each other on the bleak assessment of climate change. Professor Barrett may have toned down his rhetoric suggesting that global warming will only lead to 'the end of civilisation as we know it'[29] rather than his original claim that it will lead to human extinction, but even those attempting to be more moderate and normative can't help but be alarmist and accusatory.

[25] Sewell Chan, 'Climate Change and the 'Politics of Fear', New York Times, City Room, 31 October 2007, 12:32 pm

[26] Secretary-General Ban Ki-moon, 'UN Debates Urgent Action to Avert Global Warming', New York, 31 July 2007

[27] Professor John Houghton quoted in 'Global warming is now a weapon of mass destruction', The Guardian, 28 July 2003

[28] Professor Barrett quoted in Matt Nippert, 'Hitting Home', New Zealand Listener, 4 October 2004

[29] Professor Barrett quoted in Simon Collins, 'Global warming won't cause extinction, just civilisation's end', New Zealand Herald, 18 November 2004

The mayor of New York, Michael R Bloomberg, typifies the 'common sense' rhetoric around climate change. He points out that 'the weather seems to be getting hotter more unpredictable, and summers seem to be getting hotter... it's a reality. It's called global warming'.[30] Global warming is 'a crime for which we are all guilty, from our cars, our homes and our workplaces,' says actor Kiefer Sutherland, promoting a series of public education videos.[31] Orlando Bloom, star of 'Pirates of the Caribbean' visited Antarctica and 'saw how tragically fragile the ice caps are'[32] as 'evidence' of climate change. Everything from the Norwegian moose whose flatulence gives off 2,000 kg of carbon dioxide a year[33] to the by-products of a non-vegetarian diet[34] have been cited as direct evidence of global warming and as its causation. Such cod scientific rhetoric can be found everywhere these days. Even when it comes to scientists — people who should know better like meteorologists, climatologists, geologists, etc — all are prone to the sustainability zeitgeist. Physicist Stephen Hawking, who has been out of the headlines since receiving severe heatstroke and sunburn outside his house in 2004[35] and therefore thinks he knows a thing or two about global warming, says that 'the worst-case scenario is that Earth would become like its sister planet, Venus, with a temperature of 250 [degrees] centigrade, and raining sulfuric acid.'[36] Thanks, Stephen, that's very useful.

This book doesn't explore climate change *per se*. This is because it is considerably low down on my list of things-to-worry-about. Instead, this book seeks to deal with the poverty of ambition in political life. It looks at the issue of climate change only in as much as it aims to confront the paralysing obsession with carbon emissions and the belief that human agency has inevitably harmful consequences. This book doesn't examine global warming, but explores the fetishisation of global warming, the very thing which paralyses

---

[30]  Michael R Bloomberg, Press Release, 'Mayor Bloomberg Delivers Sustainability Challenges And Goals For New York City Through 2030', 12 December 2006

[31]  Stephen Foley, 'Jack Bauer, the hero of '24', takes on global warming', The Independent, 6 August 2007

[32]  'Polar meltdown not so cool', TheLondonPaper, 29 May 2007.

[33]  'Norway's Moose Population in Trouble for Belching, ' SpeigelOnline International, 21 August 2007

[34]  Patrice Green, 'Save the Planet with a Vegetarian Diet,' The Baltimore Sun, 19 July 2007

[35]  Stephen Hawking Denies Reports That He Is a Victim of Abuse', New York Times, 24 January 2004

[36]  Stephen Hawking, quoted in 'The 11th Hour', Nadia Conners, Leila Conners Petersen and Leonardo DiCaprio, Warner Bros, 2007

societies into an inability to provide solutions ... to anything. The never-ending stream of fear-mongering rhetoric in the media and in public and political discourse might lead you to believe that climate change and global warming are, indeed, the most important issue in the world. Wrong. One of the most important tasks today, is to undermine the fear-generating perception that human agency, modernity, growth, materialism, want, development, experimentation, technology, infrastructure, political debate and critical engagement—in a word, progress, is a problem.

It is hardly surprising that this has become the dominant perception when many sustainability advocates are happy to admit that they don't think progress is worth defending, or worse, that it is inherently dangerous. Indeed, circular 'feedback loops' are preferred to the audacity of single-minded forward thinking. Author Jay Griffiths, says that the 'key feature of modern environmentalism is to prefer the cycles of sustainability to the arrows of so-called progress.'[37] These days, people would rather go round in circles than get to the point.

Philosopher A C Grayling is so exasperated by John Gray's assertion that 'progress is a myth' that he asks: 'Does he thus mean that the movement from feudal baronies to universal suffrage and independent judiciaries is not progress? If it is not, what is it? Regress?'[38]

Actually Gray, like most anti-progress advocates, isn't in favour of a return to the past or for giving up the gains of a liberal society, he is merely frozen—petrified—by what he envisions as the inevitably harmful consequences of human actions in the future. 'We are marching, heads down, toward global ecological collapse'[39] says environmental campaigner, John Feeney, and it is this fear of the future, rather than a delight in the past, that drives the demands for social, economic and technological restraint. The solution? Well John Gray would prefer that we comfort ourselves by being 'cheerful' in our extant condition;[40] while fellow London School of Economics' professor Lord Layard advocates that everyone be encouraged to be 'thankful for what they have'.[41] Both, in their own

[37]   Jay Griffiths, 'Time Bandits', The Guardian, 3 November 1999
[38]   AC Grayling, 'Through the looking glass', New Humanist, Volume 122, Issue 4, July/August 2007
[39]   John Feeney, 'Humanity is the greatest challenge', BBC News, 5 November 2007, http://news.bbc.co.uk
[40]   John Gray quoted in Laurie Taylor, 'Going nowhere: Laurie Taylor interviews John Gray,' New Humanist, Volume 121, Issue 1, January/February 2006
[41]   Richard Layard, 'Happiness: Lessons from a New Science', Penguin, 2006, p8

way, lay claim to the Enlightenment but actually bastardise the
concept by exemplifying a position that says that progress is futile.

*** 

Each chapter looks at a particular theme (transport, energy, education, etc) and links it to one negative aspect of the sustainability
agenda (such as localism, nihilism, pessimism, etc). These aspects of
the sustainability agenda are the Enemies of Progress of the title. I
hope that readers might begin to notice how each of these enemies of
progress also affects other themes: the low horizons prevalent in
architecture, say, can also be seen in the energy and transport
debates. The doctrinal approach to environmental education today,
for example, can also be seen in the Western attitudes to developing
nations, and so on.

In Chapter 1 we look at the relentless demands for less travel,
more parochialism and greater moral condemnation for those who
refuse to accept the constraints imposed by carbon emissions, where
'energy and $CO_2$ (are) a proxy for the wider issues of sustainability.'[42]
Such all-encompassing anti-transport strategies are clearest in the
UK where protests against roads and cars have metamorphosed into
criticisms against cheap flights and the demands for 'ethical travel'.
Admittedly, there are slightly awkward debates in developed countries like Australia and America, where, over the years, inter-city
flights have become a matter-of-fact public mode of transport in
order to deal with travel across those countries' vast distances, but
scornful indignation is heaped on China when they try it. Today, one
aeroplane is being built every month in India. Two years ago the
total Indian passenger fleet had 170 aircraft, today it is double that
and is scheduled to comprise 550 planes by 2010 and peak at 1100 in
2020. Meanwhile, on the ground, Tata, the massive steel and manu-
facturing company wants to democratise mobility in the same way
that Henry Ford did for Americans, over 100 years ago. However,
the projection that 1.2 billion people might soon develop a busy 21st
century transport infrastructure in order for them to raise their living standards even higher, fills sustainability advocates with profound horror. This chapter says that more travel, better transport
and increased mobility is what progress is all about.

In Chapter 2 we look at the state of energy and the retreat from the
belief in universal provision. Today, opting out is the new in, with
Paris-based Sustainable Energy Watch advocating decentralised

[42]  P F G Banfill, A D Peacock, (2007), 'Energy efficient new housing — the UK reaches
for sustainability', Building Research & Information, Volume 35, Issue 4

systems instead of 'large plants'; and 'access to local resources' as opposed to 'more grids and networks'.[43] Typically, sustainability advocates are less interested in human efficiency, than resource efficiency, with leading American environmentalist, William McDonough, in the introduction to the Chinese edition of his book *Cradle to Cradle* points out that 'in the United States it took merely a century to turn the rich, fertile soil of the Great Plains into the ravaged landscape of the Dust Bowl.'[44] He conveniently forgets to mention that today, with only 5 per cent of the number of people who were employed on American farms in 1930,[45] agricultural productivity has risen (since 1948) by 167 per cent.[46]

In Chapter 3 we look at the miserably low horizons of architectural ambition and reveal that the UK government's pledge to build three million homes, including one million 'eco-homes' by 2020 looks a little shallow when you realise that in the first 18 months it had built precisely two eco-houses, both of which have failed the government's own tests for eco-friendliness. Stanford University's Sustainability Working Group formed in 2006, is advisory to the President and Provost and says that 'The most sustainable building is the one that is never built.'

But such self-flagellating thoughts are not novel. Arguing that that we should free 'technology from the unthinking pursuit of efficiency and economic rationality'[47] the construction of the 2005 Tokyo Expo, an extravagant exhibition of the world's most inventive architecture, criticises itself for placing a 'tremendous burden on the natural environment, exceeding its capacity for self-recovery'. In July 2008, the Zaragoza Expo boasts that it has saved the most drinking water in Spain. Compare these meagre modern 'visions' with the

[43] Sustainable Energy Watch, Global Report for RIO+10, 'Energy and Ecodevelopment, An assessment of the impact of energy policies on Planet Earth'

[44] William McDonough, 'Cradle to Cradle' quoted in William McDonough & Michael Braungart 'Foreward to the Chinese Edition of Cradle to Cradle', www.mcdonough.com

[45] Carolyn Dimitri, Anne Effland, and Neilson Conklin, 'The 20th Century Transformation of U.S. Agriculture and Farm Policy', Electronic Information Bulletin Number 3, Economic Research Service, U.S. Department of Agriculture June 2005, www.ers.usda.gov

[46] 'Agricultural Productivity in the United States', U.S. Department of Agriculture, June 2005, www.ers.usda.gov

[47] www.expo2005.or.jp

first Expo at Crystal Palace way back in 1851 at which Prince Albert sought to reflect the 'realisation of the unity of mankind.'[48]

In Chapter 4 on Education, we look at the underhand indoctrination of schoolchildren by sustainability consultants and the mainstream educational establishment. Children are no longer being taught, they're been given 'the sustainability line'. In today's schools, we have a doctrinal environmental agenda, which is not only causing schools to loose sight of their educational purpose, but leads them to believe that indoctrination *is* their purpose. Indeed, the UK's Department for Education and Skills intends to 'launch an indicator of learners' capability to contribute to a sustainable society' which will ask 'how education policy should be adjusted'[49] to meet that aim, as opposed to asking how education policy should best educate the next generation.

In Chapter 5, we look at the dynamics currently affecting China and India where, even now, the restraining influence of sustainability is in evidence. Clearly 'progress' is winning out and China is developing, but even so, the (UK-based) engineer for Dongtan, the first low carbon city in China says that, 'through the development of sustainable cities, China is trying to curb inappropriate demand.[50] The same can be said for India. Who determines 'inappropriateness' is open to question. Perhaps, the fact that 'most of Maharashtra went without electricity for up to 15 hours a day'[51] during the summer of 2006, is meant to exemplify responsible (appropriate) demand?

In Chapter 6, we look at the anti-developmental implications of sustainable development in the Third World. UK academic and environmental commentator, John Whitelegg says the important thing about the developing world is that 'they have very little, they use very little (and) they make hardly any contribution to global environmental problems'.[52] As a general critique of the rise of eco-imperialism, this chapter challenges the mainstreaming of such patronising attitudes.

[48]  Prince Albert, 'The Speech of H.R.H. The Prince Albert, K.G., F.R.S., at The Lord Mayor's Banquet, in the City of London, October 1849', The Illustrated London News, 11 October 1849

[49]  Department for Education and Skills, 'Sustainable Schools for Pupils, Communities and the Environment: An Action Plan for the DfES', 2007

[50]  Chris Luebkman of Arup's global foresight and innovation initiative, quoted in Clifford Coonan, 'Carbon-free living: China's green leap forward', The Independent, 6 February 2007.

[51]  Kalpana Sharma, 'Fuelling the fire,' New Statesman, 6 August 2007

[52]  John Whitelegg, 'Transport for a Sustainable Future: The case for Europe', Belhaven Press, 1993, p11-12

In the final Chapter 7, we look at the US as metaphor, exploring the little recognised fact that in America, sustainability and environmental consciousness dominate the political landscape and the implications that that has on a belief in modernity. Democratic senator John Edwards says that global warming 'is the great moral test of our generation'.[53] Hilary Clinton recognises it as 'one of the most pressing moral issues of our time'.[54] Senator McCain calls dealing with the environment a 'national security issue'[55] while Barack Obama suggests that unless America amends its energy policies, it is 'condemning future generations to global catastrophe.'[56] The popular view is of gas-guzzling, swaggering, nature-trampling braggarts. In reality, sustainability, and the consequent rise of self-doubt, confusion and fear, is everywhere.

This book attempts to provide some ammunition to make it possible to argue for a destruction of the mantra of sustainability, removing its unthinking status as orthodoxy, and for the reinstatement of the notions of development, progress, experimentation and ambition in its stead. The ideology of sustainable development may yet prove to be unsustainable.

[53]  Cain Burdeau, 'Edwards Calls Global Warming Moral Test', Associated Press, Sunday, 4 November 2007, www.washingtonpost.com
[54]  Hilary Clinton, 'Reducing Global Warming, Promoting Energy Independence and Protecting the Environment', Hilary for President, Fact Sheet, www.hillaryclinton.com
[55]  John McCain, 23 April 2007, 'McCain's energy policy speech', the Daily Green, 24 April 2007
[56]  Barack Obama, 'Energy Independence and the Safety of Our Planet', Monday, April 3, 2006, personal website, http://obama.senate.gov/

# CHAPTER 1

# THE NEW PAROCHIALISTS

*Transport and mobility denied*

One of the most visible signs of progress has been the development of speedy and efficient transportation. Watching a Victorian steam train travelling across the countryside in the early 19th century, Dr Arnold, the headmaster of Rugby School announced: 'I rejoice to see it, and think that feudality is gone forever'.[1] Indeed, steam opened up the world in ways unimaginable to prior generations. Ditto, the bus, the car and the aeroplane.

There is overwhelming historical precedent for believing that increased mobility has been, and is, a social good. It is tragic then, that contemporary sustainable transport policy propounds regressive demands for reduced transport opportunities. We are now told that local is good, that slow is best, that we should travel 'responsibly' or not at all. Some transport modes and destinations are now deemed to be 'unsustainable' and access to them is increasingly being criticised and restricted. So who are these new feudal arbiters of our travel plans?

## Motoring morality

Sustainability has affected transport more aggressively and detrimentally than it has possibly affected any other aspect of modern life. Starting as a relatively fringe campaign against the car and particular transport infrastructure projects in the 1980s and 90s, twenty years later sustainable transport has become a fully-fledged policy

[1]   Tony Tanner, 'So Quickly Was That Way of Life to Vanish: The World of Jane Austen', introduction, Jane Austen, 'Mansfield Park', Penguin Classics edition

discussion about whether more transport, travel or even the concept of mobility is actually a 'good thing'. From obesity to community fragmentation, from road rage to global devastation, from speed to greed, transport has been accused of each of them and found guilty in the kangaroo court of environmentalism. At the start of his premiership in 1997, for example, Tony Blair suggested that 'a new approach to transport may mean sometimes not travelling at all.'[2]

In 1959, when there were just 2.5 million cars in Britain (compared to 25 million today) and some 10 million worldwide (compared to 57 million today), The Guardian newspaper, today renowned for its critical stance on modern car driving, stated that: 'The snail's pace of modern British road-building is an unhappy reflection on our society.'[3] Indeed it was, and still is. Over the last ten years or so, transport debate in the UK has ceased to pretend that it is about the real, material, technical improvement of travel opportunities and is characterised by an absence of rhetoric about improving its speed, efficiency and reliability.

In the last decade, transport policy has become a value judgement rather than a state provision and it is common to hear it discussed in terms of its causal link in — what UK government's 'happiness guru', Lord Layard calls — the various 'failures of modern societies', including crime, low trust and mental illness.[4] One report notes that 'while new and improved infrastructure brings economic and social benefits, it can also facilitate the spread of disease'.[5] Academics tell us that more mobility has a habit of 'altering our values'[6] and can 'weaken families and communities'.[7] Increasingly then, transport pronouncements seem more concerned about family bonding, health and community engagement than in assisting people to get conveniently, comfortably and quickly from A to B. Indeed, frequently we are asked to consider whether we actually need to go to B in the first place. Logically, if mobility has the potential to cause

[2]   Tony Blair, 'Speech by the Prime Minister Tony Blair to the UN General Assembly,' 23 June 1997   •

[3]   The Guardian, 2 November 1959

[4]   Richard Layard, 'Happiness: Lessons From A New Science', Penguin, 2006, p180

[5]   'Towards sustainable transport infrastructure: a sectoral approach in practice', Director-General for Development European Commission, July 1996, quoted in Dr Lieve Fransen and Professor Alan Whiteside, 'Study of the Impact of HIV Epidemic on the Social and Economic Development of Developing Countries: Document 3 (A) HIV/Aids And The Transport Sector,' Commission of the European Communities under Contract B7.5046/94/06

[6]   Richard Layard, 'Happiness: Lessons From A New Science', Penguin, 2006, p145

[7]   Richard Layard, 'Happiness: Lessons From A New Science', Penguin, 2006, p233

harm, then it seems almost charitable to restrict it on our behalf. It is common nowadays for such restrictions to be posed as medicine for the greater good, and therefore it is often not seen as a restriction at all. In his much quoted essay, 'The Social Consequences of Hypermobility', Professor John Adams calls it 'collective self-discipline.'[8]

Today, researchers can only gingerly suggest that there is 'evidence for a positive utility for travel'[9] but it is not a view held in the public sphere with much conviction. For example, arch anti-car campaigner Mayer Hillman uses a motoring motif to suggest that 'we are on the road to ecological Armageddon'[10] while an Australian transport commentator blames the car for 'a plague of alienation'.[11] In America, influential blogger Arianna Huffington together with environmentalist Laurie David (producer of Al Gore's film 'An Inconvenient Truth') has produced hard-hitting advertisements linking SUV ownership to support for terrorism. Drive a big car (or what environmental commentator Jeremy Rifkin calls a 'death engine'[12]) and you are as good as declaring war on all reasonable, right-thinking people seems to be the current moral agenda.

So when leading architect, Richard Rogers presented his Reith lecture series and argued that 'it is the car which has played the critical role in undermining the cohesive social structure of the city', his thesis was seized upon. Never mind that he also said that 'the car remains the century's most liberating and most desired technological product',[13] his initial comments echoed an incumbent (Conservative Party) parliamentary suggestion that 'the only remaining option is to reduce mobility'.[14] One of the first things that the New Labour government did after coming into power in 1997 was to alter the direction of transport policy in order to 'reduce the need to travel'[15]

[8]    Professor John Adams, 'The Social Consequences of Hypermobility', RSA Lecture, 21 November 2001
[9]    Patricia L. Mokhtarian and Ilan Salomon, 'How derived is the demand for travel? Some conceptual and measurement considerations', Transportation Research Part A: Policy and Practice, Volume 35, Issue 8, September 2001, Pages 695
[10]   Mayer Hillman, 'How We Can Save The Planet', Penguin, 2004, p8
[11]   David Engwicht, 'Reclaiming our Cities & Towns: Better Living with Less Travel', New Society Publishers, 1993, p59
[12]   Jeremy Rifkin, 'Sorry, Mr President, homilies won't stop the hurricanes', The Guardian, 23 September 2005
[13]   Richard Rogers, 'Cities for a Small Planet', 1997, Faber and Faber, p35
[14]   'Transport and Sustainability: Post Report Summary', Parliamentary Office Of Science And Technology, November 1995
[15]   'A New Deal for Transport: Better for everyone', Department of Environment Transport and the Regions, 1998, p8

(with the subclause 'especially by car'[16]). Its avowed aim of minimising car use was accepted as 'the only show in town.'[17]

'Reducing the need to travel' sounds sensible enough. After all, if
you don't need to travel, then why do it? But over a century ago,
Henry Ford is reputed to have said that he 'had' to invent his gaso-
line buggy so that he could escape the 'crushing boredom of life on a
mid-West farm'.[18] Contrary to the simplistic worldview of government policy wonks, he didn't *need* to escape his hick lifestyle, he just
thought it would be a good idea. For him, it was a desire; a progressive step, and fortunately there is something about the human condition that led him to do it. The sustainable transport position, on the
other hand, is that he didn't really *need* to do it. Implicitly, for them, if
Ford had stayed on the farmstead the world would have been a
better place. Even the RAC (the Royal Automobile Club) suggests
that 'around 50 to 70 per cent of journeys "do not inherently have to
be made by car, or in some cases, not at all."'[19]

*Having* to travel is one thing, simply *wanting* to travel is quite
another, and it is this choice that is being denied by the framework of
sustainability. Once we accept that a third party can legitimately
deem our chosen journey to be 'unnecessary' — or, more commonly,
'irresponsible' — then we have lost the right to decide on *any* journey.
Why? Because through this corrosive process of moral attrition, we
give up the autonomy of the individual subject to decide for his/her-
self whether a journey is beneficial.

It's bad enough that sustainable transport policy prescribes erstwhile free choices of transport modes. But more worryingly, it even
forces us to consider and reconsider whether we should actually
make the journey in the first place. We are expected to weigh up
whether our journey is really necessary? What mode of transport
should I use? What is the optimal time to travel? Can I combine two
trips in one? What are the carbon implications? Should I walk?
Straightforward tasks like catching the bus or taking the car are now
turned into major moral dilemmas. Sustrans, the pro-cycling lobby,
seeks 'to encourage people to incorporate health-enhancing physical
activity into their daily routine, by choosing active rather than

[16]  'A New deal for Transport: Better for everyone', Department of Environment
      Transport and the Regions, 1998, p114
[17]  David Begg, quoted on BBC TV's 'One O'Clock News', 9 December 1998
[18]  Stephen Bayley, 'Transport in the New Millennium', ed Austin Williams,
      Transport Research Publications, 2000
[19]  RAC quoted in Christian Wolmar, 'Unlocking the Gridlock: The key to a new
      transport policy', Friends of the Earth, 1997, p80

sedentary transport modes.'[20] Changes to the UK driving test will include questions such as 'could my journey be better made by bike? Trevor Wedge, Britain's chief driving instructor says; 'There's a whole generation of people who never even think about the environmental issues surrounding the car and its use… but if we put that on the syllabus, people are more likely to give it some thought.'[21] The government seems to be developing a transport strategy that celebrates pontification. What used to be automatic decisions are now meant to be made conscious, and conscionable, resulting in time-wasting inconvenience … and that's even before we step outside the house. Once we are outside, our mobility — the act of venturing through the public arena — becomes an insular, guilt trip.

By acknowledging culpability in this heinous crime against the planet, then, and only then, are we absolved. So, for example, George Monbiot, the environmental campaigner sheepishly admits to having bought a car. This from a man who suggested that 'a car is now more dangerous than a gun; flying across the Atlantic is as unacceptable, in terms of its impact on human well-being, as child abuse.'[22] But it's OK: 'I still feel pretty awful about it,' he admits.[23] Eco-activist Laurie David, who admits to taking private planes on holiday a couple of times a year admits to feeling 'horribly guilty about it.'[24] Sin, penance and forgiveness.

Ironically, it is the church that describes the highway as 'a place where fraternity is expressed',[25] while it is left to secular pulpit campaigners to dwell on the baser side of humanity, exploring their own dystopian vision of drivers 'blazing with homicidal anger'[26] and the cars they drive as 'Satan's little run-arounds.'[27] It used to be a common sentiment that 'travel broadens the mind' but now it's left to the Pope to endorse the saying, sounding like a progressive defender of liberal Enlightenment values on transportation compared to some environmental critics today. 'We may see traveling not only as physical movement from one place to another, but also in its spiritual

[20]  Sustrans, 'Health Travel' No 8, Winter 2003
[21]  Dipesh Gadher, 'Driving test to go green with eco-questions', Sunday Times, 5 November 2006.
[22]  George Monbiot, 'Meltdown', 29 July 29 1999, www. monbiot.com
[23]  Emma Smith, 'Mr Green goes motoring,' The Times, 3 June, 2007
[24]  Ed Pilkington. 'On a mission to the stars', The Guardian, 18 November, 2006
[25]  The Bishops of France, 'Road Safety: An Evangelical Challenge', October 2002
[26]  Paul Eberle, 'Terror on the Highway: Rage on America's Roads', Prometheus Books, 2006, p28
[27]  Andrew Simms, New Economics Foundation, interviewed in Richard Black, '4x4s 'should carry health warning', BBC News, 26 November, 2004

dimension, due to the fact that it puts people in touch with each other,'[28] said the Vatican in 2007. Fifty years ago, Pope Pius XII recommended that motorists 'make the car a more useful tool for yourselves and others that is capable of giving you a more genuine pleasure.'[29] Such an argument for the putative pleasures of driving are seldom expressed in polite company these days. A group of academics at a conference at Keele University better express the current view when they describe transport today as a 'car-based regime (that) generates widespread problems—ecological collapse, war, widespread death and ill-health and economic dysfunctionality, to name but a few.'[30]

Having started the 20th century recognising the liberating potential that came with the mass produced motor car, we ended it by associating that mode of transport as the key ingredient in our unsustainable lifestyles and treating ordinary people who avail themselves of it with utter contempt. No-one made assumptions about the emotional state of Britain's 2.3 million cyclists after a man was found having sex with his bicycle[31] but it seems perfectly acceptable to pathologise all motorists' relationships with their cars. One academic suggests that transport policy is 'encouraging car worship.'[32] Author Katie Alvord suggests that drivers are in a 'dysfunctional relationship.'[33] While others simply suggest that drivers are 'complete idiots.'[34] With this in mind, the UK government's 1998 Transport White Paper has been relatively unopposed in its commitment to counsel us out of our much-vaunted 'love affair with the motor car.'[35]

Once you scratch the surface of this Freudian approach to transport, it becomes clear that it has ceased to be a genuine debate about mobility and has become one about how we *consume* transport. It is a

[28] Document Of The Pontifical Council For The Pastoral Care Of Migrants And Itinerant People: 'Guidelines For The Pastoral Care Of The Road', 19th June 2007
[29] Pope Pius XII, To the members of the Rome Automobile Club: Speeches and Radio Messages of Pope Pius XII, vol. XVIII (1956) p. 89
[30] 'Against Mobility', Steffen Böhm, Campbell Jones, Chris Land and Matthew Peterson (eds), Blackwell Publishing, 2006, p9
[31] BBC, 'Bike sex man placed on probation', BBC News Online, 14 November 2007
[32] Robin Hambleton, dean of the College of Urban Planning and Public Affairs, University of Illinois and Chicago, 'Avoiding the roads to ruin', The MJ, November 2004
[33] Katie Alvord, 'Divorce Your Car!: Ending the Love Affair With the Automobile', New Society Publishers, 2000, p1
[34] Paris bid to ban designer jeeps', CNN.com, 10 June 2004
[35] Howard Jacobsen, 'The Americans will give up their love affair with guns when we do the same with cars', The Independent, 21 April 2007

commentary about how we see ourselves. Or rather, how some of us are viewed by others. Environmental journalist, Mark Lynas has a dim view of 'us'. He admits to being in favour of lower growth, less mobility, fewer goods, and lower material standards; condemning those 'wasting their lives commuting to work in cars' and proposing that we 'liv(e) less consumptive lifestyles.' [36]

## Pedestrian developments

The early morning commute by car is an easy target because it is difficult to claim that the commuter's journey is a great voyage of discovery or an Enlightenment project for the right to travel. It is usually, mundane, solitary and tiresome. For environmentalists, commuters are the epitome of arrogance; cosseted in their anti-social bubble. When Mrs Thatcher proclaimed that any man who found himself on a bus after the age of 30 had 'failed in life', car-based commuting automatically became a symbol of economic selfishness. Even avowed petrolhead, Richard Hammond, presenter of BBC's flagship TV motoring programme 'Top Gear' who owns two Porsches, a Dodge Charger, two Land Rovers, a Suzuki, a BMW, a Morgan V6 Roadster and a 1968 Ford Mustang compains that driving a 4x4 in London is 'damaging to the environment.'[37] I hate to break it to pious sustainable transport commentators, but commuting by car has its merits over the often sweaty reality of public transport (which traditionally have been designed with a cavalier disregard for ergonomics, comfort, speed or storage space). In Britain the average car commute still only takes 21 minutes each way, which is hardly a strain but Sustrans, a sustainable cycling charity is foisting personal travel advisors on local communities 'asking people to sign a pledge to use their cars less'.[38]

Eighty-five per cent of London commuters, 80 per cent of those in Kolkata and 55 per cent in New York use public transit, whereas, for example, in Indianapolis, the second most populous city in America, that figure shrinks to 1.8 per cent.[39] Does this mean that Indianans are particularly irresponsible? Or lazy? Or are they exercising common sense by avoiding a public transit network that has 'has suf-

[36]   Mark Lynas, 'A better way to live', EcoLife, The Independent, 7 July 2007
[37]   Bo Wilson, 'Hamster's guilty secret… he prefers cycling in London,' London Lite, 30 April 2007
[38]   Ben Webster, 'Hello, I'm your personal travel adviser. Can I persuade you to get on your bike?' The Times, 31 October 2007
[39]   Les Christie, 'More than half ride subway or bus to work,' CNNMoney.com, 29 June 2007

fered from years of neglect'? In the US context at least, Americans have actually become less mobile over the past four decades and commuting is the only area where personal travel has increased.[40] Speaking of neglect, the UK government's Sustainable Transport Initiative rejects investment in major infrastructure provision in favour of smaller schemes that aim to change behaviour and attitudes. Why provide a bus, when you can encourage more people to cycle. Why provide a cycle lane when most local councils are actively working to 'promote walking.'[41]

The government's 'Manual for Streets' creates a hierarchy of travel priorities: starting with pedestrians, then cyclists; public transport, emergency services, and then motor cars.[42] For over ten years in Britain, the primary objective of transport policy has been to reduce reliance on the car for work and other journeys[43] to the extent that investment in public transport schemes *only* really occurs if it can be shown to dissuade people from driving.[44] More transport choices is good but restricting one mode of transport to force people to use another is a discreditable evasion of the need for more and better infrastructure of all transport types. The justification for restraint has been the reputed build up of 'congestion' a concept that has entered the psyche of all commentators on the subject even though there is no workable definition of it.

A decade ago, a European Commission report suggested that the cost of congestion in the UK was equivalent to 3.2 per cent of GDP. Subsequent surveys by the CBI consistently put the loss to the economy at about £20 billion a year, the Adam Smith Institute suggests £18 billion and the government's adviser said that 'eliminating existing congestion ... would be worth some £7–8 billion of GDP per annum.'[45] The costs of congestion have been taken to the nth degree, and include 'social costs' such as the monetary effect of poor

[40] Allison Tarmann on research by Kimberlee Shauman, assistant professor of sociology at the University of California–Davis, in 'Is America Settling Down' Population Reference Bureau, November 2003
[41] ww.wyltp.com (5 January 2008)
[42] Welsh Assembly Government, Department for Communities and Local Government, Department for Transport, (2007), 'Manual for Streets', Thomas Telford Publishing, Table 3.2, p28
[43] House of Commons, 'Transport - Seventh Report', Section 12, Clause 276, 14 June 2006
[44] Transport: Trends and Challenges; Issues to promote debate at the PIU Strategic Futures Seminar, 13 November 2001
[45] Rod Eddington, 'The Eddington Transport Study - The case for action: Sir Rod Eddington's advice to Government,' Executive Summary, December 2006, Item 6, p5

employee performance caused by the stress of being stuck in traffic, various environmental costs' and Eddington has even included 'personal satisfaction' and 'happiness' as a costed benefit! Even though the economic figures don't bear analysis, it doesn't stop commentators repeating that a five per cent reduction in travel for all businesses could generate £2.5 billion of cost savings (0.2% GDP).[46] These figures are simply inventions.

However, once everything is seen through the prism of congestion — and the *sine qua non* of the UK transport debate is that building roads 'would be unsustainable on a scale needed to halt the growth in congestion'[47] — we are left with the assertion that driving has to be reduced. Congestion is therefore the holy grail for transport planners and London is at the forefront of congestion charging technology. The issue has been talked up to such a degree that we see gridlock at every turn. However, the truth is significantly different to how it is portrayed. London, in fact, had exactly the same number of cars driving around it in 2003 (before the congestion charge was introduced) as there had been in 1963.[48] But that's not the point, even if congestion was a problem, the progressive solution would be to plan to provide more roads as well as more and better public transport links.

With fictions and platitudes dominating the transport agenda, it is hardly surprising that in the UK, there was a meagre 22 miles of road network completed in 2005/06. China on the other hand, with fewer qualms about the human efficiency gains resulting from swapping their bikes for motor cars, has recently announced that they will be building 5,500 miles of new roadway in the next five years. While the Indian government initiates a 15-year project to widen, resurface and maintain over 40,000 miles of national highways, British Transport Minister, Dr Stephen Ladyman recently boasted that 'from 2006–07 through to 2007–08 we expect to complete two national schemes, which collectively will deliver approximately 6.3 miles of road improvements to the network.'[49] It is all beginning to look at little pathetic. But convincing the world that low and zero growth is sustainable is the key to keeping the West, and Britain in particular, with a market advantage. Having the ability to portray the emerging

[46]   'The Eddington Transport Study - The case for action: Sir Rod Eddington's advice to Government,' Main Report: Volume 1, December 2006, Item 2.20, p24
[47]   GreenLightGroup, 'Roa'd pricing: Can the technology cope?' December 2006
[48]   Transport for London, London Travel Report 2002'
[49]   Dr Stephen Ladyman, House of Commons Hansard Written Answers, 19 December 2005: Column 2320W

economies as morally repugnant in their attitudes to the planet is a god-send.

A patronising New York Times editorial drips with righteous indignation at the cheek of the Indian small car market: 'The world has changed since Americans celebrated the egalitarian breakthrough of the Ford Model T,' it points out in exasperation. 'We know now that gas-driven automobiles do terrible damage to the environment, and the notion of loosing millions upon millions of new carbon emitters on our planet is not something to celebrate.'[50]

Well actually, it is. India's motorists have grown from 0.3 million in 1951 to 6.6 million today (in a population of over 1.1 billion). It is estimated that there'll be 15 million by 2015, allowing more and more Indian families to stop risking their necks on two-stroke scooters. Meanwhile climate change author Dave Reay is concerned that 'the sleeping greenhouse gas giant of Asia is waking up to aspirations of mass car ownership and US lifestyles. This is very bad.'[51] But it isn't. Twenty-five years ago in China, private citizens were not allowed to purchase vehicles for private use. They were stuck in their villages, up to their knees in rice water. By 2005, there were 20 million private and official cars on the roads and in 15 years there may be around 140 million. China is now the second largest auto market after the United States.[52] As families get wealthier, more than 2.5 million are taking foreign holidays, with 1.7 million Chinese tourists simply crossing the border.[53] Typically, some environmental activists are trying to halt the tide in China: 'Part of our mandate,' says one, 'is to promote bicycles as sustainable transportation in a world that seems to be hurtling toward major ecological disaster.'[54] Fortunately, China is paying little heed.

## Don't see the world?

The car has been more than just a means of physical conveyance; it has historically been a symbol of freedom and personal liberation. 'The car was the star';[55] the freedom of the open road, and all that. As we have seen, that symbol has been under sustained attack, but

[50]  Editorial, 'The Other Nano', The New York Times, 16 January 2008
[51]  Dave Reay, 'Climate Change begins at Home: Life on the two-way street of global warming', Macmillan, 2005, p31
[52]  Melinda Liu, 'Drivng Through', Newsweek, 14-21 May 2007, p75
[53]  More Chinese Taking Foreign Holidays, Xinhua News Agency, 6 February, 2003
[54]  Henry Gold, 'China: Kingdom of bicycles no more', TheStar.com, 15 January 2007
[55]  Austin Williams, ed Kate Trant and Austin Williams, 'The macro world of micro cars', Black Dog Publishing, 2004, p25

unsurprisingly the newly emerging economies are revelling in the exhilaration of the mobility revolution that the west experienced in the 50s and 60s. The latest transport revolution comes in the shape of the budget airline, and air passengers are now treated with the same ignominy that drivers have endured for years. The Organisation for Economic Cooperation and Development's criteria for environmentally sustainable transport calls for a move away from car ownership and usage; fewer long-distance flights, more local and non-motorised travel and more 'virtual in lieu of physical travel'.[56]

Sustainability advocates who have become bored with the ease with which they can express contempt for our 'lazy, pro-car culture'[57] now extend their condemnation to those who wish to travel by other means. When the Bishop of London announced his belief that flying is a 'sin against the planet'[58] he was following, rather than leading, the opinion of unelected pulpit campaigners like Friends of the Earth, who argue that cheap flights are 'immoral' and who demand a 'new criminal offence of mass murder by environmental homicide.'[59] Or the Greenskies Alliance pronouncement that 'flying around the UK and to near-European neighbours needs to be socially unacceptable'[60]. Plane Stupid, a group protesting at airport building in Britain, have issued a fatwa — via a Baptist minister — that 'people killing our planet should be put on notice.'[61]

Acceptable travel, it seems, has to have a higher moral purpose in order to be justifiable. Holidaying is now seen as an act of crude self-aggrandisement. Greenland politician, Aqqaluk Lynge, president of the Inuit Circumpolar Council flew thousands of miles to Britain with a petition to complain that Western travel patterns were directly connected to the destruction of Inuit habitat and way of life. He took great pains to emphasise his moral mission to ensure that he couldn't be judged by frivolous Western materialistic standards:

[56]  Todd Litman, 'Sustainable Transportation Indicators', Victoria Transport Policy Institute, 4 February 2003 , p7
[57]  Richard Rogers and Anne Power, 'Cities for a Small Country', Faber and Faber, 2000, p 121
[58]  Richard Chatres, Bishop of London, quoted in Becky Barrow, 'Flying on holiday 'a sin', says bishop', Daily Mail, 23rd July 2006
[59]  Brent Friends of the Earth submission to consultation on the government's report on the Energy Review: 'The Energy Challenge', www.dti.gov.uk/energy/review/consultation-submissions/april/public-and-private-organisations/page31478.html#Brent
[60]  Jeff Gazzard, coordinator Greenskies Alliance quoted in Ben Webster, 'Domestic flights take off thanks to high rail fares', The Times, 24 December 2007
[61]  Rev. Malcolm Carroll quoted in Plane Stupid Press Release, 'Sermon On The Runway', 24th September 2006

'Planes are sometimes necessary,' he said. 'I could not have come here without traveling by plane. But I came here for an important purpose. Most flights from London Stansted airport are not for an important purpose. They are mostly for holidays and leisure purposes.'[62] Today, it would seem, holidays are unimportant.

In the sustainability framework, cheap flights no longer symbolise the aspiration to explore, to open up the world to a generation (and a social group) that might previously have only read about it. Instead, Ian Pearson MP, government environment minister calls cheap flights: 'the irresponsible face of capitalism.' Whether it is the car or cheap airlines, the contemporary criticism of their use is really an attack on the people that use them. Guardian journalists describe cheap holiday-makers as 'drunken mayhem-makers' and if Sian Berry, Green Party activist and anti-car campaigner has her way, 'we may be about to send the city break and cheap-flight-stag-night the way of the 4x4'.[63] Mayer Hillman says: 'I've seen pictures of people in Bangladesh with the sea surging … How dare people then go on saying "Oh you can't interfere with people's freedom if they want to fly to Prague for a stag weekend … It's got to stop".'[64] He presents things as if there is a linear connection—a blame line—between the two events. It is also intended to differentiate between knowing, caring environmentalists—of which he is one—and the ignorant rest.

In some respects, it is the born-again converts to environmentalism who show the greatest contempt for personal freedom; those people who've had everything and now want to deny others the same opportunities. Mark Ellingham, has travelled a fair bit as the founder of travel handbooks The Rough Guides series, now wants to 'encourage travellers to travel less'. His ire is levelled at so-called 'binge-fliers'[65] and his contempt is palpable. A fellow travel journalist criticises those like Ellingham who wish to rein in travel opportunities for the budget end of the market, parodying the claims that 'hoards … in football shirts will ruin the planet, pissing in Latvian fountains, drunkenly trampling a rich cultural heritage which hardly anyone knew about until 15 years ago.'[66]

[62]  Dominic O'Connell, 'Eskimo urges airport freeze', The Sunday Times, 27 May 2007
[63]  Sian Berry, 'Is the airplane going the way of the 4x4?', New Statesman, 23 July 2007
[64]  Mayer Hillman quoted in Matthew Taylor, 'An inconvenient man,' Fabian Review, Spring 2007
[65]  Amelia Hill, 'Travel: the new tobacco', The Observer, 6 May 2007
[66]  Mark Khazar, 'Save the planet, don't see the world?', Battle in Print, Institute of Ideas, 2007

Comically, anti-airports campaigners Plane Stupid even criticise those in their own organisation who fly saying: 'the majority of our social circle ... are wealthy, middle class kids, financially supported by very nice parents, educated to one of the highest standards in the world ... who really ought to know better.'[67] Admittedly, such snobbery is nothing new. In 1921, novelist G. K. Chesterton whimsically noted that: 'They say travel broadens the mind; but you must have the mind.'[68] Today, there seems not even the belief that increased travel, experience, choice and experience does anything other than narrow the mind. The car driver represents excess, risk and speed; the cheap tourist represents cultural degradation. The pedestrian, on the other hand, is representative of moderation and public spiritedness; the cyclist is slim and virtuous. This is a gratuitous debate about the national stock, reminiscent of the century-old establishment endorsement of social Darwinism. Today, it is about cultivating the responsible citizen.

For sustainability advocates, the cheap flight user represents profligacy, a cavalier disregard for others and a symbol of national decline. Green businessman, Jeremy Leggett suggests that the day when there are 'cheap day trips to Manhattan, we can forget about our children enjoying anything approaching civilisation.'[69] Leggett has already travelled the world, you understand (as a representative of the oil industry), but with the wisdom that comes with experience, he now wants to save us all from having to do the same. Unlike the acceptable issue of business class travel, in the eyes of environmentalists, cheap flights for the hoi-polloi are socially, environmentally and culturally unsustainable. The recent rise of the 'slow travel' market is merely an expression of a luxury market's rejection of 'the vulgar hordes'[70]

To show us the way, sustainable transport advocates know no patronising bounds. Even though Al Gore has been criticised in some circles for his personal carbon-intensive, jet-setting lifestyle whereby, every month, his house uses up twice the annual energy consumption of the average US home, Gore proclaims that since

[67]  Robbie, an 'activist', writing on Plane Speaking, www.planestupid.com, 30 May 2007

[68]  G.K. Chesterton, 'The Shadow of the Shark' in 'Thirteen Detectives' (1921), Penguin, 1989

[69]  Jeremy Leggett, 'Cheap flights to extinction', CommentIsFree, The Guardian, 13 April 2007

[70]  Anna Travis, 'Put the brakes on this cult of slowness', spiked-online, 31 May 2007

2004, he 'made a decision to live a carbon-neutral life'.[71] Meanwhile, Leonardo DiCaprio told journalists at the Cannes film festival that he was doing his bit by trying 'as often as possible to fly commercially.'[72] In environmentalists' terms, better a sinner who repenteth. Others are just oblivious to the debate. On one side you have Ryanair's cheap flight impresario, Michael O'Leary, well known for his no-nonsense rejection of environmentalists' claims announcing that: 'there is no suggestion the [eco] loonies are dissuading people from travel'[73] (three weeks later, his deputy chief executive was concerned that 'people might say "maybe I will not fly on holiday and maybe I will make a different choice".'[74]). On the other extreme is the gloriously carbon-unfriendly Royal family. When Prince Charles picked up his Global Environmental Citizen Prize by flying to New York to collect it, Joss Garman, anti-airports campaigner said that Prince Charles should be getting an 'award for green hypocrisy (since) ... flying is the single most polluting way in which you can travel.'[75] Blanching at the excesses of the monarchy is one thing (the Duchess of Cornwall's decision to fly a pair of stilettos from Highgrove to Kuwait when she realised she had embarked on a state visit without them is a particularly decadent example), but it's a little sad when protests against an un-elected monarchy should focus on their mode of transport. When Queen Victoria was attacked in her carriage at the turn of the 19th century, it had little to do with her waste-depositing, methane emitting, noisy, dangerous four-horsepower carriages. All her attackers were flogged for high treason.[76] Today it is the royal family that stands accused of treasonable acts against the green orthodoxy.

It might not be a consistent argument; it might be one that is honoured only in the breach, but once the logic that $CO_2$-emitting mobility is a problem *per se*, no-one is safe. When Easyjet boss, Stelios Haji-Ioannou received his knighthood in 2006, the Queen praised him as the person who had 'made it possible for millions to fly.'[77] Six

---

[71] Al Gore quoted in Jonathan Freedland, 'Al Gore', The Guardian, 31 May 2006

[72] Leonardo DiCaprio quoted in Charlotte Higgins, 'No more private jets for me, DiCaprio tells Cannes', The Guardian, May 21st 2007

[73] Terry Macalister, 'Ryanair declares 'price war' with £10 fare,' The Guardian, 10 May, 2007

[74] Howard Millar, deputy chief executive of Ryanair quoted in Dan Milmo, 'Ryanair: climate campaigners hitting sales,' The Guardian, 31 May 2007.

[75] BBC News Online, 19 January 2007

[76] Lytton Strachey, Queen Victoria', Penguin Classics, 1991

[77] Easyjet press release, 'Easyjet founder receives his knighthood', 29 November 2006

months later, Prince Charles had sworn to reduce flights—even for the monarchy[78]. Even the Pope is in trouble for opening Mistral Air, the world's first airline for Catholic pilgrims between Rome and Lourdes.[79]

## Travelling less

Heathrow airport is the biggest terminal in Europe. It handles around 70 million passengers per year and generates lots of carbon dioxide (predicted to be around 35m tonnes by 2025). The ex-head of British Airways, and UK government advisor, Rod Eddington says 'I firmly believe that the world needs to face up to the reality of climate change, and that implies learning to live within a carbon-constrained future' and as a result, cutting carbon emissions in and around Heathrow has become a key ingredient in London's sustainability strategy. However, by so doing, the very purpose of Heathrow—i.e. carbon intensive flying—becomes more and more untenable. David Milliband MP has already announced that carbon ration books will be available by 2010, setting a cap on mobility unless you have the money to pay. It falls to the Centre for Alternative Technology to explain the policy logic. Britain, it says, could become zero carbon, if, 'people stop travelling by air and in petrol-driven cars'.[80] Admittedly, that isn't going to happen, but these constant campaigns of attrition have meant that a belief in the progressive nature of mobility for its own sake is under threat.

A recent spate of government-sponsored reports produced by allegedly impartial (read, 'unelected') financial commentators, provides the political establishment with a certain air of detachment, and an unquestionable moral authority on the issue of travel reduction. Economist Sir Nicholas Stern, for example, the author of an eponymous report on the costs of climate change, spent a considerable amount of time flying around the world informing its poorer residents about the evils of flying. His unopposed message that 'we must travel less'[81] or 'travel differently'[82] has filtered deep into the general consciousness.

[78]   Jon Land, 'Royal Family to adopt 'strict' eco-friendly travel plans', 24dash.com, 7 December 2006
[79]   Tom Kington, 'Vatican plans airways to heaven', The Guardian, 15 August 2007
[80]   Joel Taylor, 'Car-free blueprint that could save the planet,' Metro, 9 July 2007
[81]   Julia Hailes, 'How to be a green traveller', Daily Telegraph, 17 May 2007
[82]   Douglas Alexander, Secretary of State for Transport, Speech on transport and climate change, 'Transport: Acting on CO2?' Institute for Public Policy Research, European Commission Representation in London, 28 March 2007

One consequence has been that the decision to build the third runway at Heathrow, initially proposed in the 1940s is still, at the time of writing, at the 'consultation phase'. There are obviously significant social impacts to be managed, but when asked about the consequences of demolishing homes and building on farmland to construct the project, Mark Bullock managing director of BAA's Heathrow operations says 'as a human being I feel for them (the local residents), but you've got to look at the greater good for society and balance out the benefits you get for the many, compared with the problems it caused for the few'.[83] You may disagree with his viewpoint, but at least these are rarely voiced, progressive sentiments. The 'greater good' he refers to is that of society — humanity — not that of 'the earth'. Merely his rejection of the commonplace faux humility towards an anthropomorphised planet, in itself, is significant. In truth, we need to reinstate this *type* of approach and reject the notion that scientists, accountants and *carbonistas* should determine transport strategy. $CO_2$ may or may not be a problem, but it shouldn't be allowed to be resolved at the expense of freedom of movement.

Unfortunately, this is exactly what is happening. In the last ten years or so, sustainable transport has won a considerable pyrrhic victory; undermining the legitimacy of mobility and the sociability, aspiration and inquisitiveness which are contained within the desire to transport ourselves beyond the local. It has made us more parochial and helped fragment the notion of ever achieving an integrated transport strategy.

Many people insist that the transport 'problem' has become impossibly complicated, but political will — for safe, speedy, comfortable, efficient and improved transportation — has metamorphosed from infrastructural engineering to social engineering. The tendency to think small, to think local, and to reduce our societal aspiration for universal solutions means that parochialiam is now regularly promoted as a progressive action plan. The current iteration of sustainable transport advocates want to restrain even our imagination by suggesting that its boundaries should be set in the local context. Environmental campaigner, Jeff Gazzard says that 'there is only one sure way to reduce climate change impacts of aircraft exhaust emissions, and that is to fly less... Holidaying in the UK and using video conferencing are two straightforward alternatives

[83] Mark Bullock, quoted in John Harris, 'Turbulent times', The Guardian, 17th August 2007

to flying.'[84] A nostalgic desire for less hectic lifestyles combined with modern internet technologies exemplifies the potential for connectivity without the need for personal private motorised transport. Today, the futuristic sounding Forum for the Future proposes that we look forward to the time when we can use a 200-year old technology to travel across the Atlantic in an air ship. Predominantly, only those with few financial worries will be able to afford the fare and the 24 hours to get to America, and so this is the ultimate luxury escape. One executive airship, due to launch in 2020, will moor at its destinations thus saving passengers the need to book into hotels. In this way, they can literally float above the Great Unwashed. This is just one example of the New Feudal transport aspirations of sustainability proponents.

There are however, genuinely futuristic travel proposals in the pipeline — like the Spanish-financed Galactic Suite Project that plans to construct an orbiting hotel that can tap into the space tourism market.[85] But you haven't got to explore extreme examples like this to see the exciting possibilities available for those who still see travel as a social good.

Take the growth of the Indian budget airline market. Experiential possibilities have been made available to those who would otherwise not have the opportunity. Obviously, in India, all is not rosy in the garden. With 300 million Indians living on less than US$1 a day and 45 per cent of Indian under-fives malnourished, this is not a simple story of national advancement when approximately 60 per cent of Mumbai's 16 million people live in slum conditions. However, the genie is out of the bottle and demand for social improvement is filtering down the chain. It is the aspiration to escape such degrading conditions that are exemplified in the various forms of social and physical mobility. Even though there is a growing influence of the United Nations Habitat programme that hints strongly for people to stay in their villages and not move into cities, relentless poverty still drives families to seek a better life. As we will see in Chapter 5, environmentalists would rather stop their progress. Having seen the mass travel consequences of cheap mass transit provision, many now want to turn the clock back. Anumita Roychowdhury, associate director of Delhi's environmental lobby group, the Centre for Science and Environment recognises that peo-

[84]  Ben Webster, 'BA asks passengers to pay green fee', The Times, 12 September 2005
[85]  David Gardner, 'A hotel with lots of space', Daily Mail, 13 August 2007

ple want to buy cheap cars, but asks 'how easy should we be making it for them? Once they have started using cars it will be hard to get them back (onto public transport).'[86]

## Anti-transport transport policy

As we have seen, the contemporary transport discussion is not a technical debate. Technophiles miss the point: they think that it is the mechanisms of mobility — rather than mobility itself — that is under attack. Rightly, they point out that as technologies advance, so they ought to alleviate the time and effort that goes into a particular task. Increasingly they promote the eco-efficiencies of video conferencing, as a modern method of reducing the need to travel; and admittedly, there are real physical and time benefits in communicating by video-link and letting 'waves and electrons travel'[87] while the nucleus remains at home. However, even the progressive technological angle of this debate has been requisitioned for reactionary parochial ends. Protesting against Al Gore's Live Earth concert and the performers who had the audacity to fly to an event that they were taking part in, the Climate Outreach Information Network campaigned for people to have a concert in their bedrooms instead. In this way, they boasted, 'there will be no executive jets, no cars, no floodlighting, no air conditioning, no paper, no plastic, no cans.'[88] They omitted to say: 'no enjoyment' and 'no point'. Admittedly, they were simply extending the logic of Live Earth's ambition to eliminate carbon emissions. It is all neatly summed up by leading UK cynic, George Monbiot who hopes that his book *Heat* will 'make people so depressed about the state of the planet that they stay in bed all day, thereby reducing their consumption of fossil fuels'.[89]

If we view mere mobility with such scorn, it is hardly surprising that confusion reigns over whether — let alone how — we should exercise transport policy. However, if you allow yourself the luxury of common sense, to recognise that the 'purpose' of travel is more often than not for some other reason — ethereal, personal, businesslike, pleasurable, or simply wanton — then the current demands for

[86]  Andrew Buncombe, 'Global Warming: Just what overcrowded, polluted India didn't need,' The Independent, 22 June 2007.

[87]  Ernst von Weizsäcker, presentation 'Energy efficiency is a prerequisite for renewables' at 'Fueling Change with Renewable Energy', University of Illinois at Urbana-Champaign, 26/27 April 2007

[88]  http://coinet.org.uk/news/alive

[89]  George Monbiot, 'Heat: How To Stop The Planet Burning', 2006, Allen Lane, p xix

restraint can be seen for the parsimonious, anti-social 'rhetorical' device that they are.

If the criticism of the car or the cheap flight was genuinely about offering a comfortable, fast and efficient alternative choice of conveyance, that would be one thing, but usually, the alternative under discussion is one that further restricts choices and undermines the personal belief in the necessity, or innocent personal desire of a particular journey and mode of transit. The central conceit is that we are irresponsible and need correctional advice so that our overarching responsibility will be directed towards the planet, rather than towards our selfish selves. Monbiot again: 'Libertarian conservatives contend that modern humans are destined to behave well if left to their own devices; I believe that they are likely to behave badly'.[90] Or take Toni Vernelli, vegan campaign co-ordinator of the animal rights organisation, People for the Ethical Treatment of Animals (PETA), who explains that she had an abortion and sterilisation because, for her, 'every person who is born uses more food, more water, more land, more fossil fuels, more trees and produces more rubbish, more pollution, more greenhouse gases, and adds to the problem of over-population.' Now, Vernelli is able to take guilt-free holidays to South Africa because 'We feel we can have one long-haul flight a year, as we are vegan and childless, thereby greatly reducing our carbon footprint.'[91]

British philosopher Alain de Botton suggests that if we adopt the right frame of mind we could just as satisfactorily 'apply a travelling mindset to our own locales.'[92] He tells of the late 18th-century writer, Xavier de Maistre, who documented his experiences in 'Journey around My Bedroom' detailing the joys of the travelling to his wardrobe, bed and sofa. De Botton has a sneaky regard for the fact that de Maistre's holiday required only a pair of cotton pyjamas and involved minimal disruption and effort on the traveller's part, implying that that the most sustainable travel is the transportation of our imaginations. As a logical consequence of this inward-looking philosophy, we are currently being asked to imagine fewer travel possibilities. As Judy Garland put it: 'If I ever go looking for my

[90]   George Monbiot quoted in Haseeb Khokhar, 'Interview: George Monbiot Talks to London Progressive Journal', London Progressive Journal, Issue 6, 15-21 February 2008

[91]   Toni Vernelli quoted in Natasha Courtenay-Smith and Morag Turner, 'Meet the women who won't have babies — because they're not eco friendly', Daily Mail, 21 November 2007

[92]   Alain de Botton, 'The Art of Travel', Penguin, 2002, p246

heart's desire again, I won't look any further than my own back-yard.'[93] On a philosophical level today, rejecting the symbolism of mobility and reinforcing the womb-like embrace of home, has the hallmarks of a society that has given up its intervention in history: it has given up on its humanity and it has given up on its future.

This is the essence of contemporary *anti*-transport policy, one that represents a fundamental rejection of the social ambition for more and better mobility. The desire for freedom of movement, whether holidaying, commuting, relocating, up-sizing, emigrating or just travelling for the hell of it requires the same response: better infra-structure, improved networks, greater choices and more possibili-ties. Unfortunately, one of the most prestigious investigations into the future of transport into the new millennium announced that 'some of the best projects are small-scale, such as walking and cycling.'[94]

Instead of mobility, the sustainable solution put forward is that we should be 'fostering the local at the expense of the remote.' A few years ago this sentiment might have been condemned as a narrow, Little Englander mindset, but nowadays, such protectionist language is commonplace among anti-transport campaigners and associated localists. The Greens want a 'debate on sustainable popu-lation levels for the UK'[95] and Sir Crispin Tickell, leading light in the environmental movement, appears to endorse 'zero net migration' in his position as patron of the Optimum Population Trust.[96] These repugnant arguments condemn ordinary people to lower life chances than would otherwise be the case. As one writer points out:

> The surge in aviation is being fuelled—at least to a significant extent—by the large numbers of eastern Europeans coming to and from Britain since the enlargement of the EU. We are talking about the people on whom our economy is increasingly depend-ent, popping home to see their families from time to time.[97]

Good! In reality, freedom of movement means a lot more than this, but the drive by aspirational immigrants to transform their circum-stances is—writ large—exactly why mobility is an unmitigated

[93]  Screenplay, Noel Langley, 'The Wizard Of Oz', MGM (1939)
[94]  Rod Eddington, 'The Eddington Transport Study. The case for action: Sir Rod Eddington's advice to Government', December 2006, p19
[95]  Green Party, 'Manifesto for A Sustainable Society: Population,' policy.greenparty.org.uk, Spring 2003
[96]  Press Release, 'What you can do: action and politics', Optimum Population Trust, 31 July 2007
[97]  David Millward, 'The carbon footprint of Polish plumbers', 10 August 2007

good. The drive for increased mobility that needs to be championed may indeed be selfish—but so what? It might not make liberals happy but the struggle by many immigrants (whether legal or so-called 'bogus') is a shot at a better life, what Philippe Legrain rightly calls their 'zeal for self-improvement'[98]. Their inspiringly ambitious project captures the enlightened potential made possible by freedom of movement. For this reason alone, increased mobility is a mark of real human progress. We allow ourselves to be constrained by sustainable transport at our peril.

[98]   Philippe Legrain, 'Immigrants: Your Country Needs Them', Little, Brown, 2007, p19

# CHAPTER 2

# THE OPT-OUTS

*Energy and the end of universal provision*

Peter and Sarah Robinson get up early in the morning but refuse to put the lights on. They open the curtains just enough to let sufficient daylight into the room to help them navigate their furniture safely, but not so much that too much heat escapes. In the dark mornings of winter, they see by the borrowed light from a streetlamp fortuitously placed outside their window. They own no television and their children are allowed to watch DVDs only on the weekend and only if the brightness control is turned down. Most evenings, the family spends its time in the kitchen in order not to have to switch 'more lights on than necessary'[1] in other rooms. Even though this sounds like the opening lines of a particularly dystopian spy novel, the Robinsons are real people and members of a radical Carbon Rationing Action Group (CRAG). They exhibit the carbon restraint that they would like to see extended to the rest of us. Fortunately, most of us realise that emerging from the dark ages was a progressive step.

Peter's personal testimony is instructive. His conversion to radical carbon efficiency came about when he realised, he says, how easy it was to lead a frugal life. After visiting a prison with a group of psychology students, he noticed the routine, almost instinctive way that warders would unlock a door, pass through and then secure it behind them. To them, this rigorous lock-down activity became second nature, and, he says, 'when I started going round at home turning lights out it reminded me of that routine.'[2] The Robinson's personal prison may not be everyone's cup of tea, but at the time of

[1]   Robert Greenall, '8am: Shower. Save the water. Save the planet', BBC News, 15 May 2007
[2]   Robert Greenall, '8am: Shower. Save the water. Save the planet', BBC News, 15 May 2007

writing, they are but a small part of the growing carbon rationing movement. Their relentless carbon calculation is a way of measuring how much energy one uses, the better to curtail it. There are many and growing local CRAG branches around Britain, Europe, North America and Australia/ New Zealand, each with a self-flagellating cohort of members volunteering to tiptoe about their daily lives as some kind of advert for the energy efficient domestic bliss of the future. London-based consultancy, WSP Environmental has 'voluntarily' recruited 60 members of staff to the CRAG allowance system. Their members must keep their personal annual $CO_2$ emissions under an arbitrary target level and fine themselves if they exceed it. One can only guess that the Robinsons are in credit.

Energy self-restraint—actually frequently imposed by others—is catching on. The UK's Guardian newspaper has launched its own 'online community' that pledges support for a range of energy-saving measures such as turning off standbys, using low energy light-bulbs, etc. One of its hosts, Leo Hickman concludes that once you explore this subject 'you start to reach a thick, sticky conclusion that says flicking the switch on humanity itself is just about the only act that will ultimately make any difference in the grand geophysical scheme of things. But the concept of self-extinction isn't much of a vote-winner these days.'[3] Hickman almost sounds disappointed that the switch hasn't been flicked on the rest of the world's population. Admittedly, as described throughout this book, there are many people who ditch Hickman's overt vile misanthropy but still buy into the essence of his discomfiture with modern life and the people who live it.

Mathis Wackernagel, for example, of the Global Footprint Network is annoyed that 'humanity is living off its ecological credit card and can only do this by liquidating the planet's natural resources.'[4] Others have retreated from modernity. Jacqueline Sheedy, a gardener from London reads by candlelight and converts her toilet waste into fertilizer.[5] Liberal dropout Masako Neville says, 'it's nice to be free from things like energy crises and uncertain food products. I want to live in harmony with nature.'[6] She does this by nurturing her garden with human sewage.

[3]    Leo Hickman, 'Ask Leo,', The Guardian, 19 April 2007
[4]    Mathis Wackernagel, 'World slips further into the "eco-red"' New Scientist magazine, 14 October 2006, page 7
[5]    James Kantor, 'Local groups use peer pressure—and fines—to cut carbon emissions', International Herald Tribune, 16 October 2007
[6]    Masako Neville quoted in 'Waste not, want not', Kevin McCloud, The Sunday Times, April 29th 2007

Craig Simmons, co-founder and director of Best Foot Forward (described as a 'UK based footprint network') sums up the variety of lifestyle changes. 'To deliver a sustainable future,' he says, 'it is necessary to reduce demand, improve efficiency and switch to renewables.'[7] And switching to renewables has now become the never-ending entreaty from central government. Clause 4 of the Climate Change and Sustainable Energy Bill requires the UK government to set a national target for microgeneration (using renewables for small scale energy production[8]) in order to reduce carbon emissions. Local planning authorities are mandated to 'specifically encourage' such schemes as part of their local development plans[9] thus reducing their reliance on centralised power plants. And so, regardless of the revelation that they are generally useless in all but coastal or hilltop locations, hype about wind turbines continue to proliferate. Danish turbine manufacturer Vestas has crossed the 1 billion euro sale mark. While the chief executive of the British Wind Energy Association, Marcus Rand's prediction hasn't yet come true, that small windmills in residential back gardens 'could become the latest home owner's fashion accessory'[10], that's possibly more to do with the fact that they take, on average, around 35 years to pay off.

Oblivious to the well-documented inefficiencies involved in alternative energy generation, the drive towards microgeneration has become more than just an energy policy. From solar panels to geothermal; from windmills to biofuels; from photovoltaics to woodburning stoves; from labyrinths to heat sinks; each draws people into a process of fetishising their own energy requirements. Newspapers and lifestyle programming constantly encourage an incestuous debate about what type of energy we should use; which is the most sustainable; whether we should use energy in the first place, and if so, how we can reduce our essential needs. It is a constant subliminal drone of public service broadcasting all directed cynically to encouraging civic engagement in an 'energy dialogue'.[11] The

[7]   '9 October: the day humanity starts eating the planet', New Economics Forum, 9 October 2006
[8]   Department of Trade and Industry, 'Energy Act 2004', Part 2 Sustainability and Renewable Energy Sources, Chapter 1 Sustainable energy, Clause 82 (6)
[9]   Planning Policy Statement No.22, Renewable Energy, ODPM, August 2004
[10]  Marcus Rand quoted in Paul Brown, 'Home wind turbines cut bills and pollution', The Guardian, 3 May 2005
[11]  Dr Jason Chilvers, Sarah Damery, Dr James Evans, Dr Dan Van Der Horst, Professor Judith Petts, 'Public Engagement In Energy: Mapping Exercise: A Desk-Based Report For The Research Councils UK', School Of Geography, Earth

dialogue, of course, is all structured to obtain the correct result (i.e. reduction), but beyond that, the mere process of people getting involved — or becoming empowered, as they say — in deciding which jumper to wear while the thermostat is turned down a degree or two, is the real political victory for sustainability devotees. 'Climate change', say the advocates, 'can seem such an enormous issue that there is little that individuals can do about it. Micro-generation can enable people everywhere to actually 'get involved.'[12]

The microgeneration debate is situated firmly in the behaviour of fragmented individuals whereby blame for the incapacity of the system to provide sufficient energy can be allocated to inefficient users. The American National Academy of Sciences bemoans the fact that if 'divorced couples had stayed together in 2005, the United States would have saved 73 billion kilowatt-hours of electricity.'[13] (Energy policy used to reinforce Thatcherite family values?) Seldom is the debate turned around into a progressive demand for more and better infrastructure. Instead, the microgeneration conversation aims to involve people in a discussion about how to behave responsibly; to live differently; to consider the error of their wasteful ways; and to play a part in making things better by considering what they could do to reduce their energy use in the first instance and to produce the essentials more locally. As Walt Kelly put it in his infamous 1970 Earth Day poster, 'We Have Met The Enemy and He Is Us.' Unfortunately, instead of simply speaking for himself, Walt and others have a nasty habit of speaking for everyone else. It is easier for microgeneration advocates to point the finger at so-called irresponsible users for the network's failure to provide sufficient energy, than to have to argue for a grander societal project of universal supply.

A new era of self-sufficiency beckons. Who needs, so the argument goes, a centralised power station when you can have the simple pleasures of a tepid solar powered bath and a wind-up radio? Those that haven't yet bought into the joys of composting and biofuels are regularly described as representative of a 'slavish reliance on centralised solutions.'[14] The main consequence of this

And Environmental Sciences Energy Research Public Dialogue Project, Universty of Birmingham, September 2005, p18

[12]   Sarah Boyack MSP, 'The Energy Efficiency and Micro-Generation Bill Proposal' December 2005

[13]   Juliet Eilperin, 'Divorce Found to Harm The Environment With Higher Energy, Water Use,' Washington Post, 4 December 2007

[14]   Mischa Hewitt and Kevin Telfer, 'Earthships: Building a zero carbon future for homes', Building Research Establishment, p108

increasing energy insularity is that the 75-year old universalising ambition of the UK's National Grid — the inter-war plan to supply every home with centrally distributed power — is being torn up as energy policy becomes just an unconnected series of neighbourhood energy production and reduction schemes. The chairman of America's Edison Electric Institute has a novel business plan that says that 'the most efficient and environmentally responsible (power) plant you can build is the one that you don't build.'[15]

Australia's energy supplier, EnergyAustralia, has launched a campaign against singing in the shower in order to save water. Showering, it says, normally takes an average of 4.35 minutes — but if you sing while showering it takes 8.96 minutes thus wasting fractions of a kW of power. The reason why Janet Leigh's murder scene in Hitchcock's 'Psycho' was so shocking, was because taking a shower is the essence of the sanctity of individual privacy. But that is now under attack by those people who want to pry into our personal habits. A power-shower is the new social faux-pas in respectable energy-saving circles. A London-based Housing Association imposes a duty on households to reduce water and energy use by building small baths in all its new houses to reduce one's personal drain on resources. The Guardian's ethical consumer guide, Leo Hickman, advises 'not to fill baths above the bottom of your ribcage when sitting down'.[16] If you thought your private life was your private life, beware, the enjoyment police are watching. With scant regard for convenience, Australia is the first to ban incandescent bulbs in favour of energy efficient fluorescent lighting and the European Union has just declared that it will follow suit by 2010.

Across Europe, governments are advising people to turn off 'unnecessary' lights and British MP Peter Hain proposes a ban on standby buttons on TVs and other electrical appliances. Several councils in England have taken the decision to turn off street lights at night to save both energy and carbon emissions. And California's Environmental Protection Agency building has purportedly 'cut its utility bill by 8 percent by turning off its lights at night and asking its maintenance crews to work days'.[17] In all these ludicrous examples, there are hefty fines for not complying.

[15]  James E Rogers, chief executive, Duke Energy and chairman of Edison Electric Institute referring to energy saving as the 'fifth fuel' after electricity, natural gas, nuclear and renewables. Steve Lohr, 'Energy Use Can be Cut by Efficiency', New York Times, 29 November 2006

[16]  Leo Hickman, 'Do try this at home', May 27, 2004, The Guardian

[17]  Ken Silverstein, 'Saving the Planet by Saving Energy', EnergyBiz, August 9, 2006

Some government agencies try to use subtle persuasion. Brian Wilson, as Energy Minister in Blair's cabinet until 2003, set aside £2 million 'to create an awareness and involvement campaign (whose) primary goals (were) to encourage consumers, companies and individuals to consider how they can play their part in growing renewable energy.'[18] Mind you, after resigning, he became chairman of the UK Operations Board of Airtricity, the Irish-based renewable energy company constructing windfarms all over Ireland and beyond. Others like Robert Hastings of the Swiss-based organisation Architecture Energy & Environment are more forthright. We need, said Hastings, 'to instil terror in people to make them reduce energy usage.'[19] In journalistic circles, this sort of thing used to be called The Good Lie; a propaganda device that argues that truth is contingent. If the storyteller believes that he or she can induce the desired response from the audience by spinning, then so be it. Scare stories and fear-mongering are the stock in trade of environmentalists that believe that the end justifies the means. Famously, the seminal Club of Rome report, 'The First Global Revolution' in 1991 said that 'in searching for a new enemy to unite us, we came up with the idea that pollution, the threat of global warming, water shortages, famine and the like would fit the bill. All these dangers are caused by human intervention ... The real enemy then is humanity itself.'[20]

### Fear-mongering

Commenting on Sir Nicholas Stern's much criticised, over-inflated warnings of global economic devastation if nothing is done to halt climate change, Bill McGuire, director of the Benfield Hazard Research Centre at University College London said that 'the scariest thing about the Stern report is that it may not be scary enough.'[21] Britain's ex-Environment Secretary, David Miliband agrees, and advocates that 'people *should* be scared',[22] which may not be the best way to build social solidarity at home. As a result, even the monarchy was depressed. Perceiving that 'economic progress was "upset-

[18]   Brian Wilson MP, 'All-Energy Conference', speech, Aberdeen, Wednesday, 21 May 2003
[19]   Austin Williams, 'Micro Aspirations', spiked-online, 30 September 2005
[20]   Club of Rome, 'The First Global Revolution', Pantheon Books, 1991, p 115
[21]   James Kirkup, 'Blair acts, as expert warns climate change could wreck economy', The Scotsman, 31 Oct 2006
[22]   David Miliband, 'Miliband fears on climate change', BBC News Online, www.bbc.co.uk, 27 September 2006

ting the whole balance of nature",[23] Prince Charles can only mutter that it is all 'terrifying, terrifying,'[24] but it takes the Americans to rack up the fear factor: American presidential hopeful, Barack Obama really stakes out the parameters of panic. He says:

> the tyranny of oil ... funds everything from the madrassas that plant the seeds of terror in young minds to the Sunni insurgents that attack our troops in Iraq. It corrupts budding democracies, and gives dictators from Venezuela to Iran the power to freely defy and threaten the international community. It even presents a target for Osama bin Laden.[25]

Presumably such talk is meant to be a sabre rattled in the face of middle-east leaders, a shake-down of Big Oil's tax breaks, or a warning to Russian president Vladimir Putin currently expanding the Sakhalin oil fields. But rhetorically it implies that energy restraint is a democratic duty. Energy profligacy logically becomes treachery. This is a corrosive path for politicians to follow. As Mike Hulme, director of the high profile Tyndall Centre for Climate Change Research says , presenting an issue as something 'which evokes fear and personal stress becomes a self-fulfilling prophesy.'[26]

Brian Hoskins, professor of meteorology at Reading University and a fellow of the Royal Society says that 'there has always been a conflict between social behaviour and selfish behaviour'. He continues: 'It's very sad, but I actually think that we might need a whole series of disasters in different countries before people make the connection.'[27] Comments on our energy future seem almost always to be premised on a bleak assessment of the present and with a shallow, condescending view of the public. The notion that we can transform the world for the better, for them is almost inherently contradictory. In their eyes, it is our folly to try to overcome natural barriers — to transform the world — after all, that has led us to what they see as this sorry pass. As sustainability advocates they often have to talk about 'the future' (since it is written into their bible, the Brundtland Report), but they are programmatically unable to speak positively about it. One of Lovelock's homilies to parents, for example, is guar-

[23] Prince Charles quoted in 'Charles: U.S. must lead on planet', cnn.com, 3 November 2005

[24] Prince Charles quoted in 'Geoffrey Lean: Hot October days. Deadly hurricanes. A shrinking ice cap. And a wobbling PM', The Independent, 6 November 2005

[25] Remarks of Senator Barack Obama to the Detroit Economic Club, Detroit, 07 May 2007

[26] Mike Hulme, 'Chaotic world of climate truth', BBC News, 4 November 2006

[27] Quoted in Lois Rogers, 'Climate change: Why we don't believe it', New Statesman, 23 April 2007

anteed to give kids nightmares: 'Make sure that your children's generation know that there is a future for them and for humanity,' he says. 'It will be bad and many will die but that is no reason for despair.'[28]

If these self-appointed moral minorities can frighten the public into using less energy, then they are convinced that it doesn't matter whether the methods used are inherently disingenuous or not; pillorying us, as they do, for our carbon-centric lifestyles (i.e. decent standard of living) and the 'devastating impact of continuing our energy-profligate lifestyles'[29] which are 'destroying the planet'.[30] Others take this logic even further and wish ill on us all. Using a kind of 'I-told-you-so' rhetoric — as a contemptuous wake up call — some environmentalists show an exasperated contempt for humanity. In his best-selling book, *The Revenge of Gaia*, James Lovelock recommends a metaphorical, and literal retreat to higher ground to avoid what he sees as a forthcoming flood from rising tides and refugees.

It seems that those who consider themselves to be concerned for the environment, cannot help but try to scapegoat others using thinly disguised attacks on other people's apparently profligate use of energy and resources. They want to safeguard against what they deem to be a threat to their way of life. Arch-controversialist, Simon Jenkins contemptuously suggests that 'it is the availability of cheap petrol and aviation fuel that has enabled the Chinese and Indians as well as the Americans and Europeans to deluge the atmosphere with filth.'[31] Indeed, the government's ex-chief scientific adviser notes that 'we've been having cheap energy for so long and people have just seen it as a resource that they can burn'.[32] I'm no scientist, but isn't that what fuel is for?

## Energy restraint

There is definitely more than a hint of survivalism in the growth of energy self-sufficiency. The editor of Environmental Building News calls our new energy-paranoid lifestyles 'Passive Survivability.'[33] 'If the oil's going to run out before the windfarms have been built,

[28]  James Lovelock, 'James Lovelock: You Ask The Questions', IndependentOnline, 14 August 2006
[29]  Mayer Hillman, 'How We Can Save The Planet', Penguin, 2004, p180
[30]  Mayer Hillman, 'How We Can Save The Planet', Penguin, 2004, p27
[31]  Simon Jenkins, 'Save the planet: tax the poor back onto their bicycles', The Sunday Times, 5 November 2006
[32]  Sir David King, quoted in Amanda Birch, Building Design, 5 April 2005, p18
[33]  Alex Wilson, editorial, Environmental Building News, December 2005

we'd better start learning how to cope without electricity', is how one journalist explains it.[34] Other motivations for this retreat into self-imposed darkness are many and varied, but George Monbiot argues that even though we have been 'brought up to believe that it is better to light a candle than to curse the darkness, we are now discovering that it is better to curse the darkness than to burn your house down'.[35] The house, you understand, is a metaphor for the earth. Geddit? (A sentiment echoed in Christopher Hitchens' idea that we are soon to witness 'the death of the species and the heat death of the universe.'[36]) It all ends up reinforcing a sense of hopeless isolation, made bearable by the artificial creation a community of other hopelessly isolated individuals busying themselves in CRAGs, no doubt, idling their days away with carbon calculators.

It's not just eco-worriers that believe that energy restraint is a 'good thing', it has actually entered the public, and corporate, psyche. Restraint is so pervasive that Shell, an oil company, is funding a UK National Curriculum 'Education for Sustainable Development' with the express intent that students 'can understand how to reduce personal energy use.'[37] Even Wal-Mart, the hate figure of most environmentalist campaigns, has a sustainability strategy that aims to reduce its carbon emissions to zero, focusing on renewables and zero waste.

With energy *use* seen as a problem by almost everyone, to varying degrees, energy *provision* is falling apart. Exciting projects like the world's first underwater tidal 'energy farm' off St David's peninsula; or the £14 billion tidal barrage along the Severn estuary are threatened by indecisive consultative processes; and nuclear power is haunted by the inability of successive governments to stridently argue for its benefits against over-stated public opposition (led by the unelected officers of Greenpeace). Thirty years after protesting about nuclear missiles, the massed ranks of aging rockers like Jackson Browne, Bonnie Raitt and Graham Nash have made another anti-nuclear album, this time against nuclear power.[38] Everything, but everything—from nuclear power to clean coal—is seen through the prism of carbon emissions which means that arguing for power

[34]   Louisa Pearson, 'Power to the people', Scotland on Sunday, 19 August 2007
[35]   George Monbiot, 'Mocking our dreams', The Guardian, 15 February 2005
[36]   Christopher Hitchens, 'God is not Great: The case against religion', Atlantic, 2007
[37]   Centre for Sustainable Energy, 'Energy Matters: National Curriculum Links', 2003
[38]   Bernie Woodall, '"No Nukes" stars reunite to fight nuclear power', Reuters, 11 Oct 2007

production and transmission in their own terms has become marginalised. If it doesn't tick the carbon constraint box, it must be harmful. And so, every debate becomes an exercise in self-justification, playing rather cynical games to 'prove' that one energy source is as morally legitimate as another. All the while, we waste more energy producing more bullshit reports, while energy provision stagnates.

Take one example: for the officials of Burgess Hill town council in West Sussex, the problem seemed straightforward enough. How could they maintain the free heat gain benefits from the sunlight streaming in from the window while reducing glare at their employees' desks? After setting up a committee, holding three meetings, several feasibility studies (included installing computer-controlled blinds with wind sensors to the outside of the office window and treating the glass with a solar reflective glaze), preparing a report and spending six months exploring the options with contractors, the council has decided on a way forward: it has moved the desks away from the window.[39] This story which appeared in The Daily Telegraph describes a system in thrall to environmentalism: whereby it is deemed important to reduce every sort of energy expenditure ... except our own physical expression of energy: human labour.

Environmentalists act as if natural systems provide 'free work',[40] i.e. energy for nothing. Solar power is one of the most often cited examples of energy provided without emissions or detrimental impacts. It is undoubtedly an 'abundant source of free energy'[41] but even that misunderstands that sunlight is nothing unless humans harness it. And sometimes, this human effort makes a mockery of the notion of labour-saving free work. Human exertion, human labour and human time spent on these relentless penny-pinching activities is automatically deemed to be worth it but actually, it is the drive to minimise the amount of human labour time embodied in a given resource that is the key to human progress. It is the minimisation of human effort, not external energy, that is the key to progress: the freeing up of labour so that humans can do other things. In India, for example, some commentators observe that 'there is no question that a developing country ought to look for labour-intensive

[39]  Stewart Payne, 'Council takes 6 months to come up with bright idea', The Daily Telegraph, 12 March 2002
[40]  Daniel E Williams, 'Sustainable Design: Ecology, Architecture and Planning', John Wiley & Sons, 2007, p16
[41]  David A. Crocker, Toby Linden, 'Ethics of Consumption: The Good Life, Justice, and Global Stewardship', Rowman and Littlefield, 1998, p33

solutions rather than capital-intensive ones.'[42] Even though this may seem economically commonsensical and environmentally benign, this attitude is a recipe for greater human suffering. The environmental lobby seem to have a sneaky regard for the cruel physical exertions of cheap labour. Fortunately real industrial energy manufacture and power generation are still being commissioned, but not as quickly as might otherwise be the case.

## Dropping out

In Manhattan, Colin and Michelle Beavan are another eco-couple trying to do their bit. They have turned off the electricity, play Scrabble in the dark, brush their teeth with baking powder, keep a wormery in the kitchen and refuse to use toilet paper. Unsurprisingly, Colin will be writing a book of his experiences, which presumably he will ship to bookshops on the back of a zero-carbon donkey. Called 'No-Impact Man' he wants it to be an example of how things could be in a sustainable future.[43] In Britain, there's Channel 4's flagship makeover programme 'Grand Designs' which featured Nigel and Karen Lowthrop's 'highly commendable' commitment to their self-sufficient way of life, having built a house that 'isn't connected to any mains utilities, including drains and sewers.' Another programme, 'Dumped' placed eleven people in a rubbish dump with no mains power supply. In London's Borough of Tower Hamlets, the poorest borough in Britain, the council gives tenants bags of 'micro-organisms, bran and molasses'[44] to mix with their rubbish to aid biodegradation, increase recycling and save energy.

There are many examples of carbon-constrained lifestyles — of people choosing to reduce their consumption of energy and opting out of what they characterise as a reliance on energy. As an editorial in The Independent put it, 'small actions such as putting on an extra sweater instead of turning up the heating … will help the planet.'[45] Undoubtedly, woolly jumper sales will increase given that the Financial Times describes how, 'for the first time in a thousand years

[42]   Darryl D'Monte, 'There's wealth in waste', InfoChange News and Features, www.infochangeindia.org, March 2007
[43]   Kim Ghattas, 'US family tries life without toilet paper', BBC News, 19 September, http://news.bbc.co.uk
[44]   Sophie Verhagen, 'The worm has turned', The Guardian, 30 June 2004
[45]   Julia Stephenson, 'Seeing The Green Light,' The Independent, 'Your Planet' supplement, 20 September 2005, p4

that there are more people moving into the Highlands than are moving out'[46] each coming for a slice of the simple, energy-lite life.

Nick Rosen is author of yet another personal testimony entitled *How to Live Off-Grid*, a book that promotes the right to live without mains water and electricity. He boasts that there are over 24,000 people in the UK opting to turn themselves off from the mains infrastructure. Not so long ago, the idea that a significant number of people had no running water, or who hadn't been connected to the mains in the first place, would have been a local and national scandal. Nowadays, Rosen et al, think it's a scandal that so many of us are hooked up to it.

Actually, in 21st century Britain, there are still around 2.8 million, mainly rural households, that are still not connected to the mains network (many of them in Cornwall). The small campaigning group National Energy Action, who want to extend energy provision, describes this situation as 'a significant problem'[47] but, for an increasing minority of carbon critics, this shocking energy deficit is characterised as some kind of liberation. Rosen, who admits to being an off-grid 'lifestyle tourist' who relishes 'creating (his) own Noah's Ark,'[48] says that his style of self-sufficiency 'is about escaping the rat race, bucking the system, and virtually disappearing—becoming untraceable.' [49] His website states that 'two billion worldwide are living without mains power, water or phone ... (and) many of those people are happy as they are.'[50] Happiness may undoubtedly be the state of mind of the 31,000 Glastonbury tent dwellers who venture off-grid for one-week-a-year—it could also be true for the 10,000 barge-dwellers able to afford the mooring fees on Britain's canals, or weekend holiday-homers—but for the remainder of those two billion, happiness doesn't come into it. Those billions of people to which he refers, are unconnected to mains services in developing countries: they have not opted out, they just haven't been offered the chance to opt in.

The fact is that less than a third of India's homes have a toilet and fewer than 50 per cent of its 500,000 villages are connected to the electricity grid,[51] and this should be viewed for what it is—a global out-

[46]  Professor James Hunter quoted in Rob Blackhurst, 'The hills are alive...', Financial Times, 12 January 2008
[47]  Martha Buckley, 'Rural struggle without mains gas', BBC News, 25 October 2006
[48]  Anna Shepard, 'Pulling the plug on modern life,' The Times, 2 June 2007.
[49]  Nick Rosen, summary to 'All Planned Out' conference, 18 May 2007
[50]  http://www.off-grid.net/index.php
[51]  George Arney, 'India Rising' World Agenda, BBC World Service

rage. In Mumbai alone, some '125, 000 villages still have no electricity and roughly 23 million households, including some in cities, live without any electrical power.'[52] What these people want is development without the 'sustainable' prefix. The energy deficit faced by many in the world is nothing other than a disgrace, but still the condescending 'back-to-nature' romantics, or sustainability devotees in the West continue to endorse what they see as its charming simplicity; what respected environmentalist Amory Lovins calls 'liv(ing) with more elegant frugality.'[53] The fact that Rosen et al suggest that doing without can be 'fun', or even liberating, is even more patronising. Energy opting out, sums up the decadent mood of our times.

### Search for meaning

There is something profoundly disturbing going on in this clamour to opt out. It represents a palpable crisis of meaning among some sections of the public in the West who would prefer to play no part in mainstream modern society. US actor Sean Penn says 'I've always felt like I love mankind, the problem I have is with man.'[54] His latest movie 'Into the Wild' is the true story of a youngster who decides to live and die in the great American wilderness. More and more, this kind of social absenteeism is interpreted as a worthy adventure, and as such empty gestures are imbued with meaning. Environmental writer, John Laumer, describes off-grid living as 'a symbolic act of rebellion for counterculture members wanting to disconnect from high-consumption society.'[55] Obviously, when you read of examples of the Australian man who married his TV because it was the thing he loved the most, then even the most hard-bitten materialist has to recognise that there is obviously something wrong with the over-celebration of consumer products.[56] However this is, as they say, is an extreme example.

For Laumer though, getting out of the technological rat-race reflects a desire for a pioneering spirit. He harks back to the days when people sought challenges rather than the modern comforts of

[52] Kalpana Sarma, 'Fuelling the fire', New Statesman, 6 August 2007, p31
[53] Ernst Ulrich Weizsäcker, Amory B. Lovins, L. Hunter Lovins, 'Factor Four: Doubling Wealth, Halving Resource Use—A Report to the Club of Rome', Earthscan, 1998, p78
[54] Sean Penn quoted in Ravi Somaiya, 'Sean Penn: Mr Congeniality', Daily Telegraph, 14 October 2007
[55] John Laumer, 'Living Off-Grid – 3 years in the Life of a New Pioneer', Treehugger. 19 April 2005, www.treehugger.com
[56] Anthony Dunne and Fiona Raby, 'Design Noir: The Secret Life of Electronic Objects', August/ Birkhauser, 2001, p8

urban life. For some people today, life has no challenges, no meaning, and this type of 'lonesome cowboy' nostalgia represents an
ironic craving for a society of active subjects rather than passive
objects. Many of those opting out are simply contemptuous of modern political life and want to reforge new challenges. Recognising
that contemporary life is fearful of the future, some seek to immerse
themselves in virtual reality hardships of the past. Contestants on
BBC Wales' reality TV series 'Coal House', for example, who will
live as a typical early 20th century mining family in Blaenavon, look
forward to renouncing modernity. The show's producer says that 'as
a typical 21st century family they will have to come to terms with life
lacking the luxuries we take for granted in our modern lives. All
traces of creature comforts will be removed from the house. There
will be no TV, PC, washing machine or microwave oven. They will
have to live without the benefit of central heating and hot running
water. Dad will have to bath in the front of an open fire or outside in
the back yard.'[57] In this scenario, the material comforts of modern
Western societies are portrayed as devoid of real substance, while
the past is reinvented as 'real living'. He forgets that the grinding
poverty of the past is what the 20th century mining family was trying to escape. This contemporary, self-indulgent, post-modern angst
is an insult to the material progress made over the last 100 years
because there are still plenty of intellectual and material improvements for which to strive, but at every turn, we are told that the
energy necessary to attain them is unsustainable.

Whereas many adults in the past endured hardship to create a
better society and material conditions for their children, so today we
hear nothing but the mantra that whatever we do, ours is the first
generation that will leave he world in a worse state for our children.[58]
It's no wonder that we seek solace in the past rather than strive to
create a dynamic engagement with the present. But the idea that we
disengage from society, the better to learn how to create a more
engaged society, is a contradiction in terms.

Living off-grid is, in fact, simply a retreat. It is nothing more than
an evasion from meaningful civic engagement — with people giving
up on the struggle for improvements. If they want more civic participation by seeking the simple fragmented life, they are actually
undermining the very thing that they seek to create. Even Tom and

[57]  Colin Davies quoted in 'Coal Reality TV contestants hunt', BBC News Online, 12
      March 2007, www.bbc.co.uk
[58]  Former senator John Edwards quoted in Ahra Cho, 'John Edwards Speaks At
      Dartmouth', CBS News, Nov 13, 2007

Barbara's sphere of influence in BBC's hit 70s sit-com 'The Good Life', the programme of two down-sizing Londoners living off their domestic allotment, amounted to nothing more than social dislocation; with human contact nothing more than occasional chats with the neighbours.

Opting out of energy provision is actually a metaphor for social and political disengagement. Ironically, for the self-satisfied, down-sizing, chattering classes of middle England, opting out is being presented as a meaningful political statement. Whereas, in the past it was generally assumed that you had to get involved to change things, nowadays it seems, you can change things by doing nothing at all. It is the ideal message for today's non-political age. Instead of standing outside the tent pissing in, or standing inside the tent pissing out, in this scenario, everyone's simply pissing off. Funnily enough, given that the national political scene is as un-engaging as it is, and with UK's parliamentary leadership increasingly introspective and self-absorbed, it's hardly any wonder that the polity is disengaged. The British energy strategy for the 21st century, for instance, includes Prime Minister Gordon Brown's pledge to ban plastic bags, eradicating 'short-life electric bulbs' and 'eliminating standby'.[59] Even his curious grammatical attempt at conveying gravitas can't cover up the fact that the gesture politics of sustainability have taken over from meaningful engagement. At the 2007 Liberal Democrats' annual conference in Brighton, delegates opted out of air conditioning in the main hall to save energy. The Labour Party conference has decided to phase out light bulbs. And Tory leader David Cameron famously has a wind turbine on his roof to reduce reliance on the national grid. But whether it's doing without altogether, or whether it's some ridiculous party political stunt, it is fashionable to pretend that reduced energy consumption is some kind of positive political engagement.

Nowadays, energy-saving doesn't mean building more efficient power-stations; it doesn't even mean producing energy locally to minimise distribution inefficiencies. It means recycling—sucking the last remnants of embodied energy out of an already existing product. This is surely the low-point of the politics of energy provision. A typical high point of political intrigue seems to be the front page news that the then Environment Minister Ben Bradshaw had 'blatantly broken his own rules by putting recyclable waste in with

[59] 'Homes must be greener, says Brown', BBC News, 12 March 2007

his general rubbish.'[60] After rummaging through Bradshaw's bins, the press could reveal that 13—yes, 13—items were found that should have been put in some other container for recycling. This is about as inconsequential as politics gets. If this is the 'big political idea' then it's no wonder that people are fed up. But with no clear belief in a bolder vision, and with no-one confronting the dogmatic stranglehold of environmentalism, these petty issues are held up to be the only framework for debate. But there are other ways of doing things.

### Energy innovation

As we will see in Chapter 5, while the UK pontificates, China imported 165 million tonnes of oil (in 2006) and is expected to account for 59 per cent of global oil supply use by 2015. But, without making a song and dance about it, it has also imposed a requirement that power companies generate a tenth of their electricity from renewable sources by 2010 and a fifth by 2020. It is already the world's leading user of solar power for water heating[61] and accounts for 80 per cent of the world's thermal photovoltaic market with 65 million $m^2$ of solar panels already installed on rooftops and 90 per cent of Beijing's street lamps are now powered by solar.

China's targets call for expanding wind power almost as much as nuclear energy over the next 15 years. It has required certain important 'state-owned enterprises and provincial governors to sign contracts pledging to reduce energy consumed relative to economic growth by 20 per cent over five years.'[62] But this sits in the context of producing 2.3 billion tonnes of coal in 2006. China recognises that the priority is to keep the wheels of industry turning, and so 'renewables', for them, have not yet become a code word for restraint in the way that it has in the West. In fact, China's biggest renewables project, the Three-Gorges dam is one of the modern masterpieces of the modern age. Characteristically, Western environmental campaigners seldom praise this environmental wonder, preferring instead to suggest that it is environmentally 'unsustainable'. One scientist spent six whole weeks to declare that the dam

[60]  Martin Beckford, 'Environment minister caught out breaking own recycling rules,' Mail on Sunday, 28 October 2006
[61]  Jiahua Pan, vice president, Chinese Society for Ecological Economists, 'China is part of the world and we are all earth citizen,' in 'Greening the Dragon: China's search for a sustainable future', Green Futures Special Issue, 2006, p4
[62]  Shai Oster, 'China Tilts Green', The Wall Street Journal, 13 February 2007

was culpable in the extinction of the Yangste River dolphin.[63] Like it or not, the Chinese have bigger fish to fry. While there are undoubtedly environmental and social issues to address, the dam will produce 84.7 billion kilowatt hours of electricity annually, equivalent to burning 40 million tons of coal.

In the same way that sustainable energy proponents cannot bring themselves to endorse Iran's ambitious, zero-carbon plans for nuclear power, their sour grapes towards China's Three Gorges dam shows that they are primarily concerned with exporting a conformist ideology of restraint and a capitulation to nature, than with the progressive ambition for efficient, useful and essential universal provision for the benefit of a modernising society. India already leads China in wind power, and they too are keen on keeping the wheels of industry going with conventional fossil fuel based resources, while the renewable market can expand.

The mechanics of energy production isn't the issue; it's sustainability's lack of ambition to realise them that is the problem. This is no more clearly summed up than in the cautious Western support for energy restraint and microgeneration. There's nothing wrong with a solar panel, you understand — that is simply a piece of technology — but it is a symbol of a retreat from a belief in the progressive nature of universal supply, over and above personal self-generation. Contrast the UK's infatuation with microprojects with real expressions of innovative ambition today: Japan, for example, states that, whereas America's ambitions were historically realised by going towards the stars, Japan will drill downwards to meet its growing energy needs. With no natural fuel resources of its own, it is tunnelling up to 17 km into the earth's crust to tap into limitless geothermal heat sinks. Russia has ambitions to mine the moon for helium-3. China is looking to exploit its huge reserves of under-sea combustible ice. Each example, wonderfully, creatively exploits natural resources for mankind's benefit. While all that exciting stuff is going on, in 2004, prime minister Tony Blair spoke of Britain's future energy policy. He had, he said, 'a healthy instinct that if we upset the balance of nature, we are in all probability going to suffer a reaction.'[64]

This risk-averse attitude is stifling exploration and leading to ever-lower ambitions. Getting involved in politics as it presents

[63] Ian Sample, 'Yangtze river dolphin driven to extinction', The Guardian, 8 August 2007

[64] Tony Blair, 'PM's speech on climate change', www.number10.gov.uk, 14 September 2004,

itself today, is by turns boring, confusing and hopeless, all reflected in the fact that the parameters of political dialogue seem to begin and end with carbon counting and climate change. It's no wonder that people want to switch off more than just their standbys.

By definition, opting out en masse represents a tacit collapse of identification with social life and the political agenda. It is at odds with the collectivised concept of the body-politick. The sustainability conceit, as we have seen, is that the mere process of opting out is meant to be a political act intended to transform society into more sustainable energy behaviour. However, with no real belief in the transformative capacity of society, nor any real desire to engage in meaningful, progressive transformative change (after all, all change is automatically assumed to have negative consequences for future generations) — then the political act is one of defeat. This is the very kernel of political nihilism. Given the terrible consequences facing society and global politics more generally, it is ironic that political disengagement is increasingly being given official sanction. As one commentator notes, 'we could say that the eco-lobby has become the militant arm of the government's own attack on energy consumption.'[65] It is therefore essential that this fragmentation into anti-social, self-sufficiency be combated to be replaced by a progressive vision of universal supply. We need to celebrate the fact that the automatic, unthinking ability to alter our relationship with nature at the flick of a power switch, is as profound an achievement as is the actual manufacture and transfer of energy down the power lines.

Individuals are not to blame for using too much energy; rather the powers that be are responsible for not providing enough. If that provision can be supplied more efficiently, cheaply and sensitively then that is a good thing (and reflects the progressive reality of the way energy supply has improved throughout history). We should reject the call to reduce our ambitions and instead increase supply in order to meet the world's real energy deficit. Demanding more energy to create a better world should be our starting point.

[65]   Dave Perks, 'Drax protestors: Radicals for austerity,' spiked-online, 6 December 2006, www.spiked-online.com

CHAPTER 3

# THE LIMIT-SETTERS

*Architecture's loss of humanity*

The American Institute of Architects currently identifies sustain-ability 'as the most important change affecting the future of the profession'.[1] In Britain, Alex Michaelis, the eco-architect to opposi-tion leader David Cameron, predicts that 'sustainability is going to be the most important word in architecture in the next 20 years.'[2] Speaking on the theme of urban design, Prince Charles, says that the 'one of the greatest challenges we face today is that of sustainability.' They are undoubtedly right. But rather than that being a good thing, it is an un-mitigated disaster. Unless something is done, the retro-gressive impulse contained within sustainability is going to be the death of architecture.

Since time immemorial, individual architects have wanted to change the world for the better, depending on their particular world view, and architecture reflected and generated a robust political debate about its ability and desirability to foment such a change. Le Corbusier's Modernist edifices for the new city of Chandigarh in post-colonial India, represented democracy and included a futuris-tic 'Museum of Knowledge', all designed as a 'unique symbol of progressive aspirations'.[3] Oscar Neimeyer's plans for Brazilia were designed to encompass '50 years of progress in five'. The Sixties radicals, Archigram, believed that 'an architecture based on mobil-

[1]  The American Institute of Architects, 'Environment/ Sustainability', www.aia.org (accessed 11 January 2008)
[2]  Alex Michaelis quoted in Stuart Jeffries, 'The renovator', The Guardian, 15 July 2006
[3]  'Urban and Architectural Work of Le Corbusier in Chandigarh', Department of Tourism, Chandigarh Administration 23 October 2006

ity and malleability could set people free.'[4] Nowhere today do we hear architects profess such a human-centred ambition; nor to we often hear of contemporary architects with such progressive aspirations. Gone are the days of visionary urbanists like New York's Robert Moses, for example:

> The city is endlessly fascinating, and that is why so many families gravitate to population centers, why suburbs continue to be suburbs and satellites, why the vast hinterland may talk against the big town, deprecate and deplore it, minimise its attractions, but somehow can't keep away from it, why our domestic critics carp, groan, crock, vent their spleen but are unable to tear themselves away … why, in spite of analogies with Babylon and Babel, traffic and other congestion, it will never be dispersed, decentralised and abandoned.[5]

Love these comments or hate them, that's not the point: the vision is the thing. Where once these and other architects had a belief that they could construct a new world, now they want to limit construction *to reduce* their effect on the world. Where once they wanted to maximise their impact, today they want to minimise it. So no-one bats an eyelid when Lord Rogers, architectural adviser the London mayor, says that 'cities have become parasites on the landscape.'[6]

How can a profession that builds structures reconcile itself with such a contemporary philosophy of low or zero growth? How does architecture — one of the most humane of the liberal arts — fit into the misanthropic public dialogue exemplified by commentators like John Gray who compares humanity to 'slime mould'; or that kindly old James Lovelock, who complains that the world is suffering a 'plague of people.' With sustainability as a dinner-party euphemism for Malthusianism, architecture has not risen to the challenge to defend human creativity. In this all-pervasive moral onslaught, architecture will not be able to maintain the illusion of a creative profession if it continues to refuse to challenge the widespread belief that human actions are inherently or inevitably destructive. For the moment, architects see themselves engaged in damage limitation. This is a shameful way to see one of the most creative of all the professions.

Australian Pritzker Prize-winning architect, Glenn Murcutt made a name for himself with the borrowed aboriginal saying that he

[4]   Exhibition notes, 'Archigram Architects (1961-1974)', Design Museum, 2005
[5]   Robert Moses, quoted in ed Hilary Ballon and Kenneth T Jackson, 'Robert Moses and the Modern City: The Transformation of New York,' WW Norton & Co, 2007, p96
[6]   Richard Rogers, 'Cities for a Small Planet', Faber and Faber, 1997, p27

wants to 'touch the earth lightly'. It is now regurgitated by everyone from Japan's Shigeru Ban to Professor Richard Horden[7] (designer of the minimal impact micro-compact home) to the Commonwealth Association of Architects. One American architectural firm, EDAW, has a Director of Ecology, who notes that the architectural project should be to 'move towards life within natural limits'.[8] Working 'with the grain of nature'[9] has taken over from imposing one's vision on nature. A new film 'Last Call for Planet Earth' by Jacques Allard encourages architects to '(work) differently in order to build differently and do everything in order to protect our vulnerable environment.'

To put it mildly, this mentality doesn't lead to the most progressive appreciation of the creative impulses of architecture. What it does do, is imply that architecture should be reined in to whatever arbitrary limit we ascribe to nature. Accepting it can only constrain architectural ambition and lead to a presumption that those built environment practitioners who don't play eco-ball, are in some way morally culpable for nature's despoliation. So the commonplace assumption underlying even the most anodyne architectural discussions is that human activity causes harm and should be reined in to suit whatever nature's limits will allow. Janine Benyus, author of the architecturally influential 'Biomimicry' advocates that we should 'respect nature's limits'[10] and, in many ways it is this sort of assumption that has resulted in a crisis in the architectural profession, although many may not recognize it.

Some pussyfoot around in the search for the 'least damaging way to erect a house'[11]. William McDonough has been commissioned by Fortune magazine to design a skyscraper that has 'a 100 per cent positive impact on people and place … (and) would do just about everything a tree can do except self-replicate'.[12] One designer actually wills the destruction of her own work saying that a 'straw-bale house with a timber frame and lime render will eventually return to nature, but the plastic and concrete in conventional houses won't

[7]   Quoted in Jon Cockle, Ping Magazine, Tokyo, www.pingmap.jp, 5 Sep 2005
[8]   Gary Grant, 'Green roofs and facades', HIS BRE Press, 2006, p ix
[9]   Prince Charles, 'Respect the Earth: 6: A Royal View', BBC Reith Lectures, 2000
[10]  Janine M Benyus, 'Biomimicry: Innovation Inspired by Nature', Quill (William Morrow), 1997, p 46
[11]  Yenna Chan, Sustainable Environments', Rockpool Publishers, 2007, p14
[12]  William McDonough quoted in Press Release, 'Design visionary to present futuristic "building for today" at Abu Dhabi world future energy summit', World Future Energy Summit, 7 January 2008

biodegrade.'[13] Mayer Hillman, environmentalist and author of 'How we can save the planet' has taken it to its logical conclusion having given up his early career as an architect because he couldn't reconcile himself to ruining the countryside. He may be an extreme example, but increasingly, this is the alienated context that architects find themselves in. Speaking of her low carbon footprint, architect, Lucy Pedler, who is also a ClimateCare trainer, says: 'Jumping on a plane should be an architect's last option. At my firm ... we don't do any jobs abroad.'[14] Only under the label of sustainability can one's lack of an international portfolio be used as a badge of honour.

Sustainability's misanthropic mindset affects the simplest ideas, even notionally environmental ones. A 'green roof,' for example, is the idea of transforming otherwise vacant roofscapes into pastures by covering them with soil and planting grasses and shrubs, etc. Visions of office staff lazing on freshly mown grass, several storeys in the air, are definitely appealing and it seems like a sensible move to utilise wasted space and bring a little bit of the country air into the city. However, such is the fanaticism for biodiversity that roofs are now regularly given over to invertebrates and songbirds at the expense of humans. Almost by definition, if nature is being pro-tected, human access to those areas — especially since man is indicted in the negative effects on nature — must be restricted. Suddenly, the lazy, grass-roofed parkland for human enjoyment has turned into a 'haven for wildlife'[15] and a no-go area for people.

### Ceding to nature

With half the world's population living in urban areas, there is clearly no sense of exhilaration in the increasing urbanisation of a planet for six, seven or eight billion people, and more. Such a moment in history demands maximum engagement, but architec-ture has become paralysed in its acceptance of the orthodoxy that humanity is a problem and nature is sacrosanct. Nowhere is the paralysis better exemplified than New Orleans, where the urgency of rebuilding a new city is held back by doubts about the legitimacy

[13]  Barbara Jones, founder, Amazon Nails, quoted in Jenny Knight, 'America inspires Yorkshire to create houses of straw', The Times Focus Report, 30 March 2007

[14]  Karen Glaser, 'How green is your footprint?', Building Design, May 18th 2007, p21

[15]  Dusty Gedge, Nigel Dunnet, Gary Grant and Richard Jones, 'Living Roofs', Natural England, 2007

in building near 'fragile areas'[16] at all. Three years on from Hurricane Katrina, and displaced residents continue to live in trailer parks.

Across the globe, from Bangladesh to The Netherlands to London's Thames Gateway, instead of attempting to overcome natural barriers (a mindset which seems to have exemplified previous generations of architects and sums up the social role of architecture), we now have the concept of 'managed retreat'.[17] If architects accept the principle that 'nature knows best' they may as well give up. To a certain extent they already have. The (lack of a) response to Hurricane Katrina is a good case in point.

Not to be too blasé about it, 150 miles of prime New Orleans' development land became available after the devastation. What was remarkable was that 'progressive' architects, loosely defined as those leading architects regularly seen clamouring for inclusion in most international competitions — were noticeable by their absence. In effect, architects lost their nerve. The unwillingness of such leading progressive architects to engage with this historic redevelopment challenge has cleared the way for New Urbanism — the reactionary, happy-clappy architectural movement for urban stasis — to fill the void.

New Urbanism gave us the town of Seaside in Florida (best known in Britain as the picket-fenced setting for 'The Truman Show') and Disney's wholesome urban paradise, Celebration (Celebration, ironically, was built on swampland). New Urbanism primarily advocates close-knit communities based on 'neighbourhoods (that are) compact, pedestrian-friendly, and mixed-use (which) bring diverse ages, races, and incomes into daily interaction, strengthening the personal and civic bonds essential to an authentic community.'[18] Unfortunately, New Urbanism tends to maintain its community values through an 'urban policy agenda of proscriptive practices and social restraint'.[19] A more fundamental criticism is that New Urbanism makes a virtue of allowing itself to be dictated to by social norms and natural topography. In each case, human agency is devalued.

By contrast, when Chicago flooded in the mid 19th century, the solution was to lift the city up to five metres into the air, out of harm's

[16]  June Arney, 'Flirting with disaster', Baltimore Sun, 11 September 2005
[17]  Mark A. Kulp, Duncan M. FitzGerald, Shea Penland, 'The Impact of Hurricanes Katrina and Rita in Louisiana: America's Coasts Under Siege,' The Geological Society of America, The Pontchartrain Institute of Environmental Studies, University of New Orleans, February 2006
[18]  Charter for the New Urbanism,http://www.newurbanism.org/pages/532096/
[19]  Austin Williams, 'New Orleans, New Urbanism', Future Cities Project, www.futurecities.org.uk, 9 February 2006

way. Famously there are reports of the Tremont Hotel, a six-story building, being jacked up while the guests occupied their rooms. This was one of the most amazing engineering feats of modern times, a solution that virtually eliminated future flood risk. 150 years later, the dominant reaction to a similar threat in New Orleans has been to suggest that 'some areas should, in effect, be given up'.[20] This meta-phorical fear of *la Deluge* is almost contagious. In Adrian Geuze's 2005 Rotterdam Architecture Biennale the theme was 'The Flood' and Peter Edidin of the New York Times said that 'the Netherlands has strategically begun to uncreate itself'[21] with contributors speaking of the need to cede land to the sea, turning back 700 years of land recla-mation. The winner of the History Channel's 'City of the Future' com-petition 'shows New York's street grid taken under floods of biblical proportions.[22] Two hundred years ago, the founders of New Orleans dared use the motto, 'built where God never intended a city to be built.' Nowadays, there is a cowardly perception that nature, rather than god, never intended man to settle there. And rather than display the same resistance of old, they are preparing to head for the hills. The hurricane, in some people's eyes, was retribution for man's folly. Anywhere in the world, sea level fluctuations are now automatically interpreted as punishment for daring to build in coastal regions.

## Carbon constraints

Strangely though, the architecture of limits is a growth industry. Crystal ball-gazing, eco-author, Sue Roaf argues that 'everyone needs to "future proof" themselves against what lies ahead'[23] as if, whatever it is, it's bound to be bad. This precautionary approach is derived from 1992 Rio Declaration which states: 'where there are threats of serious or irreversible damage, lack of full scientific cer-tainty shall not be used as a reason for postponing cost-effective measures to prevent environmental degradation.'[24] International architect Ken Yeang says 'we must secure commitment at the high-

[20]  Lord Robert May, president of the Royal Society, 'Threats to Tomorrow's World', Anniversary Address, Royal Society, 2005
[21]  Quoted in Austin Williams, 'Floating Architecture', The Architects' Journal, 16 February 2006
[22]  Scott Geiger, ARO quoted in Samantha Topol, 'Waterworlds', The Architect's Newspaper, 11 December 2006.
[23]  Sue Roaf in Sue Roaf, Manuel Fuentes, Stephanie Thomas, 'Eco-Homes', 3rd edition, Architectural Press, 2006, p5
[24]  United Nations, 'Report Of The United Nations Conference on Environment and Development' (Rio De Janeiro, 3-14 June 1992): Annex I, Rio Declaration on Environment and Development', Principle 15, 12 August 1992

est level in order to make our cities green, or this millennium will be our last'.[25] It falls to John Reader, in his useful book *Cities*, to point out that an 'unrelenting emphasis on the negative aspects of environmental issues creates a sense of helpless inertia.'[26]

Unfortunately, aside from a few notable exceptions, this inertia completely dominates architecture, opening the door for a remarkable number of bodies, many unelected, to influence how, where — and whether — we build. Rules, regulations and guidelines which may have lain fallow in the bottom drawer of council offices for years are now being dusted off and set in stone as the standards to which local authorities, designers and clients are now obliged to comply.

In 2000 in the UK, Nottingham City Council put itself on the map with its Declaration on Climate Change, urging other councils to make a public commitment to the delivery of carbon reduction programmes. This was trumped by the Merton Rule, the 10 per cent renewables policy which has been described (by Merton Council) as a 'groundbreaking planning policy'. The Joseph Rowntree Trust has the Lifetime Homes Initiative which, in the name of sustainability, encourages people to stay in the same home for life. These non-statutory tiers of bureaucracy have a disproportionate influence on the practice of architecture and urban design. But there are many others. From WWF's One Million Sustainable Homes initiative to BioRegional's Zero Carbon strategy, architects are regularly brow-beaten by officialdom into compliance.

This green mire that architecture finds itself in today can only get worse unless it begins to break free of the low aspirational, anti-progressive, sanctimonious, petty-minded, misanthropic miserablism that sustainability represents. When, as an example, Anjana Ahuja, the science correspondent of The Times can report that 'the worst mistake in the history of the human race, let alone Britain, was the replacement of hunter-gathering by agriculture, which fuelled rapid population growth, urbanisation and disease'[27] where is the response from architects daring to advocate 'development' — without prefixes — as a way out? Consequently, at the very time that it is enjoying a resurgence in the media and in popular opinion, architecture has actually managed to reduce itself to nothing more than a

[25]  Ken Yeang quoted in Max Thompson, 'Ken Yeang sounds Eco-warning', Architects Journal Architects' Journal, 23 November 2007

[26]  John Reader, 'Cities', William Heinemann, 2004

[27]  Anjana Ahuja quoted on Danny Finklestein, Comment Central, 'The greatest mistake in British history', The Times, 7 February 2008, timesonline.typepad.com/

sustainability index, an environmental impact assessment and a carbon calculator.

Practically all architectural debate now centres on zero emissions and environmental auditing: from green roofs to brownfields; from no-car housing to solar panels; from urban compaction to microflats; from mud bricks to local labour, from Eco-Homes to HIPs.[28] Carbon reduction is king but no-one really knows what it all means. The government states that it is committed to a '20 per cent reduction in carbon dioxide emissions on 1990 levels by 2010.' Meanwhile, the Royal Commission on Environmental Pollution reports that the UK needs to achieve a 60 per cent reduction in $CO_2$ emissions by 2050'. Al Gore says it has to be 90 per cent by 2050. The Green Party says 90 per cent by 2030. Take your pick. In such a morally-charged debate, scientific and statistical clarity is of secondary importance, I guess. Within these totals, houses are deemed to be responsible for a hefty proportion of total carbon emissions and an obvious place to start the programme of reductions. Depending on whom you believe, the housing sector causes 27 per cent (Energy Savings Trust) of total carbon emissions in the UK, or 30 per cent (National Statistics Office), or 'almost 59 per cent of the UK's building-related carbon output'.[29] In reality, of course, houses and their occupants produce hardly any $CO_2$ at all, the vast amount of it coming from industry and energy generating plants. But let's not have facts stand in the way of a moralistic assault on individuals who dare to turn up their thermostats instead of donning a thick woollen jumper at home.

It's no wonder that architects—that is, commercially motivated businessmen and women—are jumping on the bandwagon when Paul Hyett the ex-president of the Royal Institute of British Architects (RIBA) says that 'if sustainable design isn't a moral imperative, what is?' Architects need to comply or be portrayed amongst their peers—and by default, their prospective clients—as 'immoral.' Thus more and more architects find themselves caught up in nonsensical environmental claims-making. Just because buildings are blamed—however inaccurately—for carbon emissions, energy profligacy or merely as a blot on the landscape, architects are becoming polarised into adopting either the role of guilt-ridden apologists or eco-zealots. At every turn, the very thing that architects do is being cited as inherently harmful. Instead of rejecting this insulting parody of the

[28]  A 'HIP' is a Home Information Pack (Department of Communities and Local Government), 2007

[29]  Davis Langdon & Everest, Oscar Faber, 'Building Regulations—Cost model', Building, November 2001, issue 48

architects' role, most believe that they have to adapt, and work within its limitations. Allison Connick of major British developers CB Richard Ellis claims to specify everything from 'sustainable furniture, through to sustainable carpets.'[30] British architects Wilkinson Eyre claimed 'socially sustainable' credentials for its Stirling Prize-winning Gateshead Millennium Bridge because it joined two 'communities', previously separated by the river (an elementary requirement for a bridge, I would have thought). Timber, in itself, is now said to be 'ethical.'[31] These 'sustainability' claims tend not to be cynical but merely pragmatic — after all there is no other prism through which architects allow themselves to see the world and therefore they get shoe-horned into this framework. But it's about time that the profession stopped celebrating the need for limits and rediscovered their critical faculties and creative ambitions.

Even tall buildings are now defended in terms of the minimal amount of land area they take up; energy they use; or carbon they emit. As a result, mainstream architecture finds itself hiding behind climate chaos or community consensus to justify itself. Where once architects revelled in stamping their vision on the world, now they make excuses for the size of their footprint.

Too many have signed up to the Faustian pact which says that 'sustainable architecture' is unquestionably good; and 'good architecture' is inherently sustainable. From this supine formulation, judgements about the credentials of architects and their architecture need only be justified against the latest sustainability indicator; benchmarked against an energy reduction target; or self-audited against one of the many hundreds of cod ecological indices.

Leading American architectural journalist, Witold Rybczynski claims that there are two high profile buildings vying for the honour of being labelled Manhattan's first green skyscraper. One is Foster & Partners' Hearst Building, a facetted 42-storey office on top of Joseph Urban's original Art Deco block. It is deemed appropriate for consideration into the sustainability fold because, says Rybczynski, it has been engineered to use 20 per cent less structural steel. Notwithstanding the slight desperation in this arbitrary determinant of sustainability, it begs the question: what self-respecting engineer would have designed it with twenty percent *more* steel than was

[30] Allison Connick, Director of Safety and Environment at CB Richard Ellis, 'ISO14001', The Architects' Channel, NBS Broadcast (previously The Einstein Network), www.nbs.com
[31] Gary Ramsay, 'Timber — the gold standard', Sustain magazine, volume 8 issue 06, 2007, p45

thought to be necessary for the design parameters of the project. This appropriation of everyday practices in order to rebrand them with an environmental prefix is galling. Over the years there has been a gradual improvement in structural efficiency and in the ability to realise that efficiency. This has nothing to do with overt eco-considerations, even though there may be some environmental by-products.

The real fact is that the engineer did a 20 per cent better job in terms of saving his client money, which is a hallmark of a noble, professional approach that one would expect on a scheme of this magnitude and profile. But in the world of environmental sustainability that is too simplistic — and too unbelievable. That can't possibly be the reason: design choices, they assume, *must* be governed by sustainability quotas. It seems that for an avowedly ethical philosophy, sustainability seems to have, at its heart, a very shallow appreciation of people's motivations.

Actually, achieving more with less has always been a badge of honour for architects. Comparing two equivalent buildings, where one has been designed with more resources, it is usually the one using fewer materials that will elicit the plaudits, reflecting an understandable appreciation of imaginative creativity and efficient use of materials. The problem is when this becomes a principle. The first criteria in the Waste & Resources Action Programme (WRAP) encourages 'using less material'.[32] Even though Buckminster Fuller coined the phrase 'ephemeralisation'[33] fifty years ago as the concept of doing more with less, he still used that as a starting point for doing yet more. That is not the premise today. Architects are now enjoined to use limited resources 'imaginatively'. Today, not only do they not realise that they are confined, but, because there is no alternative, no criticism and no debate, architects seem to find solace in this restricted universe.

### Green default

The second building considered as the contender for Manhattan's green crown is the 52-storey 7 WTC designed by commercial architectural practice Skidmore, Owings & Merrill. Apparently, it gains its eco-credentials 'by using highly transparent glass (to increase daylighting).'[34] Clearly, the desperation to claim ecological creden-

[32]  www.wrap.org.uk
[33]  J Baldwin, 'Bucky Works: Buckminster Fuller's Ideas for Today', John Wiley & Sons, 1996
[34]  Witold Rybczynski,' Green Unseen: Environmentally Friendly Buildings Don't Need To Look Like Cheese Wedges', Slate, 16 July 2007

tials has caused erstwhile sensible commentators to lose a sense of perspective. What, in the past we might have labelled 'hogwash', we now know as 'greenwash'.

Greenwash is defined as the process of people 'portraying themselves and their causes as pro-environmental even when they are not'[35] or as 'disinformation disseminated by an organisation so as to present an environmentally responsible public image.'[36] So an accusation of green hypocrisy only reveals that someone is not doing something that they ought to. It is not really a criticism of the thing itself; it's a criticism of failing to live up to it. In his new book *The Hot Topic*, Sir David King, the ex-government scientific advisor, criticises those who make people feel guilty about their energy use because it 'makes them less likely to act, not more'.[37] The purpose of this type of 'criticism' is actually to reinforce the need to prioritise environmental objectives more effectively.

For example, campaigners at the University of Princeton critique greenwash stating that, for any architectural project, 'environmental performance should be the organising principle.'[38] This so-called criticism simply reinforces the importance of honestly meeting strict environmental criteria; but more importantly, it sets up the need to monitor the professed attainment of those criteria. Thus it actually increases mistrust within and outside the profession and it creates a bureaucratic discipline whereby everything has to be checked off to ensure compliance.

There are many other examples where the gloss of sustainability trumps meaningful critical engagement with the result that, even though architecture is more popular than ever before—it has also never been more vacuous, pliant, parochial and insular. Even though there are more public architectural awards ceremonies, competitions, personality-led conservation campaigns, TV programmes, as well as ministerial statements on the value of design, public sector design conferences, and op-ed pieces on everything from prefabrication, procurement and planning policy, with few notable exceptions, there is an almost total lack of critical engagement with architecture. For instance, the Bank of America tower at One Bryant Park, New

[35]  Chris Park, 'Oxford Dictionary of Environment and Conservation', Oxford University Press, p200

[36]  Oxford English Dictionary, 1999

[37]  Sir David King, 'The Hot Topic', quoted in Oliver Burkeman, 'Science chief: greens hurting climate fight', The Guardian, 12 January 2008

[38]  Victoria Whitford, 'In the planet's service?' DailyPrincetonian.com, 7 November 2006

York, designed by Cook & Fox, has been described as taking '"sustainability" to a point just short of growing its own food'.[39] What is less known is that these green measures are reputed to have added $60 million to the cost[40] (with the energy efficiency measures paying for themselves in approximately 20 years). With sustainability as a self-justification, no-one raises an eyebrow.

In this and other ways, the insidious, self-congratulatory, uncritical nature of the broader sustainability agenda is let off the hook precisely because its restrictive nature is seldom acknowledged. Many architects content themselves in the belief that they are exercising a freedom of choice because they are self-regulating rather than being 'forced' into decisions by some outside agency. The irony is that the framework of self-censorship is absolutely determined by others. The result is increasingly anal.

Stephen Hill of sustainability consultancy Beyond Green says, 'the focus should be on energy-efficiency — aesthetics come a long way down the line.'[41] Wired magazine recently described Arup's masterplans for the Chinese eco-city Dongtan as 'hundreds of pages of maps, schematics, and data — (with) almost nothing to say about architectural style.'[42] Where's the outrage? Where's the professional realignment in favour of good design in its own terms? Nowhere, it seems. Dongtan has become one of the most celebrated schemes in Western architectural magazines, not for its architecture you understand, but for its attempt to rein in Chinese development.

## Quantity not quality

Instrumentalism in the guise of social sustainability has become second nature to architects. For several years, urban designs have been created as a mechanism to 'unify urban neighbourhoods'[43] or to 'reduce cultural and racial tensions, cut down the incidence of anti-social behaviour and encourage the local community to become more involved.'[44] Seldom are parks, buildings or urban spaces designed and defended for the simple fact that they are 'exciting' or 'pleasant' or 'beautiful'. We now have quantity not quality justifica-

[39] Jerry Adler, 'Why Environmentalism is Hot', Newsweek, 17 July 2006
[40] Adam Aston, 'Bank of America's Bold Statement in Green', Business Week, 19 March 2007
[41] Rory Olcayto, 'Eco-homes fail final test', Building Design, 9 November 2007
[42] Douglas McGray, 'Pop-Up Cities: China Builds a Bright Green Metropolis,' Wired magazine, Issue 15.05, 24 April 2007
[43] Katheleen Conti, 'Grants expected to unify cities,' Boston Globe, 1 November 2007
[44] CABESpace, 'Parks Need Parkforce: A report on the people who work in our urban parks and green spaces', CABESpace p4

tions, whereby hospitals with a view of a tree are praised for the belief that they encourage people to get well more quickly.[45] Schools are feted because 'students in classrooms with openable windows had a 7 to 8 per cent advantage over those with fixed windows.'[46] None of these ridiculous pseudo-scientific interpretations are worth anything, you understand, but they simply provide an evasion tactic for designers who no longer have the confidence to justify their work in its own terms. In fact, in the aforementioned hospital, some patients found a non-natural scene 'more stimulating and hence more therapeutic'[47] but even contradictory results don't seem to stir the suspicions of pliant architects. Either way, these examples prove absolutely nothing but have established, in the minds of some architects, the self-flattering notion that designers are nature's healers.

Prince Charles claims that good urban design creates a 'nurturing environment'. On the other hand 'poor design has been found', he insists, 'to contribute to ... delirium.'[48] Spurious research and anecdotal waffle has become an orthodox way of legitimising the social role of architects at a time when they have lost the confidence to do it through rational and intellectual means. A dental surgery in Chelmsford 'has calculated that the building's design gains an extra hour in work efficiency each day ... producing a significant return on the investment.'[49] On this basis, the design of an African sweatshop must be worthy of architectural prizes.

Quantification is everywhere in the world of sustainable architecture leading to unwitting charlatanism by architects and their overseers. The Commission for Architecture in the Built Environment (CABE), the UK's leading urban design quango, makes the claim that 'a walk in the park ... has been proven to reduce the risk of a heart attack by 50 per cent'. Instead of this nonsensical claim being ridiculed by the profession, it is regularly used to justify the design of any old landscaping project or other.[50] (Whenever you hear the words 'it has been proven' used by sustainability advocates, healthy

[45]   CABE, 'The Value of Good Design: How buildings and spaces create economic and social value', CABE, p3

[46]   BBC, 'Education: Putting learning in a good light,' BBC News, 14 October 1999

[47]   Roger S Ulrich, 'View Through a Window May Influence Recovery from Surgery,' Science, Volume 224, Issue 4647, 1984, pp. 420-421

[48]   Prince Charles, 'A speech by HRH The Prince of Wales at the Enhancing the Healing Environment conference hosted by The Prince's Foundation for the Built Environment and The King's Fund, St James's Palace, London', 26 January 2006

[49]   CABE, 'Buildings and spaces: why design matters,' CABE, 2006, p8

[50]   Natural England, (Country Parks),'Country Parks: A breath of fresh air', www.countryparks.org.uk, accessed 14 January 2008

scepticism wouldn't go amiss.) The aforementioned heart attack figures were actually ripped from a study of 700 non-smoking,
non-drinking septuagenarian Japanese-American men in Hono-
lulu[51] (which makes it hard to generalise causal links with healthy 20
year olds in Hackney) but the quote has already been used in a variety of inappropriate contexts. A genuine argument should propose
that, regardless of the putative health benefits, parks should be built,
maintained and cherished for less deterministic reasons. Some of us
like to visit parks not as part of some kind of healthy lifestyle regime,
but because they are relaxing places to be. The authors of 'The Gardens of Amsterdam' point out that during the Dutch Renaissance,
laying out a green space was part of the 'search for universal harmony ... where one could reflect on one's attitude to science and
nature.'[52] No qualification needed: a park was a place in which to
relax and ponder. But designers no longer seem to have the confidence to make that straightforward claim.

Under the ever-doubting rubric of sustainability, good design
must be measurable. Everything has to be evidence-based, however
fatuous, to show that the design has tangible returns on investment.
A classroom study concludes that it 'cannot prove that daylighting
actually causes the students to learn more or perform better'[53] but
that doesn't stop it being quoted as such. Planning policy in New
York, for example, is being steered towards 'healthy urbanism' to
reduce obesity. On the other hand, The Times 'reveals' that 'young
women who grow up in cities or move there from rural areas are five
times more likely to suffer from bulimia.'[54] Rather than showing up
the silly, often-contradictory nature of the claims, conflicting
interpretations such as these serve only to reinforce the perception
that the harmful effects of design are not yet fully understood. The
result is even more cautious architecture.

If architects are riddled with doubt about what they perceive to be
the putatively detrimental impact of their work, then it is understandable that they hide behind spreadsheets to prove their innocence.

[51]  Amy A Hakim et al, 'Effects of Walking on Coronary Heart Disease in Elderly
      Men: The Honolulu Heart Program', Circulation: Journal of the American Heart
      Association, 1999; 100; 9-13
[52]  Koen Kleijn, in Renate Dorrestein, Keon Kleijn, Harold Strak, 'Behind the Façade:
      Gardens of Canal Houses in Amsterdam', Hunsthistorisch Bureau, D'Arts/
      Architectura & Natura, 2005, p38
[53]  Lisa Heschong, 'Daylighting in Schools: An Investigation into the Relationship
      Between Daylighting and Human Performance, Condensed Report', Heschong
      Mahone Group, 20 August 1999
[54]  Nigel Hawkes, 'Why city life can bring on bulimia,' The Times, 1 December 2006

## Engineering correct behaviour

When deputy prime minister, John Prescott MP outlined his vision of progressive architecture in 2002 it all sounded so promising. 'Improving the quality of our public space,' he said, 'is not about creating a sanitised, sterile, shrink-wrapped world. It is about creating communities where people feel they have a stake in their future.' He then went on to spell out that vision: 'tackling failure, such as litter, graffiti, fly-tipping, abandoned cars, dog fouling, the loss of play areas or footpaths, for many people is the top public service priority.' The problem with communities apparently, is the people who populate them. Such a shallow view of humanity leads to the conclusion that getting rid of anti-social behaviour is the first step towards building public space and civic values. In a Catch 22, anti-social behaviour is frequently defined as that which doesn't accord with civic values. The UK government's Sustainable Communities plan, 'People, Places and Prosperity' had the idea that 'people's sense of belonging and pride in their community (would) be renewed and revitalised' through a number of urban interventions, but was unsure whether this would actually created the right sort of communities if left to their own devices. The government thus felt obliged to introduce a so-called 'multi-agency approach' whereby officials were drafted in to document certain communities' activities to make sure that they all played ball, metaphorically-speaking. Civic space is now being fashioned to engineer the 'correct' behavioural response. Thankfully it won't work of course, but it's bad enough that they are trying — and that no-one is complaining.

Contrary to the accepted deterministic norm in the West, it is not the built environment that generates social capital, self-esteem or a more meaningfully engaged civil society but the other way round. Unfortunately, think-tanks, lobby groups, career politicians and media pundits are all too happy to look for simple solutions to complex problems. In one major UK riverside development, the sustainable initiatives include 'a sustainable living centre and lifestyle officer' to ensure that residents 'improve their lifestyles.'[55] In January 2008 the Academy for Sustainable Communities is offering twenty bursaries to subsidise individuals to become professional community activists.[56] Speaking of historic global trouble spots like

[55]  Steffie Broer, 'Ask Green Jeeves', Building Services Journal, Vol 28, November 2006
[56]  Academy for Sustainable Communities, News, 'Community activists supported to study new foundation degree', 8 August 2007, www.ascskills.org.uk

Belfast, Beirut, Dr Ralf Brand, lecturer at the Manchester Architecture Research Centre believes that making urban spaces less 'unfriendly' can create 'stable social conditions'. In reality, designing social harmony is about as likely to succeed as imposing democracy.

The 2007 president of the American Institute of Architects, speaking about architecture schools in the US, says that it is 'imperative that we design the next generation of schools to teach about a more sustainable way of living'.[57] Note: not 'designing', but 'living'. Instead of wanting to change the world, many architects want to amend our behaviour and are toeing official government policy line on social engagement strategies. Others, like CABE, present itself as 'a public inspiration ... essential for decision makers who are looking for a strong public mandate to back up tough decisions and motivate changes in behaviour.'[58] It masquerades as an independent body that lobbies and challenges the government's urban and architectural policy. It forgets that it is, to all intents and purposes, a government agency, funded by the state and simply interpreting its social policy agenda. For all of their radical talk, it seems as if most architects are not breaking boundaries at all. A radical, challenging, public intellectual engagement with design ideas no longer exists and they are going along with any old guff, as long as it keeps them in the corridors of power. Architects have been out of public favour for too long, it seems, for them to want to upset this new-found popularity. This is a sign of weakness not strength.

In Britain, the notion of zero-carbon development is uncritically acclaimed as the way forward for the UK housing crisis with Eco Homes as the latest carbon-neutral fad. Their layouts encourage walking, cycling and use of public transport. All wastewater is recycled on-site; and any energy generated on-site from waste, sun, and wind is used to treat rainwater and grey water and provide residents with high quality potable drinking water. Even food waste and landscaping waste will be converted into energy to power residents' homes. Constructed wetlands and swales collect and treat water for reuse, serving the dual purpose of enhancing the aesthetic value of each neighbourhood and creating green waste that can be transformed into energy within an on-site anaerobic digester.[59] No, this is not a screenplay from the Flintstones, but a UK government spon-

[57]  R K Stewart, 'Green schools: Color them healthy places of teaching and learning,' Seattle Post-Intelligencer, 13 September 2007
[58]  Commission for Architecture in the Built Environment, 'Briefing: Sustainable design, climate change and the built environment', CABE, 2007, p2
[59]  Lara Abrams Melman, 'Eco-Cities Take Root,' GreenBiz.com

sored programme for the future of housing in the 21st century. Maybe architects have been in poor environments for too long, but if they think that this is progressive architecture, they are suffering from Prince Charles' aforementioned delirium.

Pritzker Prize-winning American architect, Thom Mayne says: 'I fought violently for the autonomy of architecture ... Architecture with any authenticity represents resistance. Resistance is a good thing.'[60] It's a shame that more people don't agree as contemporary architecture blithely replicates government social programmes and refuses to challenge the instrumental motivations of funding agencies and sustainability wonks. It regurgitates think tank edicts on sustainable communities, sustainable design or any other unofficial sustainability piffle without the merest hint of a challenge. In the main, contemporary architecture accommodates to environmental criteria without any sense that it has reconciled the needs of humanity over nature. As Financial Times architectural critic Edwin Heathcote says: 'sustainable architecture is the big cliché of the era, a glib mantra that can be used to justify anything and which has decimated intelligent debate.'[61] It produces what architectural critic Tom Dyckhoff admiringly calls architecture that is 'radical in its reactionariness.'[62]

The state sponsored Academy of Urbanism bemoans the 'earlier traumatic era of competing ideologies'[63] but seems perfectly content with the cosy sustainability consensus that allows it to dominate the field of urban discourse without having to win any arguments. Its moral authority comes by appointment rather than rigour. I do not wish a return to the past, but the current dearth of competing societal visions is a real problem. More free-thinking critics might actually lead to a healthy, robust creative dialogue.

A more arrogant and future-oriented cadre of architects and designers might begin to challenge the new consensus, and in this way could lay the ground rules for overcoming the disorientating rut in which architecture now finds itself. To do so requires a stance against the prevailing culture of pessimism, so that a new, more

[60]  Thom Mayne quoted in Robin Pogrebin, 'A Defiant Architect's Gentler Side', The New York Times, 19 December 2007
[61]  Edwin Heathcote, 'What's so good about British architecture?', Financial Times, 31 August 2007
[62]  Tom Dyckhoff, 'Slow architecture that tastes good', The Times, 21 December 2007
[63]  Keith Murray, director, Academy of Urbanism, 'Whither and Academy of Urbanism', in ed Brian Edwards and Frank McDonald, 'Learning from Place 1', RIBA Publishing, 2007, p012

exciting, more challenging, more assertive architecture can emerge as part of a more strident society.

It's not all doom and gloom. Assessing ten years of Chinese juris-diction in Hong Kong after hand-over, one commentator notes that 'reassuringly, the skyline still bristles with ever-taller buildings.'[64] In Dubai, while there are enough architectural marvels (and horrors) being created to keep most architectural magazine editors busy for many years, a new 'Dynamic Architecture' is envisaged by Floren-tine architect David Fisher 'which not only adapts to its surround-ings but also to the tenant's needs and ... caprices'.[65] It has voice-activated floors that can rotate independently of the structure to suit whichever view is best for that particular day, and it comes with a retractable heliport just for fun. Love it or hate it, it is clear that social and economic development frequently gives rise to expres-sions of confidence, civic pride and urban experimentation. In less developed regions, it enables members of that society the luxury to consider more ethereal and cultural matters. People may disagree about how successful they are at it, but as Kazakhstan's energy-fuelled economy matures, some point out that it is able to pay 'increasing attention to aesthetic appeal.'[66] And even though 'Progressive Architect' magazine folded in 2007, it still hosts the Progressive Architecture Awards celebrating the 'profession's faith in progress — the unceasing, collective desire to question, rethink, and improve on the status quo.'[67]

There is hope, but unfortunately many of these new developments in non-Western countries are borrowing from the Western sustainability agenda in their apparent break with materialism. Such changes are spelled out by Malaysian architect Jimmy CS Lim: 'Corbusier,' he says, 'was in India at the right time and filled a vacuum, but the mindset lineage to Corbusier needs to be broken'. That's fine, but such a break sometimes carries with it an ideological rejection of the more progressive aspects of Western-style material development.

Symbolically, many high-rise buildings — traditionally seen as the expression of architectural arrogance — now resonate with lower and lower ambitions. Arrogance has been replaced with humility;

[64]   Gerard Baker, 'One country, one fear', The Times, April 13 2007
[65]   'Italian creativity brings new era of architecture to Dubai', AlaqariyaNews, 12 April 2007
[66]   Alec Appelbaum, 'Kazakhstan: new architecture reflects rising prosperity', EurasiaNet.com, 20 July 2007
[67]   Ned Cramer, Editor in Chief, 'Architect' (previously known as 'Progressive Architect'), ARCHITECT Magazine, 1 January 2007

not the best advert for a profession that needs to build where nature never intended. Nowadays, tall buildings frequently embody small thinking to chime with the sustainability zeitgeist and one of the key proponents of tall buildings with small footprints is internationally renowned architect Ken Yeang who claims that 'buildings should imitate ecological systems'.[68]

He is wrong. There is a fundamental need for architects to prioritise human creativity as sacrosanct. This will only come about if architects are prepared to kick against the mainstream orthodoxies that currently infect and misinform current practice, because to realise a new, progressive, human-centred architecture we must have the confidence to assert a belief in human creativity to transform nature, not kow-tow to it. Restrictions on architects are severe enough and calling for more is perverse. Having lots of materials, time and money at your disposal might not *necessarily* produce good architecture, but it certainly provides better *opportunities* for more progressive architecture ... by definition. It doesn't mean that those potentials will be realised, but volunteering to use fewer materials will narrow the possibilities for the best design solution.

This doesn't automatically mean a demand for more and more technological solutions to architecture. Criticism of those technophiles who say that technology is the whole answer are essentially correct — even though the technophobes who say it are equally misguided. Both miss the fact that a debate about technology is nothing without taking into account the socio-political framework in which it is created and utilised. The contemporary climate of sustainability discussed throughout this book, means that technological advances are developed with a social agenda of restraint built in; these technologies are often then used to legitimate or encourage the replication of that low-growth agenda. For example, the only clear debate in architecture today is that promoting energy savings; and the reason for energy saving technologies is to encourage further energy restraint. Real technological research should come with no agenda.

Having a 360-degree view of what the solutions to a problem are, is potentially — significantly — a more positive way of coming up with design solutions, than having a tunnel vision of pre-determined acceptable considerations. Today, innovation, experimentation and modern methods of construction are parodies of what they could be, bogged down in the demand that through the course of their develop-

[68] Ken Yeang, www.cnn.com

ment, no harm be done to the environment. We have to see potential gains in human development, rather than potential harms.

Not only is it right to experiment with new forms, processes and materials, it is essential, *regardless of their environmental provenance*. As the new progressive architectural manifesto, ManTowNHuman says: 'a progressive approach to design is one in which architects have the self-assurance to fail.'[69] To attain that status, architects must be confident in the concept of architecture for architecture's sake, asserting their trained eye for design rather than falling back on clichéd pseudo-scientific justifications. The manifesto concludes: '"good architecture" need not have a prescribed ethical dimension'... but to provide architecture with a progressive kick-start, will require that the guardians of our architectural and public morals step aside and that we start to sharpen up our critical faculties.

As acclaimed architectural journalist, Hugh Pearman notes, an architectural ambition for 'a better, healthier, fairer, more rational world' ought to be seen as a step forward.[70] Unfortunately, the bean-counters of sustainable architecture take us two steps backwards.

[69]  Austin Williams, Alastair Donald, Richard Williams, Karl Sharro, Alan Farlie, Debby Kuypers, 'Manifesto: Towards a New Humanism in Architecture', ManTowNHuman, March 2008

[70]  Hugh Pearman, 'Modernism—or should that be Modernwasm?', New Humanist magazine, March/April 2006

# CHAPTER 4

# *THE INDOCTRINATORS*

## *Environmental educators' underhand tactics*

Amazon, the book distribution company, advertises a 'young adult edition' of Al Gore's 'Inconvenient Truth', in which 'the text has been edited down from 320 to 192 pages, with younger readership in mind.' It says that sections aimed specifically at adults (e.g. the sections on insurance, investing in energy and political material) 'will be omitted in favour of clear text, appropriate photographs and easily understandable graphs.'[1] The 'political material' that has been exorcised from the kiddies' version is the posturing on environmental matters between Republicans and Democrats. It is deemed inappropriate it seems, to inculcate such a party political viewpoint into ones so young. This attempt to 'protect' children from some of the more lightweight of Al Gore's polemical opinion rests on the belief that they need their innocence protected from the shadowy world of vice-presidential party politicking. However, it has become perfectly acceptable to inculcate an 'environmental' message as if it is the very essence of non-political impartiality. What does it matter what political colour you are, as long as you're green. After all, on this issue don't all politicians, all scientists, all right-thinking people agree? They also seem to agree that imbuing children with sustainable mindsets is the responsible thing to do. Nowhere is the green indoctrination of the young more prevalent than in the education system.

---

[1] Online review of 'An Inconvenient Truth: The Crisis of Global Warming (Young Adult Version)', www.amazon.co.uk, August 2007

It may come as no surprise that today's teaching methods have been politicised. University of Kent's professor Frank Furedi says: 'Increasingly the curriculum is regarded as a vehicle for promoting political objectives and for changing the values, attitudes and sensibilities of children'.[2] It almost goes without saying that there have been many attempts in the last 50 years and beyond, to try and inculcate values, norms and beliefs in its students. However, the contemporary situation is shocking for the vacuity of its value judgments and the corresponding hollowing out of its educational content.

Effectively critical thinking has been redefined, especially around the 'givens' of sustainability and environmentalism. Now there is an automatic assumption of a prior knowledge that climate change is the problem and the only point of classroom learning is a fine-tuning exercise to work out what to do about it. From nursery to university, from science to geography, education has primarily become a route for teaching political environmentalism. Criticising this shift in The Times newspaper, Mick Hume correctly pointed out that ex-prime minister Tony Blair's much-vaunted promotion of 'education, education, education' has, in reality turned into 'indoctrination, indoctrination, indoctrination'.[3]

To help with this indoctrination in the UK, the Climate Change Resource Pack containing a copy of Al Gore's film, 'An Inconvenient Truth' has now been sent to more than 3,500 schools aimed at key stage 3 pupils (11–14 year olds). Teachers are provided with subject notes that are supposed to reflect impartiality on this subject. However, the notes imply that opposing views are risibly contrarian as they 'do not accord with the weight of scientific opinion'. It is one thing to discourage dissent in order to encourage scholarly discipline within a school, but surely quite another to hide from intellectual ideas without engaging with them.

It has been left to a lone parent, a Mr Stewart Dimmock, to voice his opposition in the courts to his children being 'subjected to political spin in the classroom'[4] and to accuse the government's 'Thought Police' of 'brainwashing' young minds with a politically-loaded film containing 'serious scientific inaccuracies'.[5] Meanwhile, the undis-

[2]    Frank Furedi, 'Introduction: Politics, Politics, Politics' in Robert Whelan, ed, 'The Corruption of the Curriculum', Civitas, 2007, p3
[3]    Mick Hume, The Thunderer, The Times, 22 May 2007
[4]    Stewart Dimmock, quoted in Joshua Rosenberg, 'Lorry driver to challenge Gore school film', Daily Telegraph, 20 September 2007
[5]    'Labour is brainwashing pupils with Al Gore climate change film' says father in court,' Evening Standard, thisislondon.co.uk, 28 September 2007

closed royalties from the schools' pack will compliment Gore's share of the $1.5m 2007 Nobel Prize receipts, his alleged £15 million Google stock options, future book deals of around £4 million and speaker's fees of £85,000 a time).[6] Who says that education doesn't pay? Or environmentalism, for that matter?

## Education with a message

Green propagandising is now a core aspect of the curriculum and, as such, a pilot study of 30 British schools will be used to develop what the government calls 'their leadership approach to enhance sustainability'. Note that the need to *enhance* sustainability is a given, the question is simply *how* to do it. In some sense, it has become apparent that 'to *promote*' has taken over from a schools' core responsibility 'to *teach*.' Kingston University, for example, has an entire department dedicated to 'embedding sustainability principles within our curricula'.[7]

These trends aren't marginal or simply confined to the UK. The Foundation for Environmental Education (FEE), for example, is a non-governmental, non-profit organisation promoting sustainable development through environmental education across 38 countries. It coordinates Eco-Schools which, it claims, have been recognised by the United Nations Environment Programme as a 'preferred school-based, children and youth global model programmes for environmental education, management, sustainability and certification at the international level.'[8] In America, consultant Bob Kobet says that 'modern education is gesturing toward an effective environmental curriculum in which we can use our educational facilities to much more effectively teach children what they need to know to be more competent citizens.'[9]

The American Cloud Institute for Sustainability Education, has educational programmes that have been implemented in over 130 New York City public schools influencing over 30,000 students. Senator John Kerry says that 'every single university and college in America has an absolute responsibility to adopt a completely carbon neutral, if not negative footprint, and engage in green sustainable

[6]  Steven Swinford, 'A convenient £50 million for green guru Gore', The Sunday Times, 9 December 2007

[7]  Centre for Sustainable Communities Achieved through Integrated Professional Education, www.c-scaipe.ac.uk

[8]  www.eco-schools.org

[9]  Eva Steele-Saccio, 'Education by Design', Good Magazine, 13 August 2007

technologies'.[10] Greenpeace USA organises a $3,800 university train-
ing semester that earns credits for communication and 'leadership
skills'.[11] And on January 31st 2008, a US organisation known as
Focus the Nation, co-headed by Senator Gary Hart (previously co-
chair of the US Commission on National Security for the 21st Century
which overhauled US national security structures and 'policies for
the post-Cold War new century and the age of terrorism'[12]) organised a 'teach-in' where schools, colleges, faith groups, etc 'put aside
business as usual ... and focussed the full weight of campus engagement on one topic ... brainstorming global warming solutions.' The
coordinating plans make a mockery of academic enquiry, educational
expertise, impartiality, and even free will:

> The faculty will say yes to involvement for two reasons. First,
> (they) do not have to be climate change experts to participate,
> nor invest heavily in preparation ... Most critically, thousands of
> students will attend, because faculty will require them to go, or
> give them extra credit, because other faculty will 'focus' their
> classes, and travel with them to attend the sessions ... Using this
> model, we view 2 million students nationwide as a realistic
> participation goal.

Blasé indoctrination to change pupils' behaviour seems to have
taken over from the notion of knowledge for its own sake (a concept
famously described by a previous UK education secretary, Charles
Clarke MP as 'a bit dodgy.') In these circumstances, with the education system losing its belief that it can teach pupils 'the best that is
known and thought in the world'[13] and to encourage them to
develop a confidence to decide the most appropriate course of action
for themselves, education writer and theorist, Alex Standish has
pointed out, there is a tendency instead 'towards the replacement of
knowledge with morality as the central focus of the curriculum.'[14]

[10]  John Kerry quoted in Dina Awerbuch, 'Senator John Kerry Speaks at HLS on
      Climate   Change',   College   Publisher   Network,   31   January   2008,
      http://media.www.hlrecord.org/home/
[11]  www.greenpeace.org/usa/
[12]  Senator Gary W Hart personal biography on The Wirth Chair in Environmental
      and Community Development Policy, University of Colorado at Denver &
      Health   Sciences   Center,   The   Graduate   School   of   Public   Affairs,
      www/thunder1.cudenver.edu
[13]  Matthew Arnold, 'Essays on Criticism' in M. Arnold, A.C. Clough and J.
      Thomson, 'The Cambridge History of English and American Literature in 18
      Volumes, Volume XIII, The Victorian Age, Part One', New York, Putnam, 1907-21
[14]  Alex Standish, 'The Anti-Democratic and Anti-Intellectual Consequences of
      Global Citizenship in the Geography Curriculum', July 2006

So values, indoctrination and behaviour modification have moved centre stage.

At a time when many liberals are concerned about the rise of faith schools and religious indoctrination, it is curious that preaching an environmentalist message in classrooms is one thing that no-one seems to abhor, and which seldom even pretends to have anything to do with 'teaching' in the true sense of the word.

## Do the right thing

We are currently in the UN Decade of Education for Sustainable Development (2005–2014) in which, unsurprisingly, the theme of Children's Book Week 2007, co-ordinated by Booktrust, was 'the environment'. The theme of International Walk to School Month was 'the environment'. The theme of the UK's National Council for Graduate Entrepreneurship's Student Technology Competition 2008 is 'the environment'. The national poetry competition which runs across all UK primary schools is based on the theme of 'the environment'. Eco Schools, run by ENCAMS (previously known as 'Keep Britain Tidy') want 'children (to) become more effective citizens by encouraging them to take responsibility for the future of their own environment'. I could go on. It's called 'reorienting education'.[15] As such, the Department for Education and Skills intends to 'launch an indicator of learners' capability to contribute to a sustainable society.' [16] So let's take a look at some of the typical ways in which environmental messaging is being used in schools around the UK.

Bridport Primary School in Dorset boasts a vegetable garden and compost heap helping schoolchildren to plant an orchard so that they can stock their Fruit Tuck Shop with low carbon footprint fruit. This Personal, Social and Health Education (PSHE) lesson uses the garden to display a continuous environmental message, the stated outcome of which is an 'increased consumption of fresh food'. This educational masquerade reinforces both the UK government's healthy eating programme and the food miles debate to proclaim that local is good. This is not education — worse, it's not even true, it's simply a social policy objective. Unfortunately, there are many examples of similar tunnel vision 'subjects,' pushing a political per-

[15] Rosalyn McKeown with Charles Hopkins, Regina Rizzi, and Marrianne Chrystalbridge, 'Education for Sustainable Development Toolkit' University of Tennessee and the Waste Management Research and Education Institution

[16] Department for Education and Skills, 'Sustainable Schools for Pupils, Communities and the Environment: An Action Plan for the DfES', 2007

spective to the detriment of any educational benefit. This gardening activity might perhaps have had some educative merit if the teacher had taken time out to explain the contrast between the school's labour intensive farming techniques with, say, Stalin's collectives farming methods, but that would be hoping for too much. That would definitely deviate too far from the environmentalist line.

In Beech Hill Primary School, music lessons involve children matching different rhythms to suit pictures of nature and of people. The consequent cacophony will 'provide a springboard to consider the effect that humans have on the environment.' Notwithstanding the underlying message that humans are somehow environmentally dissonant, the main tragedy is the unquestioned belief that even the creative arts can be massaged to encourage a 'correct' political interpretation. To make sure that the pupils reach the desired conclusions, this subject is taught with the assistance of WWF (previously known as the World Wildlife Fund).[17]

Another case involves Angela Lloyd, lecturer in conservation at Park Lane College in Leeds who has devised a ten-week course called 'Reduce Your Carbon Footprint.' She says that 'although we look in detail at the science behind climate change, we try to keep things hands-on and practical. Debate is a key part of the course and we look at arguments which deny we have a problem with climate change.'[18] By stating that she will be looking at arguments that 'refuse to accept' climate change, we automatically know which side is the right one. Even that bias wouldn't be so bad if the intention was to educate them into a better understanding of science; but, she suggests, 'debate' is seldom the best educative tool for mastering the intricacies of the scientific method. On two levels this is a poor excuse for education: firstly, it is an ideological assertion, which takes a principled stand on one side of the argument to the detriment of critical enquiry, and secondly, it is a practical guide for activism rather than intellectual development. In fact, Lloyd is obviously proud of the fact that the course is practical; after all, she is chairing a therapy group rather than a classroom. Lloyd's conservation lectures show that 'the students have already reduced their carbon footprint. They usually find it easiest to make changes in waste disposal, trans-

[17]  WWF (ex-World Wildlife Fund) is the unelected quango that has helped draft the sustainability strategy for the 2012 Olympic Games, and is at the 'cutting edge of the evolving environmental agenda in schools', www.wwflearning.org.uk
[18]  Angela Lloyd, quoted in Janet Murray, 'The conservation lecturer', The Guardian, 25 September 2007

port and shopping ... and (sharing) what they have learned with their family, (to) help influence change in the community.'

A recent UK survey pointed out that a small sample of children think that cars are 'something to be admired'. So appalled were the 'researchers' that they concluded that they had a duty to 'prevent this "love" of cars' meaning that 'children need to be educated at a very early age of the negative effects of the car; the age at where (*sic*) it may be too late is approximately six years of age.'[19] Unsurprisingly, the UK's National Curriculum now states that children should have a knowledge of the environmental impacts of transport from the age of five. By which they mean—obviously—transport's 'harmful' environmental impacts rather than the fantastic benefits that transport can provide. Even children's TV puppet Bob the Builder has been enlisted in the hope that 'by seeing what I'm doing, children will realise there's another way of living on this planet—a way which will help look after it.'[20] 'Ich bin Umweltfreundlich' (I am environmentally-friendly) is one of the first phrases learned in German classes in a north-east school in the UK.

Pupils in another primary school in the north-east studied the landfill implications of disposable nappies, exploring how their own behaviour can have consequences. This science curriculum subject hopes to broaden the investigation into the consequences of 'nappies around the world.' The benefits, convenience and time-saving benefits of disposable nappies is not on the curriculum. But neither is the question about what nappies—their use and disposal—have to do with education in the first place. As ever, this type of lesson plan is nothing more than a behavioural change device: mixing parenting classes, citizenship education and recycling policies under one umbrella masquerading as a science topic. Presumably, they genuinely believe that investigating the contents of a nappy provides some profound education insights, rather than simply peering into a morass of intellectual diarrhoea.

## Manipulation

Education has become less of an arena to learn, to be challenged, to critically analyse, to develop abstract thinking, and to lay the ground rules for a genuine sense of intellectual enquiry, and instead has become a means of winning the hearts and minds of a compliant

[19] Simon Kingham & Sarah Donohoe, 'Children's perceptions of transport', in 'World Transport Policy & Practice Volume 8, Number 1', 2002, p10
[20] Bob the Builder quoted in press release, 'Friends of the Earth, www.foe.co.uk

future generation. Unfortunately, this means that any lessons that could be learned are missed in the blinkered attempt to see everything in a framework of the morally-loaded sustainability orthodoxy.

An exchange programme links students from Oxfordshire with those from Rwanda so that they can both 'appreciate the importance of sustainable resource use — rethink, reduce, repair, re-use, recycle.' These messages are disseminated via science and geography lessons.[21] Maybe there are other lessons to be learned about the Rwandan geo-political situation than the amount of plastic they reprocess. Lest we forget, nearly two thirds of the Rwandan population live below the poverty line and life expectancy is still around 42 years for men and 27 per cent of children between the ages of 5 and 14 years were working in Rwanda in 2000[22] including those working at waste disposal sites.[23] Using Rwanda to teach the value of recycling, looks a little sick.

In a similar example, cited on the Qualifications and Curriculum website, Year 6 pupils in an unnamed primary school in the south-east, explored 'the role of the caretaker, the amount of oil used by the school, and the school's fuel and electricity bills' as part of a sustainable science project. Presumably, this type of education also saves on test tubes, books, and intellectual energy. In another school, students are advised to become a Power Saver, a person who goes around the classroom 'checking that everything is switched off.'

These are more than just money-saving gimmicks, they represent the acceptance of an insidious environmental promotion through the prism of education. Mandatory, doctrinal sustainable school practices like these have become orthodoxies and outside environmental agencies, lobby groups and NGOs are getting in on the act and hijacking the curriculum. For instance, the Design of the Times (Dott) is a cultural project that includes a curriculum–based ECO design challenge, which in 2007 was targeted at Year 8 school students telling them to 'redesign some aspect of their school making it more user-friendly, with less impact on the environment and the planet's natural resources'. It clarifies the terms of the debate suggesting that they 'think about how much water you use, how you deal with waste, how you get to school or where your food comes

[21]  www.voicesfromrwanda.org
[22]  UCW analysis of ILO SIMPOC, UNICEF MICS, and World Bank surveys, Child Economic Activity and School Attendance Rates, March 1, 2007 quoted in US Department of Labor, Bureau of International Labor Affairs, www.dol.gov
[23]  Republic of Rwanda, National Policy for Orphans and Other Vulnerable Children, Kigali, 2003, 33,

from—then think of a way design can help you do it more effectively.'[24] For 'effective', read 'better for the environment'.

Environmentalism in schools is a brazen attempt to manipulate children into the new green morality. In her book *Brave New Schools*, American author Berit Kjos explains how things have changed: 'Most parents and teachers still believe that critical thinking refers to *factual, logical thinking*. But they have been misled. It actually means the opposite ... It encourages myths, imagination, and group synthesis—the tools for manipulating a child's values system'[25] leading to a pernicious relativism in educative standards. Furedi notes that 'at a time when traditional institutions find it difficult to connect with popular concerns, environmentalism is still able to transmit ideas about human responsibility through appealing to a sense of right and wrong (which is) why the authors of children's books and school officials also use environmentalism as a vehicle for socialising youngsters.'[26]

Tragically, that socialisation is prefaced on a mistrust of society; that responsibility is contextualised within a narrative of man's irresponsibility to nature. Whatever the underlying objectives, little positive can come from these misanthropic messages. Here, for example, are just some of the recommended readings for youngsters in American schools, with a brief description taken from the Scholastic Corporation—the world's largest publisher and distributor of children's books and a leader in educational technology:

*Why Should I Recycle?* in which 'Mr. Jones takes his students on a class trip to a recycling plant'; *Long Live Earth* comprising rhyming verses describing 'what people have done to pollute our planet'; *Winston of Churchill: One Bear's Battle Against Global Warming* drawing attention to 'the polar bears' plight'; *The Earth Is Good: A Chant in Praise of Nature* consisting of 'short phrases that enumerate parts of the natural world and declare them good'. Then, for the very young, there's Brian Patten's *The Blue & Green Ark: An Alphabet for Planet Earth* which is 'a poem to the earth'. For older schoolchildren we have: *This Moment on Earth* introducing the authors' 'environmental policies by providing examples of the dangers facing the environment and the solutions that concerned people have found'; *Worms Eat*

[24] Dott 07 ECO Challenge, 'Who Designs Your Life?', Designs of the times, www.dott07.com

[25] Berit Kjos, 'Brave New Schools: Guiding your child through the dangers of the changing school system', Harvest House Publishers, 1995, p109

[26] Frank Furedi, 'In search of eco-salvation', 27 September 2007, www.spiked-online.com

*My Garbage*, described as 'the definitive guide to vermicomposting', and; *One Well: The Story of Water*, which 'warns about pollution and the need for water conservation'. There are many, many more, each one gently reminding the reader of humanity's causal role in the environmental catastrophe that we are taught—by rote—to recognise is happening all around us.

One other book on the curriculum is written by Jonathon Porritt. Entitled *Captain Eco and the fate of the Earth* it includes the line 'Your parents and grandparents have made a mess of looking after the earth. They may deny it, but they're stealing your future …'[27]

From indoctrination to fear in one simple step. Such is the concentration in schools on the potential for ecological Armageddon[28] or global catastrophes[29] that pupils are being terrified by sustainable education. A London teacher received an essay by one of his 12 year old pupils. Notwithstanding the worrying belief that this is actually considered to be an 'essay' (the teacher was equally unimpressed), it is an interesting example of how mainstream environmental fears seep down through society. Asked to write on what life will be like in 20 years' time, this is her full essay (with original spelling errors, etc):

> Big floods people dieing no way out people use to much energy to much TV, light, cars and much more people in other countries die for no reason now we are to. How can we stop this? Stop watching TV and walk to places. Play less video games watch less video use less electricity stop using cars how make global warming happen we get a lot of global warming from factories to many products come out like game hair products and stuff like that they try on animals first is not fair.

In a review of the children's version of 'An Inconvenient Truth' in New York's Schools Library Journal, John Peters points out that it 'plainly intend(s) to disturb readers rather than frighten them'. Apparently that's alright then. But disturbing pupils into behaviour change so that they develop the correct green attitudes is what's really disturbing. But I leave head teacher Jim McManners to sum up on his strategy for pliant, environmentally-responsive children. After receiving the plaudits for being the first school in the UK to install a functioning wind turbine he explained his motivational strategy as: 'you don't want to frighten them to death so they think

[27]  Jonathon Porritt, 'Captain Eco and the Fate of the Earth', Dorling Kindersley, 1991
[28]  Bill McGuire, 'Surviving Armageddon: Solutions for a Threatened Planet', Oxford University Press, 2007
[29]  Bill McGuire, 'Global Catastrophes: A Very Short Introduction', Oxford University Press, 2006

there's no point in doing anything.'[30] Implicitly, you just have to frighten them enough.

## Official endorsement

For the new unabashed coterie of environmental educationalists, one of the central tasks of education is to 'inculcate a deep and broad understanding of sustainability in learners and equip them to be able to, and to want to, live their lives in a sustainable manner,' says Dr Mary Joy Pigozzi, Director, Division for the Promotion of Quality Education at UNESCO (United Nations Educational, Scientific and Cultural Organisation). She goes on to explain that 'quality education is a relative term' but that teachers and educators must 'ensure (that) education *for* sustainable development includes, but is not limited to, education *about* sustainable development. It must include the practice of the principles of sustainability'[31] (my italics). So how has this happened?

It goes back to the days of the Rio Summit in 1992, which resulted in the pragmatic policy paper known as Agenda 21, the stated aim of which is to 'ensure that education ... incorporates the concepts of environmental awareness and sustainable development throughout the curricula.'[32] Those educationalists, therefore, who consider themselves as cutting edge advocates of radical change, should realise that they are, in fact, just the voice-pieces for establishment views on the best way of creating social cohesion. For those who think that the ends justify the means, it is worth noting just one of many, many examples cited in the UN Agenda 21 package. Paragraph 35.3 explicitly states that in science education, 'scientific knowledge should be applied to articulate and support the goals of sustainable development.'[33] Suddenly, the erstwhile impartiality of science had been given parameters which are little more than a promotional campaign for the goals of sustainable development. Science ceases to be an important education topic because of its desire to research and inquire, but because it 'articulates and supports' a pre-ordained position.

[30] Richard Garner, 'Honour for first wind-powered school', The Independent, 22 October 2007

[31] Dr Mary Joy Pigozzi, Director, Division for the Promotion of Quality Education, UNESCO, 'Sustainable Development Through Education', UK NATIONAL COMMISSION FOR UNESCO' Report the UK Launch Conference for the UN Decade of Education for Sustainable Development, Second Keynote Address, 13 December 2005

[32] UN Department for Economic and Social Affairs, 'Agenda 21' Chapter 25: Children and Youth in Sustainable Development, para 25.9 (d)

[33] UN Department for Economic and Social Affairs, 'Agenda 21' Chapter 35: Children and Youth in Sustainable Development, para 35.3 (d)

After the Rio Conference in 1992, the UN policy framework machine published a series of Agenda 21 initiatives with UNESCO leading the charge on education policy. It aims to reorient educational systems and curricula towards sustainability and stability and its political, as opposed to educational goals are fairly explicit. It says that education and educational establishments need to enhance 'public sensitivity to environment and development problems and involvement in their solutions and foster a sense of personal environmental responsibility and greater motivation and commitment towards sustainable development.'[34]

Suddenly, the purpose of education has been transformed from a learning environment into a political arena. The government's Department for Children Schools and Families suggests that part of the citizenship agenda is to explore 'how the school community could participate in, and contribute to, future Local Agenda 21 priorities'. Note: not 'whether' they should participate, not 'criticise', 'critique', 'reject', 'renounce', 'assess', 'question' or any other such bipartisan, critical or open-minded approach. The starting point is that Local Agenda 21 is a good thing; the only question then is to assess how it can be made 'better.' One of the learning 'outcomes' is that the schoolchildren organise 'school assemblies to explain the local issues and inform other pupils'. This is not education, this is peer pressure. Or, at worst, simply prejudicial gossip.

### Young messengers

As we have seen elsewhere in this book, environmentalism and sustainability have tended not to have had to confront any arguments about their legitimacy; they seem to have been elevated to the dominant philosophy of our age by default.

Seldom, have environmental advocates ever had to confront a counter-position or to have won an argument; their pre-eminence has been 'won' through mere assertion and showing contempt for (and demonising) anyone who might dare disagree. Without much intellectual substance, it is hardly surprising that sustainability advocates and environmentalists prefer to focus on soft environmental niceties such as composting, energy-saving light-bulbs, and the eating habits of its pupils. It simply means that by indoctrinating kids, they hope to influence parents in the more difficult *political*

[34]  UNESCO, 'Promoting education, public awareness and training', Chapter 36, Agenda 21, 1998, United Nations, Clause 36.8

sustainability messages — of low growth, of restraint, of social conformity — by the back door.

Environmental activist authors Laurie David and Cambria Gordon have written 'The Down-to-Earth Guide to Global Warming' which, they say will be targeted specifically at a younger audience. They are after the unsullied naiveté of youngsters and are up front about it. 'Kids,' says David, '... are the number one influence on their parents, so if you want to reach the parents, go to the kids.'[35] It would be churlish at this point to use Adolf Hitler's famous speech in 1933 where he chided those adults that opposed his ambitions:

> When an opponent says: 'I will not come over to your side,' I calmly say, 'Your child belongs to us already ... You will pass on. Your descendants, however, now stand in the new camp. In a short time, they will know nothing else but this new community.'[36]

In February 2007, Education Secretary, Alan Johnson said that educating children out of their desire for fashionable consumer goods 'is as important as the pressure they put on their parents not to buy a gas-guzzling car.'[37] This type of approach is becoming very popular for educationalists and political lobbyists who find it difficult to convince intelligent adults, primarily because they realise that adults may have one or two inconvenient questions of their own to ask. So while labelling critics as 'deniers' and likening them to Flat Earthers[38], it is much easier to invade adults' lives using their own children. Journalist Emily Bell says: 'Children these days are the miniature Nazi storm troopers of moral rectitude ... in search of signs of parental decadence and turpitude.'[39] After all, what parent is going to dare undermine what their child learns at school.

Where, once, children were perhaps overly protected from the nefarious influences of adults with political agendas, nowadays schools erstwhile *in loco parentis*, are willingly offering up their charges to be used, manipulated and made to manipulate others. Essex County Council are happy to encourage schoolchildren in this role, boasting that they are being 'asked to use their "pester power"

[35] Quoted in Nathalie op de Beeck, 'A Green Call To Arms', Publishers Weekly, 2 August 2007

[36] Adolf Hitler, 6 November 1933 speech quoted in Ralph Berry, 'The Research Project: How to Write It', Routledge, 2000, p93

[37] Alan Johnson, quoted in Richard Garner, 'All pupils to be given lessons in climate change', The Independent, 2 February 2007

[38] David Miliband, quoted in 'Miliband fears on climate change', BBC News Online, http://news.bbc.co.uk, 27 September 2006

[39] Emily Bell, 'Green-eyed monsters', Broadcast, 12 January 2007.

to encourage their communities to recycle their rubbish.' Anna Reid, head teacher at Willingdon Primary School, which is taking part in the initiative, says: 'This is a great opportunity for schools to influence their communities for the better. Residents are used to the County Council asking people to recycle more but when the message comes from schoolchildren, who are the future decision-makers and captains of industry, I think they will really listen'.[40]

Madhav Subrmanian is a 12-year-old Indian boy who sings on the streets of Mumbai/ Bombay to collect for conservation projects. He was named as one of the Guardian newspaper's 50 people who can save the planet, because, they say, 'conservation awareness is growing … largely through young activists like him.'[41] American architect, Claire Weisz has re-orientated a recycling facility in South Brooklyn 'to make it a kind of classroom'. Why? Because, she says: 'Children are fascinated by recycling, and "kids tell their parents", which increases family involvement in recycling.'[42]

Mainstream politicians are delighted to find this new simple method of getting their message across without having to canvass amongst awkward punters. New Labour's Tony Blair recognised the benefits of this sneakiness: 'On most issues we ask children to listen to their parents. On climate change, it is parents who should listen to their children.' [43] All then that is needed, is a means of indoctrinating children who will use their (socially responsible) pester power to drip feed the moral message into the home. After all, part of the new curriculum requires children to 'develop social and moral responsibility.'[44]

Not so very long ago, some of those very people who now endorse this morally-correct green pester power, were arguing that it was a reprehensible intrusion on parent/child relationships. Ten years ago, Friends of the Earth demanded a ban on TV advertising aimed

[40]   Press Release, 'Schools to ask neighbours to recycle,' Essex County Council, 30 March 2007
[41]   '50 people who could save the planet', The Guardian, 5 January 2008
[42]   Thomas D Sullivan, 'Changing our ways with waste,' Oculus, Winter 2006/ 07, p39
[43]   Prime Minister's speech to the 10th Anniversary of the Prince of Wales' Business & The Environment Programme, Banqueting House, September 14, 2004, http://www.britishembassy.gov.uk/
[44]   Advisory Group on Education for Citizenship and the Teaching of Democracy in Schools, referenced in Qualifications and Curriculum Authority, 'Citizenship: Programme of study: Key Stage 4', 2007, p41

at children before 9pm.[45] By 2005 it was producing an advert that 'feature(d) children aged 3-11 speaking about climate change' and organising conferences with the express aim of answering the question 'how to get into schools'.[46]

The mathematics staff at Moorfield School in the West Midlands, for example, have been congratulated for getting parents to attend an energy evening, which highlights pupils' work, but which also presents every parent with a compact fluorescent lamp donated by the Energy Efficiency Advice Centre to help them understand how to reduce energy use in the home. Basically, the driver for this initiative was the headmaster's '(concern) about the increasing cost of energy' (i.e. wanting to reduce the fuel bills) which has then become a manipulative way to draw the pupils into unnecessary concern about the running of the school's boiler system. It finally ends up with an intrusive and patronising presentation to their parents about duty and responsibility. It begs the question, what the hell has an adult's choice of light fitting in their own home got to do with their children's teachers? Discuss.

[45]  Press release, 'Parents Protest At Pester Power: Survey Shows Parents Angry as Kids Bombarded With TV Ads,' Friends of the Earth, 28 Nov 1998
[46]  Conference Workshop on working with young people, 'Conference Workshop: Education — in schools and youth clubs', Friends of the Earth, 10 September 2005

# CHAPTER 5

# *THE PESSIMISTS*

*Putting the brakes on China and India*

What if all the Chinese wanted to get off their bikes and jump in a car? What if India's population continues to grow past the 1.5 billion mark all wanting a Western standard of living? It's obvious, comes the response, it would be devastating! And what if China wants to continue using coal at an ever increasing rate, or what if India continues to build five aeroplanes a month for the next five years? Surely, say the environmentalists, it shouldn't be allowed! For devotees of sustainability, it's simply common sense that such rapid growth and the accompanying rise in aspiration and expectation are far too unsustainable. The tipping point is being reached, we are told, and China and India could be on the verge of pushing things over the edge. Something must be done.

With the rise of sustainability and its relentless logic of entropy, limits and demand management, it is clear that population reduction lobbyists, anti-growth environmentalists, and all other kinds of critics of man's existence have gained a new lease of life in the paranoid rhetoric around China and India. For the WorldWatch Institute, Sunita Narain, director of the Centre for Science and Environment in New Delhi says that 'The western model of growth that India and China wish to emulate is intrinsically toxic.'[1]

China, with its 'five hundred and sixty-two coal-fired plants by 2012, is expected to overtake the US as the world's largest carbon emitter around 2025.'[2] Or is it '850 new coal-fired plants.'[3] Or is it 'a

[1]  WorldWatch Institute, 'State of the World 2006: Special Focus: China and India', January 2006
[2]  Elizabeth Kolbert, 'The Climate of Man: III', The New Yorker, 9 May 2005
[3]  Katherine Ellison, 'Turned Off by Global Warming,' New York Times, 20 May 2006

new coal-fired power station every week.'[4] No matter, for what the critics are really criticising is the relentless growth of the Chinese machine to point out the terrible risks that China is prepared to take with all of our futures. As the New York Times headlined, China is 'choking on growth'.[5] But for those of us who would rather see society advance in its energy supply for the sake of its productive capacity, then it is hardly surprising that China is going down the non-renewable route, given that there is no non-renewable alternatives on offer on such a scale as would be needed.

Meanwhile, India, with its cheap 'People's Car' is going to create an extra one million drivers per year. Unveiled at the 2008 Delhi Auto Expo to music from '2001: A Space Odyssey', its company chairman Ratan Tata said: 'I hope this changes the way people travel in rural India. We are a country of a billion and most are denied connectivity.' Costing one lakh (100,000-rupees or around £1300) it should transform personal mobility, especially given the fact that Transport minister, K H Muniyappa, recently announced that 'The Golden Quadrilateral' — a massive roadbuilding project linking Delhi, Mumbai, Kolkata and Chennai — will be completed by 2009. The British Independent newspaper however, saw fit to headline the story 'Global warming: Just what overcrowded, polluted India didn't need … the $3,000 car.'[6] What it failed to note was that Delhi is also constructing a new Metro system described as a 'shining symbol of definite progress'[7] showing that a progressive transport strategy is based on an integrated, not conflictual, relationship between different modes of transport. Responding to criticism from Greenpeace, Tata said: 'We need to think of our masses. Should they be denied the right to an individual form of transport?'

## Material advancement

With economic growth rising at around 10 per cent per annum, and China's latest Five Year Plan laying down an average target of 7.5 per cent growth until 2010, the economic bubble may soon deflate a little, but so far it has managed to fund a dizzying array of social and infrastructural improvements, not least the fact that China's average

[4]    David Miliband, MP, 'Speech by Rt Hon David Miliband MP at the WWF One Planet Living Summit "One-Planet Security",' London, Department for Environment, Food and Rural Affairs, www.defra.gov.uk/ 27 March 2007
[5]    'Choking on growth', New York Times, www.nytimes.com
[6]    Andrew Buncombe, 'Global warming: Just what overcrowded, polluted India didn't need … the $3,000 car', The Independent, 22 June 2007
[7]    Sandy Howard, 'Moving On', New Statesman, 6 August 2007, p27

life expectancy has grown from 35 years in 1949 to 72 years today. Society progresses almost by default. Absolute poverty (admittedly classified as earnings of less than one dollar a day[8]) has reduced from 42 per cent in 1981 to seven per cent today. Between 2000 and 2005, China's GDP tripled to $2.25 trillion and counting. National income per capita has almost doubled over the past five years. But even though this is impressive, let's not get too carried away. Per capita figures are averages (and in this instance they are bolstered by around 310,000 millionaires and 106 billionaires, although admittedly they represent only one per cent of the total number of Chinese households). All of this economic growth in China has still only moved it from the 132nd richest per capita country in the world in 2002, up to 129th in 2006[9]. There's still a long way to go.

In India, that other 'rising civilisational giant'[10] had an average growth rate of 8.6 per cent between 2004–2007[11] compared to China's 10–11 per cent. Two hundred of the world's 500 biggest organisations have their computer operations based in India and, by '2010, India's computer software exports are expected to soar to over $50 billion—more than the country's entire exports in 2005.'[12] Not bad for a country with the highest illiteracy rate in the world. But once again, it's easy to be swept along by statistics about the growing Indian economy. Edward Luce reminds us in his book *In Spite of the Gods*, that 'an improvement of 1 per cent a year is fine if you already have a developed economy, but when almost 300 million people continue to live in absolute poverty, it is painfully slow.'[13]

That's right: too slow. While the sustainability orthodoxy suggests that things are proceeding at far too fast a pace, the needs and desires of the developing worlds throw their inequalities into stark relief; and improvement—material improvement—cannot happen fast enough. Even as India is poised to take over from Japan as the world's third largest economy, it contains a population equivalent to that of the United States surviving on less than US$1 a day (com-

[8]   Johan Norberg, 'In Defense of Global Capitalism', Cato Institute, 2003, p26
[9]   Lu Yuliang and Cheng Yunjie, 'The New Chinese Millionaires', The Wall Street Journal, 2 November 2007
[10]  Mira Kamdar, 'Planet India: The turbulent rise of the world's largest democracy', Simon and Schuster, 2007, p96
[11]  IBEF Essay, 'India in the fast lane', India Now — A Perspective, Vol 4 Issue 2: July 11, 2007
[12]  John Farndon, 'India Booms: The Breathtaking Development and Influence of Modern India', Virgin Books, 2007, p153
[13]  Edward Luce, 'In Spite of the Gods: The strange rise of modern India', Abacus, 2007, p336

pared to only 85 million people in China, which at the moment has a bigger total population than India). In India, 45 per cent of children under the age of five are malnourished. Between 32–52 per cent of its population, are economically and socially disadvantaged, and therefore described as members of the 'backward classes'.[14]

But with its recent forward thinking, India is finally developing a more confident approach to its place in the world, and the Mohandas Gandhi myths ('the incessant search for material comforts and their multiplication is an evil'[15]) are finally being laid to rest. Indian Prime Minister Manmohan Singh talks of India's 'march of progress' and interprets 'protecting the environment' merely as a way of developing 'an environment which is conducive to rapid growth.'[16] No more sackcloth and ashes for the Indian sub-continent hopefully. Similarly, the Chinese are 'not prepared to sacrifice the present generation for the generation 100 years hence'[17] either. In fact, rather than these two countries responding to the environmental hectoring approach from the West, China and India seem to be getting on with it.

In China, the central government has invested a total of £40 billion providing 26,000 miles of expressway between 1990–2005, compared to the 2,200 miles of motorway in Britain built since 1959. The ambitious aim of the Chinese government is that by 2010, over 95% of rural areas will have access to asphalt or cement roads. Meanwhile, British roads, on average, were last resurfaced 74 years ago.[18] UK newspaper headlines frequently bemoan the fact that China has 'given in' to the motor car at precisely the same time that 12 tuk-tuks (open-sided, motorised three-wheelers) went into operation in the UK as a 'sustainable means of traveling around cities.' (These have subsequently been withdrawn as inappropriate for a modern transport network, with no compensatory increase in modern vehicles.)

Two years ago the total Indian passenger fleet had 170 aircraft, today it is double that. It is scheduled to comprise 550 planes by 2010 and peak at 1100 in 2020. But even this masks the growth in the numbers of passengers. Between April and September 2006 there

[14]   National Commission for Backward Classes Act, 1993 (Act No. 27 of 1993)
[15]   M K Gandhi, 'Young India', 30 May 1929
[16]   Prime Minister Manmohan Singh, 'Speech to the Confederation of Indian Industry by the Indian Prime Minister', 29 May 2007
[17]   Nigel Lawson, in William Keegan, 'Watch out, Nigella: dad's back in town' The Observer, Sunday May 13, 2007
[18]   Alarm Annual Local Authority Road Maintenance (Alarm) Survey 2007, Asphalt Industry Alliance

was a 44 per cent growth in internal flights and it is predicted that by 2020, 400 million Indians will be flying regularly. As India's civil aviation minister, Praful Patel says, this is certainly an 'air travel revolution.'[19]

China has recently completed the audacious high altitude railway to Tibet travelling over the highest and most inhospitable terrain to 'unify' countries and peoples along its route. For all the negative hype, even on the terms set by environmental campaigners, China's railway to Tibet has had no 'deleterious' effect on the environment and more importantly, regardless of whether it has or it hasn't, it is a magnificent piece of technical and engineering excellence. The 710 mile (1,140km) Qinghai-Tibet service, costing Yen 35 billion (€3.7billion) includes sealed cabins to protect passengers from the high altitude including a back-up oxygen store and anti-ultra-violet windows to protect passengers from the sun's glare. Chinese President Hu Jintao said it showed China's people were 'ambitious, self-confident and capable of standing among the world's advanced nations'[20]. With undue modesty, Zhu Zhensheng of the Chinese railway ministry simply called the new line a 'major achievement'.[21]

In India, veteran BBC reporter Sir Mark Tully says that its railway charts a 'middle way between progress and tradition.' But while these poetic paeans to steam travel pepper the Western press, the drive for progress on the Indian sub-continent has caught up with, and rapidly overtaken, tradition. The Shatabdi Express — known as the 'bullet train' of the Indian network — travels at a top speed of 90 mph between Delhi and Agra, not far off the UK's tilting train's modest average 88 mph (top speed 125 mph). China introduced the world's first commercial passenger Maglev (magnetic levitation) — a Sino-German project — in Shanghai.[22] Four years later, and India is taking bids for the introduction of a £3.75 billion Maglev train network around Mumbai and has even hinted at a Maglev route from Mumbai to Delhi which would shorten the current journey to just 3 hours.[23] Meanwhile, Britain has just completed 85 miles of Channel Tunnel rail track, the first new passenger railway built in the UK for

[19]  Praful Patel quoted in Anupma Bindra, 'Civil Aviation in India: Flying Higher', Civil Aviation Week, 4 January 2006

[20]  BBC News 24, 'Hu opens world's highest railway', 1 July 2006, http://news.bbc.co.uk

[21]  BBC News 24, 'Hu opens world's highest railway', 1 July 2006, http://news.bbc.co.uk

[22]  Paul Amit Bhandari and Ravi Ananthanarayanan, 'Shanghai operates first commercial maglev', Times of India, 30 December 2002

[23]  Animesh Singh, 'Mumbai to Delhi: 3 hours by train', India Express, 14 June 2005

over 100 years. Ironically, the Victorian 'can-do' mentality in its creation of infrastructure projects is the nearest thing to the current phase of development in modern China and India.

## Degraded interpretations

However, in terms of the general debate around China's 'economic miracle' over the last decade or so, there has grown a creeping cynicism around its rapid rate of development. These dynamic images of China's economic development and its urban expression have been well documented, but, some say, these physical representations still don't mean that China has progressed one jot from its reactionary Maoist heyday. Behind the façade, they argue, it is still repressive and authoritarian: environmentally and socially unsustainable. Mao's proclamation that man must 'use natural sciences to understand, conquer, and change nature'[24] is now regularly cited as the beginning of the troubles for China. The phrase is widely interpreted as an allegory of Mao's megalomania, but also of humanity's arrogance and socialism's folly leading to the desertification of over one third of the country. What is missing in this equation is that Mao's collectivised farming was a bureaucratic, non-scientific, labour- intensive disaster that resulted in the starvation of millions of people that no-one with any democratic mandate, or sense of humanity, would support. But all of a sudden, Britain and others in the Western sustainability coalition have developed for themselves a moral mission. As British establishment environmentalist Sir Crispin Tickell argues, by giving up on the idea of attempting to impose dominion over nature, 'the Chinese now have the chance to re-establish that traditional harmony with Nature.'[25] Western sustainability advocates are hoping to influence the outcome of China's next phase of development in the name of environmental protection.

Clearly, debate in the West about China is fairly polarised these days. On one hand, China is held up as a beacon of economic and material progress, on the other it is condemned as a smog-ridden sweatshop. With around 120 million people having moved to its Special Economic Zones in the last ten years, China is either portrayed as a symbol of hope … or of despair. Depending on who you talk to about China's modernisation, its ever-changing skyline is, on

[24]  Mao Zedong, quoted in Peter Ho, 'Mao's War against Nature? The Environmental Impact of the Grain-First Campaign in China', The China Journal, No. 50, July 2003, p37

[25]  Crispin Tickell, 'Mao's War Against Nature', www.crispintickell.com

one hand, a metaphor for progress and social advancement; or on the other, proof of a society growing out of control and producing and consuming at an unsustainable rate. As one environmental journalist put it: 'the single biggest uncertainty on the path to a bright green future can be summed up in one word: China.'[26] As Will Hutton says, it is a 'gigantic dilemma'.[27] But behind the confusion and sniping, there can't help but be some sneaky admiration. Beijing is now regularly held up as the very paradigm of progress by some, with new buildings emerging every day.

As such, the debate concerning China and India's development reflects a completely degraded interpretation of progress. The Financial Times points out that 'the urban/rural divide is intensifying — farm incomes have been growing at half the pace of urban incomes for the past decade'[28] and CSR specialists are appalled, noting that 'While China has succeeded over the past 25 years to lift 250 million people out of poverty, income inequality has doubled.'[29] Well hold the front page. No-one, not even hard-nosed Chinese apparatchiks claim that this is some kind of socialist experiment, and so the iniquities and inequalities of the market will undoubtedly be real and profound. But to criticise the general level of social development because of the particularities of that development is like throwing the baby out with the bathwater. A society emerging out of a peasant economy and into the glare of hi-tech industrialisation will inevitably provide scope for a widening income gap, but the important thing is that rather than stabilising at some median level, more and more people are aiming for the top. Most of them won't all get there, but at least they want to. While we in the West are trying to invent fatuous sustainability benchmarks, the Chinese are dissatisfied with their lot and are striving for betterment. The World Bank points out that between 1981 and 2001, 'the proportion of the population living in poverty fell from 53 percent to 8 percent.'[30] Leaving to one side the fact that the World Bank uses a pathetic measure of poverty — less

[26]  Alex Steffen, 'Dongtan and Greening China', WorldChanging, www.worldchanging.com, 1 May 2006
[27]  Will Hutton, 'China and the West in the 21st Century', Little Brown, 2007, p339
[28]  'Lex: Chinese income disparity', Financial Times, 19 February 2006
[29]  'Ethical Insight', Issue 33, 11 January 2006. p13
[30]  Martin Ravallion and Shaohua Chen, 'Learning from success: Understanding China's (uneven) progress against poverty', Finance & Development December 2004

than one dollar a day, or 300 Yuan per person per year at 1990 prices[31] — it is still a remarkable societal transformation.

The little known city of Suzhou is spending $13 billion on a light rail system. Shanghai's subway network has been designed, constructed and is operational in the same time that Los Angeles has taken to discuss the construction of a single new subway line (that is, in the same time that London has been engaged in a consultation about a discussion about constructing a new underground line). The Chinese budget for the Olympics in 2008 is 2.5 times that for London's Olympics in 2012.[32] Meanwhile, Shanghai has built more skyscrapers in the last decade than already exist in New York, and is reputed to be building 20 cities a year for 20 years. Architect Richard Rogers once complained that in the time he had been interviewed, commissioned and had sketched out a new sustainable city in China, they had built most of it. He was peeved that they wouldn't slow down. But China is clearly a country in a hurry.

As a result, cheap labour, or 'in-migrants'[33] are undoubtedly brutalised. About 20 per cent of Shanghai's population have moved from rural areas into the cramped, unpleasant surroundings of its workhouses. A progressive answer would be to support demands for worker's rights, decent pay and conditions which have been the staple of working class organisation for years. That would be an enlightened response. But environmentalists instinctively focus away from enticing people to the city in the first place. No-one with an ounce of progressive humanity can doubt, or relish, the squalid conditions in which many of these people have to work and recognise that they are a scandal[34] but engagement with a view to transforming things for the better — rather that evasion — is the real answer.

Looking at a static snapshot of the undoubtedly harsh conditions in which the poor survive leads many campaigners to express righteous indignation and to claim that it represents a situation which is unsustainable. One report concludes that 'despite the putative benefits of urbanisation, the evidence supports the view that urbanisation, especially when its pace is rapid, can impede development and

[31] Martin Ravallion and Shaohua Chen, 'China's (Uneven) Progress Against Poverty', Development Research Group, World Bank, World Bank Policy Research Working Paper 3408, September 2004
[32] John Farndon, 'China Arises: How China's Astonishing Growth Will Change the World', Virgin Books, 2007, p151
[33] Deyan Sudjic, 'The Speed And The Friction', Shanghai Overview, Urban Age, www.urban-age.net
[34] Amnesty International, 'People's Republic of China: Internal migrants: Discrimination and abuse. The human cost of an economic 'miracle',' March 2007

exacerbate environmental problems'.[35] The United Nations UN-Habitat calls it 'premature urbanisation', defined as urbanisation without the economic base to support it, as if people should be more circumspect in their ambition. On this basis, presumably every city was urbanised prematurely. In the African context, the UN suggests that 'sustainable urbanisation is ... a quest for balancing rural and urban solutions'.[36] In China, knowing that there is little that they can do about it now, even the UN has all but given up on this kind of direct advocacy of restraint. Admittedly urbanisation has, and will continue to lead to slum formation, but like poverty this ought not be irresolvable. In truth, it is a major advance that in today's China, migrants from rural areas are now able to travel freely and work in the cities, unlike during the Maoist era when their access to the city was strictly regulated.[37] We look on the squalid conditions many find themselves in with admirable empathy, but sometimes that blinds us to the positive developmental impulse conveyed in the in migration of people who already know that the streets aren't really paved with gold, but are prepared to suffer for the benefit of their families and their future generations.

It is only 20 years since the vast majority of peasants (as they were self-consciously called) survived predominantly on subsistence farms (what environmentalists today might call low carbon footprint, self-sufficient, sustainable, local production units). They were effectively denied entry to the city (what environmentalists today might call a sustainable congestion policy). The liberation of free movement is clearly an advance and ever has it been thus. Parents want a better world for themselves and their offspring and are prepared to endure hardship so that their children won't have to. It's usually called 'self improvement' and is a fantastically positive, progressive impulse. Similarly, auto- didacticism, entrepreneurship or simply acquisitiveness have been part of the heroic story of human development since the chains of feudalism were broken.

Looking back to the Victorian era in Britain, the influx of rural poor into the hovels of London would now be seen as a snapshot of squalid repression. In many ways it was. But the torch of liberation shone through. As Ford Madox Ford wrote of those times, 'One

[35] David E Bloom and Tarun Khanna, 'The Urban Revolution', F&D: Finance and Development magazine, IMF, September 2007, Vol 44, No 3

[36] The United Nations Human Settlements Programme, 'the UN-Habitat Strategic Framework', Nairobi, Kenya, May 2003

[37] Workers' Liberty, 'China and Independent working-class politics', 30 September, 2001

would, quite literally, never get any for'arder if one stayed to inquire to the end of every tragic-comedy of which, on one's road, one caught a glimpse'.[38] His magnificent social anthropological study *The Soul of London* identifies the ambition, the dynamic, the inventiveness, the personal and social drive in Britain at the turn of the 20th century which outshone the dark reality for many people. He, and they, recognised that this was a struggle from which poor people would emerge, if not exactly triumphant, at least better off; healthier; more socialised; and even more demanding.

In America too, many of the poor downtrodden masses arriving in the new world in the 1800s were in for a rough life in the ghettos, but each invigorated with the American dream knew that things were on the up. Science analyst George Wand has a slightly harsh take on the price of progress, but outlines an important dynamic when he observes that 'all the workers who made radio and television tubes lost their jobs over time when electronic devices were developed. What's more, all the persons who built carburettors were displaced when fuel injection became the norm in the automotive world ... this is what we consider progress. However, life will always go on and get even better than before, for all those who have been affected.'[39]

### Infrastructural advances

Let's take a snapshot of India and China's road to material, infrastructural progress:

India has been blighted by bureaucracy — a legacy of colonialism — which has served respective governments well, while improving the country's infrastructure not one jot. By the end of the 1980s, for example, an estimated 1.5 million ha (out of 6.1 million) of irrigated land in Andhra Pradesh alone went out of irrigated production because of mal-administration resulting in a lack of funding to complete the necessary infrastructure.[40] But with the newly acquired economic dynamism that has freed up investment opportunities, suddenly, India has a chance of fulfilling its promise of universal supply. In the world's largest democracy, the services and utilities that we take for granted in the west are being democratised.

Most importantly, Prime Minister Manmohan Singh has announced his government's commitment 'to providing access to

[38]  Ford Madox Ford, 'The Soul of London', Everyman, 1995, p43
[39]  George Wand, 'Fuel Cell History, Part 2', www.fuelcelltoday.com, 19 January 2007
[40]  Bala Raju Nikku, 'World Bank and Irrigation Reforms: Case of Andhra Pradesh, India', Draft, 2007

electricity in every village in the country by 2009' exceeding the previous ambitious target of 2012. That means supplying electricity within five years to an additional 78 million rural homes across 125,000 villages, at the cost of Rs.160 billion.[41] Currently, around 60 million (44 percent) of Indian households have access to electricity. To put it in perspective, the extended provision will be three times the size of the household supply coverage of the British National Grid laid over a country fifteen times Britain's land area. An impressive feat, even if it takes until 2012.

The government expects to harness its full potential of hydropower (148,700 MW) by 2027 (up from 30 MW today) 'with a whopping investment of 5,000 billion Rupees'[42] In the last two Five-Year Plans since 1997, India has added more than the total hydro-generated capacity installed there in the first 30 years since Independence with 220 big, medium and small dams proposed for construction along the Ganges in the state of Uttarakhand alone.

Not only that, but in 2000, the nuclear and hydroelectric shares of the Indian market was just 1.5 and 6 per cent respectively but this is scheduled to grow significantly. At the moment, India has 14 nuclear reactors in commercial operation providing around 3 gigawatts and a further nine under construction. The total nuclear supply will grow to 30 GW over the next generation, literally transforming the lives of many millions of ordinary people. It's a reminder of the benefits that centralised energy provision can bring.

A similar story of societal progress through infrastructural provision can be told of China. In 1887, the Yellow River flooded and killed between 1 and 2 million people. Admittedly, that's a pretty wide margin of error for fatality statistics, but with such a poorly developed infrastructure not only could they not be saved, but they couldn't even be accounted for. Such was the end of the Qing dynasty. But half a century later in 1931, between 1 and 4 million people died as the river flooded again. Time does not necessarily — automatically — bring progress and these tragedies give the lie to the simplistic notion that progress is a simple, fatalistic, linear continuum. Chinese society had undoubtedly changed in those turbulent intervening years between these two events, and not necessarily for the better, but there were outside forces to contend with, from agricultural collapse to Japanese invasion. Seventy five years later, and

[41]  BBC News Online, 'All India "to have power by 2009"' 4 April, 2005, http://news.bbc.co.uk

[42]  Avilash Roul, 'India's Hydro Power — Can India Achieve its Potential?', EcoWorld, www.ecoworld.com, 17 October 2007

China is more able to control its own destiny. Shanghai has now constructed a barrier that can rise to 6.9 metres (based on a 1 in 200 year storm) and is planning to construct another one at 8.5 metres height and a cost of £350 million. Notwithstanding this technological development, China Daily reports that marine information experts in Shanghai are monitoring the sea levels once every five minutes to guage whether anything untoward is going on. Maybe that's overkill, or maybe, in a country of circa 1.5 billion people, there's a place for a proportion of them to stare at the waterline, but it just goes to show that breaking free from feudal chains, and overcoming a subsistence economy has enabled Chinese society to develop the tools to command where and how they live ... and to deal with the climate.

## Western condemnation

As China and India march onwards with their double digit growth, the West desperately hopes that something will rub off on them. Trend commentator, Mark Dziersk says, 'it's not a matter of creating a future advantage so much as staying around and competing at any level'.[43] British prime minister, Gordon Brown can only hope to hang on to coat-tails:

'We cannot dismiss these changes ... Already China and India are turning out more engineers, more computer scientists and more university graduates than the whole of Europe and America combined.'[44] Brown hopes against hope that while most people acknowledge that 'the 21st Century will be China's century ... if we show the skills, the inventiveness, the creativity and the spirit of enterprise, we can make it a British century.' But the only big British export idea left, it seems, is sustainability.

Professional sustainability consultants at One Planet Living, for example, an organisation co-produced by WWF (the former World Wildlife Fund) that advises business and governments suggest that China is following the 'unsustainable western development model'[45] while political commentator Mark Leonard has predicted that Europe will help 'China redefine ideas of its own national interests, security and even identity'.[46]

[43]  Mark Dziersk, 'Sustaining an Advantage', FastCompany.com 7 November 2007
[44]  PM Gordon Brown, 'Speech by the Prime Minister Gordon Brown to TUC Congress,' TUC, www.tuc.org.uk, 10 September 2007
[45]  One Planet Living China, www.oneplanetliving.org/china
[46]  Mark Leonard, 'Why Europe Will Run the 21st Century', Fourth Estate, 2005, p119

The principal Western influence — the primary intellectual export — seems to be the miserable Western sustainability industry. In the last few years, nearly 3000 environmental organisations have been created in China, many advised or funded by individuals with a Western education, a zero-growth mentality and irritating personal sustainable credentials. Notwithstanding the fact that China seems to be outstripping the 'Western model' in terms of GDP growth at least, after relentless lobbying, even the Chinese leadership is reported to be buying into the Western mantra of the 'four "Un's"…(it is) unstable, unbalanced, uncoordinated and unsustainable.'[47] If it catches on, not only will British expertise be at the forefront, but it'll legitimise slowing down the competitiveness of China. Win-win for UK it would seem: getting paid by your competitor for undermining your competitor's productivity.

Sustainability advocates are free — and should be free — to condemn the construction of dams, roads, airports or whatever for the peripheral damage that they do to outlying areas, communities and lifestyles. Indeed, it is good that there are concerned citizens monitoring and criticising the excesses of capitalist privateering. And the pollution in China is a serious problem. Linfen, China's coalmining powerhouse is described by one reporter as 'like a month smoking filterless cigarettes, going down the pit and eating asbestos for tea.'[48] Writing of the Huai River where water quality is unsuitable for drinking or irrigation, one commentator says that 'cleanup costs are now estimated at more than $100 billion, and the number is rising … the full economic toll of illness and death is incalculable'.[49] China stands accused of trying to shut down a report that states that environmental degradation in 2004 cost over 3 per cent of GDP and that 2005 was even higher.[50] Protest is clearly essential.

However, when protest becomes a condemnation of the developmental impulse and hence a celebration of stasis, i.e. when sustainable development advocates posit the ethereal (and somewhat mythical) qualities of unsullied nature at the expense of structural improvements which will benefit a wider public, now and in the

[47]  Wall Street analyst, Stephen Roach quoted in Clay Chandler, 'Stephen Roach on China's "Unstable" and "Unsustainable" Economic Model', Chasing the Dragon, Fortune, CNN, 28 March 2007
[48]  Adam Lee-Potter, 'Dirtiest place on the planet', Sunday Mirror, 4 February 2007
[49]  Elizabeth C Economy, 'The River Runs Black: The Environmental Challenge to China's Future', Cornell University Press, 2004, pp8-9
[50]  Chris Buckley, 'China silences Green GDP study, Report says,' Reuters, via Environmental News Network, 23 July 2007

future — that is when the argument has gone too far. There is a difference between arguing for compensation payments or for sensible advocacy of human rights; and for preserving the so-called merits of traditionalism in aspic. The world moves on regardless of the nostalgia of the sustainability lobby.

In a 47-nation survey of 'global public opinion' the 'image of China has slipped significantly'.[51] With mounting opprobrium, China is feeling the pressure and WorldWatch can argue that 'rising demand for energy, food, and raw materials by 2.5 billion Chinese and Indians is already having ripple effects worldwide'.[52] And they don't mean a positive ripple effect. Sustainable development pressure is beginning to force their hand. So Chapter 6 of China's latest (eleventh) five year plan is titled 'Building a Resource-Conserving and Environment-Friendly Society' and is so full of eco-platitudes that is sounds as if it might have been written by a British freelance sustainability consultant: 'Give priority to conservation in the short term, following the principle of "reducing, reusing and recycling"', it says, endorsing something called 'green lighting.'

When it comes to its announcement to reduce 'chromium slag pollution control', or to aid the 'Beijing-Tianjin sand source control'[53] (to alleviate the creeping desertification of the Tengger and Badain Jaran deserts), it all seems perfectly sensible. [54] (As an aside, to do this the Chinese authorities have forcibly evicted thousands of farmers in order to construct a Green Wall of China — a band of desert-stabilising plants cultivated at the expense of edible crops — in order to hold back the shifting sands.) In is obvious that there are legitimate concerns about environmental pollution and its consequent harm to humans, which require urgent practical actions.

Unfortunately, many Western commentators unequivocally celebrate the growth of any environmental protest voices in China, simply because they act as 'a locus for broader political discontent

[51] Pew Research Center, 'Rising Environmental Concern In 47-Nation Survey Global Unease With Major World Powers, 47-Nation Pew Global Attitudes Survey, 27 June 2007, p5

[52] Christopher Flavin, Worldwatch, 'State of the World 2006', 2006

[53] The Outline of the Eleventh Five-Year Plan: For National, Economic and Social Development of the People's Republic of China', National Reform and Development Commission, People's Republic of China', 2007

[54] NB: To put desert encroachment into perpective, one third of China's landmass is the Gobi desert, which is reputed to be shrinking by 7,600 sq km every year, although there may still be a net increase in total. The total natural area of the Gobi desert alone is 1,295,000 km². (Reference: Xinhua News Agency, 'China calls for cooperation in combating desertification', china.org.cn, 23 January 2008)

and ... political reform, as it has in other countries.'[55] On Earth Day in 2004, it was reported that 100,000 Chinese college students in 22 provinces participated in environmental activities organised by university groups. What is less well known is that many of these groups are state sponsored and run by party functionaries. Also, as China expert Elizabeth C Economy points out: 'China's NGOs remain heavily reliant on international funding for their work ... (and) remain open to political criticism down the line that they are actually foreign-directed enterprises ... (and) some donors have likewise voiced the opinion that some Chinese NGOs have taken money and not delivered on what was promised.'[56] So, we can add 'underhand' to the list of criticisms of the Western sustainability industry. Even though they may not be succeeding to influence events as thoroughly as they would like, the Chinese environmental lobby is largely an artificially created movement torn between the restrictive practices of its own government and the demands for restraint from outside. With those two alternatives, it's hardly surprising that the idea of restraint is catching on. Pan Yue, a minister of China's State Environmental Protection Administration (SEPA) warns that 'The [economic] miracle will end soon because the environment can no longer keep pace'[57] implying that the brakes should be applied as much from within as without.

But it's worth noting that the real progress towards participation, engagement and the rumblings of a democracy free from the grip of Chinese state power are coming from outside the 'radical' environmental movement. It is the progressive developers that are creating the conditions for democratic disquiet through the empowered ranks of the emerging working classes. An organised protest by them would be relatively unstoppable unlike the tame, insider radicalism of the environmental lobby — organised as much to detect and mis-direct political protest — as it is to encourage safe, unchallenging clean-up campaigns in time for the Olympics. And some erstwhile environmental voices see 'an advantage' in the one-party state if it gets them what they want.[58] As society materially develops, the

[55]  Elizabeth C Economy, 'China's Challenge — Beyond the Economy', The Globalist, 1 June 2004

[56]  Elizabeth C Economy, C V Starr, 'China's Environmental Movement,' Council on Foreign Relations, 7 February 2005

[57]  Pan Yue quoted in Elizabeth C. Economy, 'The Great Leap Backward?' Foreign Affairs, September/October 2007

[58]  Geoff Mulgan, 'China's great green leap forward?' Times Online, 27 November 2007

demands for a free, democratic electorate gets louder and a harder to ignore, even for the most hardline members of the National People's Congress. Some tell-tale after-effects of economic development and liberalisation are sneaking into other political systems too.

In India, for example, progress towards social equity is a potential byproduct of societal development. Currently, the Dalits (the lowest caste, to whom Gandhi gave the label Harijans [children of God], later renamed) are revolting. They are beginning to strain at the artificial boundaries of the anachronistic caste system and want some of the action that is coming India's way. Whichever country, when liberated from the scramble for survival, humanity can aspire to create a better society for itself. Only sour-faced environmentalists would see this as a recipe for wilful destruction.

## Malthusian attitudes

For observers on the ground in India and China, the dynamic humanistic drive for social progress is almost palpable. Robert L Paarlberg, the eminent professor of Political Science at Wellesley College, notes that 'For those trying to imagine how all the people of the world will be fed in the 21st century, Malthusian visions have their place. But that place is not China.'[59]. GM crops such as maize and cotton are already reasonably established in India, China and some parts of Indonesia. China's latest five-year plan sets aside around £1 billion of direct state investment in the research and development of agricultural biotechnology.[60] But even by positing it in this way, Paarlberg acknowledges that Malthusianism is certainly making a comeback and nowhere is this clearer than in Western debate about China and India's growth.

For two hundred years, Malthus' theories were ridiculed and dismissed. In its current manifestation, intelligent criticism or emotional contempt for Malthus' views are notable by their absence. With over 120 million people moving into Special Economic Zones over the last few years, and a continuing inward annual migration from the countryside of over 10 million, China has the biggest urban population in the world. Therefore, China cannot escape 'the population question'.

[59]  Robert L. Paarlberg, 'Rice Bowls and Dust Bowls: Africa, Not China, Faces a Food Crisis', Foreign Affairs, May/June 1996
[60]  Economist Intelligence Unit (EIU) 21 October 2003, cited in Robert L. Paarlberg, 'Technology Adoption In Developing Countries: The Case Of Genetically Modified Crops', 23 October 2003

Even though China's annual population growth is only 0.59 per cent, leading environmentalists like Jonathon Porritt can assert that it is causing—or has the potential to cause, or might cause some time in the future—a demographic nightmare. There is, he says, 'an ecological apocalypse unfolding in China right now.'[61] Unbelievably advocating a 'one-child policy' for the West (at the very time that China seems to be relaxing its grip somewhat on its historically authoritarian intervention in matters of personal reproduction), Jonathon Porritt states that 'the fewer there are of us, the greater our personal carbon budgets.'[62] For him it is a simple equation. It is 'the cold, unyielding calculus of climate change'[63]: more people, more consumption, more energy use, more problems. Once you see humans as a problem instead of a source of creativity, sociability, innovation and hope, then every problem can be easily interpreted through a misanthropic prism. Journalist, Justin Rowlatt (the self-appointed Ethical Man from BBC TV's Newsnight) agrees that 'when it comes to the environment, people are the problem and it is not hard to see why.'[64]

When Time magazine can promote an op-ed called 'Will Malthus Be Right?'[65] which actually criticises Malthus' for having too narrow a preoccupation with humanity's needs—i.e. Malthus condemned for being too humanist—then you have to worry. When Chris Rapley, the new head of the British Science Museum wants the population reduced by one million clarifying that: 'I am not advocating genocide … (but for) fewer people to drive cars and use electricity'[66] then we should be concerned. Humanity, in this equation is a problem rather than a solution. Dr Jonathan Newman, an ecologist at Oxford University's Department of Zoology representing the (allegedly) Humanist Association states that the rise to six billion people on the planet is an inherently bad thing:

> If we are not careful, it could double again in the next forty years, and all these extra people will need food, water, shelter and fuel. Many of them will want far more than this. Although humans in

[61]  Jonathan Porritt, 'Greening the Dragon: China's search for a sustainable future', Green Futures Special Issue, 2006, p3

[62]  Jonathan Porritt, 'If I was in government….Jonathon Porritt makes population his number one issue', Ecologist Online, April 2007, www.optimumpopulation.org

[63]  Jonathon Porritt, 'Ecologist Online', April 2007

[64]  Justin Rowlatt, 'How Ethical is my Baby?', Talk About Newsnight, BBC News Online, 30 March 2007, www.bbc.co.uk

[65]  Niles Eldredge, 'Will Malthus Be Right?', Time magazine, www.time.com

[66]  Robin McKie, 'Science chief: cut birthrate to save Earth', The Observer, 22 July 2007

the past, and other animals, have also damaged the Earth and its atmosphere, modern population growth and technology have speeded up the process. Increasingly, human beings can control their own, and other species', fertility and evolution, and this places considerable responsibility on us.[67]

Calls for population reduction are reprehensible but mainstream in modern environmental discourse. The real responsibility on progressives is to tackle these anti-humanist sentiments. The enlightened response to population growth is to celebrate it. More people is a good thing: the more we attach value to humanity the more human we become. The progressive humanistic imperative requires that we renounce the view that humanity has a malign impact on the planet, otherwise, the argument is as good as lost in today's climate. If it is agreed that people are the problem, then the argument for fewer people is won. But the 'population question' is not a Malthusian mathematical problem, in the same way that global warming is not a scientific one: these are political arguments that need political solutions.

There are clearly many Western interpretations of China and India's perceived dilemmas, which seem to sum up the paradoxes of progress in the modern era. They weigh, on one hand, the frantic development which has drawn people from the penury of the paddy fields into urban environments with potentially improved living standards, and on the other, an authoritarian regime concerned only with devil-take-the-hindmost materialism. Do progress and development reflect purely material improvements such as a rapid rate of urban transformation, productive capacity and technological know-how? Or does progress need a less tangible element, such as well-being, happiness and community? Does growth necessarily equal progress and advancement?

Well, there are various levels of answer to those questions, but in general, material improvements do not appear in isolation from the social forces which give, or allow them rise. There is, as even the old Maoist autocrats would recognise, a dialectical relationship between material development and social organisation. Maverick environmental activists Nordhaus and Shellenberger recognise that 'like the progression from material needs to postmaterial needs, higher, inner-directed needs do not appear until people first meet their prior outer-directed needs.' Even though this is a slightly mechanistic

[67] Dr Jonathan Newman, 'A humanist discussion of ... Environmental Issues', www.humanism.org.uk

way of looking at it, it is useful enough to challenge that old shibbo-
leth that says that people protest about inequality when they are
poor; but as they become more affluent, they grow out of it. Historically, the opposite has been shown to be the case. It is almost a
human predisposition to attain the means to overcome basic needs
… and then demand more. People strive and in so doing, benefits
(and challenges), successes (and failures) manifest themselves.

So as to the question: Does progress simply mean material
improvements? The answer is undoubtedly 'no'. It's surely a good
thing if there is a meaning to one's life, but meaning and materialism
are not in direct opposition to one another, as those who show obei-
sance to anti-consumerism and sustainability insist. They suggest
that meaning should be found in blind opposition to materialism.
Crucially, the tendency to fetishise a search for meaning in isolation
to material improvement, as we have seen in the chapter on Energy,
is a significant problem these days. Those who privilege 'well-being'
above all else have completely denigrated the material and invert
the concept of development. The opposite is not the case: those who
clamour for material progress frequently also develop or sharpen
their cultural appetite, and find free time in which to enjoy it.

While it is not a simple equation, defining progress is not as difficult as some people make out. Economic growth and increased productivity have a liberatory potential to free individuals from the
subservience of their labour. It is not that technology reduces exploi-
tation, but that it creates the conditions for humanity to have no
exclusive sphere of activity forced upon it, i.e. it ought to offer the
*potential* to liberate. While sustainability gurus interpret progress in
a million and one different ways, each more abstract than the next, I
am happy to assert that the ability to improve the material lot of a
society, to free people from the constraints of nature, to increase
their socialisation and to provide them with the physical means of
not having to be reliant on the whims of weather, land and seasons
is exactly what progress is. Almost inevitably, with that, comes
social advancement.

As people have more time in which to think about issues beyond
their immediate self-preservation, so they can begin to consider that
the continued material improvements are only limited by the very
nature of the prevalent social relations. Historically, that is when
demands are raised. Social and economic progress allows people to
revel in the opportunities thrown up by that development. We can
see this already in the Chinese model. The apparent iniquities

endured by peasants relocating from village to city in Beijing, Mumbai and a hundred and one other different cities across the developing world, are not the full story. In the first instance, they are striving for personal and familial betterment. That striving is a heart-warming aspirational instinct that has the potential — but only the potential — to begin to challenge the grinding inequality of that society for others. The aspiration itself is a liberation, but the fact that many people will not have their full ambitions realised can result in an even greater intention to overcome the societal barriers that are put in their way.

By 2020, India's population will be 50 per cent urban.[68] Suketa Mehta, author of the evocative 'Maximum City' writes of the lure of Bombay/ Mumbai: 'It's a place where your caste doesn't matter, where a woman can dine alone at a restaurant without harassment, and where you can marry the person of your choice.' This neatly sums up the progress between the urban experience and the rural. The tendency to congregate in cities is, as historian Michael Woods says, the very 'process of civilisation'.[69] Some might — and do — argue that this undermines the traditional values of India, but for progressives, this is usually a good thing. Regardless of the historically fictitious nature of these so-called traditional virtues, Mehta neatly sums up the nature of the unambiguous social advance that is currently happening in India. 'For the young person in an Indian village', he says, 'the call of Mumbai isn't just about money. It's also about freedom.'[70]

[68] Sheela Patel interviewed in 'Empowering Slum Dwellers', Development Gateway, 7 September 2004

[69] Michael Wood, 'India and Pakistan 07: The Story of India', BBC2 TV, 24 August 2007

[70] Suketu Mehta, 'Dirty, crowded, rich and wonderful', The International Herald Tribune, 16 July 2007

# CHAPTER 6

# *THE NEW COLONIALISTS*

*The Developing World's sustainable underdevelopment*

In September 2007, it was announced that President Gadaffi will be building a zero-carbon eco-tourism resort in the ex-pariah state of Libya which will be committed to using locally sourced labour, food and energy (and) curbing unsustainable human activities'.[1] The following month, Libya, once *persona non grata* in the West, was elected onto the United Nations Security Council. Coincidence? Possibly, but it still reflects the fact that a sustainable route to respectability seems to be the new big idea in international relations. What better way to re-enter the Western model of the 'civilised' group of nations than to buy into its primary export business: 'sustainability'. This chapter aims to explain that as in any business, sustainability is not meant to be egalitarian and in global terms, it is still a club dominated by Western interests and the profit motive. As parts of the developing world show signs of social and economic progress that offer them the potential to realise their social and economic independence as never before, sustainability has the potential to keep them in thrall to the established world order for a while longer and to act as yet one more brake on development for the poorest countries in the world.

Sustainable development appears to be the only option for the developing world. Unfortunately, it is a disaster for the meaningful progress of those countries for three main reasons. In the first

[1]  Richard Vaughan, 'Gaddafi's Green Revolution,' The Architects' Journal, 13 September 2007

instance, sustainable development redefines the concept of progress and development to pretend that those in the developing world should be happy with less developed status. The United Nations Habitat Declaration — the formal document on global strategies for human habitation — concludes that 'those living in poverty are, in fact, rich in innovative faculties'.[2] Some might say that it's incredible what people can do with a tarpaulin and a sheet of cardboard, but relativising the issue of underdevelopment has had serious consequences for the Developed World. But not just for them. This kind of relativising process is confusing the Western model of development. Once progress and development are questionable advances for the third world, the West, too, loses a certain clarity of purpose.

Secondly, underdevelopment is increasingly portrayed as a natural state of affairs, where the economic and political status of the underdeveloped world can be blamed on natural events or cultural relations; from global warming to local traditions. Sustainable development is ruinous for the underdeveloped world, which, as the name suggests, needs 'development' and not 'sustainable development' to progress, but it hides the real political challenges behind the mask of 'nature'.

Thirdly, the patronising imposition of sustainability on aspiring economies is simply ethical colonialism designed to keep them in their place. William Easterly, author of *The White Man's Burden*, writes that 'Western stereotyping ... manages to snatch defeat from the jaws of some current victories, fueling support for patronising Western policies designed to rescue the allegedly helpless African people while often discouraging those policies that might actually help.'[3] In this chapter, we look at each criticism in turn.

### Redefining poverty

Redefining 'progress' and 'development' into a relativistic value judgment goes back a long way. Two years after Gro Harlem Brundtland coined the phrase 'sustainable development', the 1989 Caracas Report on Alternative Development Indicators suggested that 'if governments of the South can create a consensus amongst themselves around lists of indicators (such as "net forest destruc-

[2] United Nations, 'Istanbul Declaration on Cities and Other Human Settlements in the New Millennium', Report of the United Nations Conference on Human Settlements (Habitat II), Istanbul, 3-14 June 1996 (United Nations publication), chapter. I, resolution 1, annex I

[3] William Easterly, 'What Bono doesn't say about Africa', Los Angeles Times, 6 July 2007

tion", "extinction of species", "secondary school enrolment" ratios, etc) which are ways of measuring social development and environmental quality and sustainability, they will be creating something which can rival orthodox ways of measuring "progress", such as growth in GNP.'[4] This erstwhile academic debate has now become the accepted wisdom. As environmental activist Susan George puts it: 'Growth is not the solution but the problem'.[5] Low growth, by this definition, is sustainable and thus, in many cases, preferable.

For example, the World Bank's impressively ambitious-sounding campaign called 'Lighting Africa' aims to ensure that people can have sufficient ability to read even after the sun goes down — a basic aspiration that we in the west have not even had to think about since Edison. However, the sustainability agenda means that the low-energy light bulbs offered to illuminate homes in Africa will only go ahead if they are powered by solar, wind power or by 'mechanical means like hand-cranking and pedal power'[6] Even Trevor Bayliss, the inventor of the wind-up radio recognises that 'a large amount of human effort is required to generate even a modest amount of power,'[7] (60 seconds of radio hand- cranking earns you 3–5 minutes of digital audio broadcasting), but when it comes to sustainability, that is not high up the list of considerations. Primarily, sustainability's goal is to minimise the so-called energy impact that humanity has on the planet. 'The alternative,' moans Jonathon Porritt, 'is the whole of Africa, the whole of South East Asia, the whole of South America, China, India will be covered by central grid based systems.'

Without any apparent need to excuse his anti-developmental worldview, Porritt says: 'Massive large power stations, connecting up every single individual wherever they are in that country, to a centralised distribution system of large-scale energy generation. That's it, that's the end of the world.'[8] Obviously, for an African having to expend time and energy on a treadle so that a family member can read a book is apparently of no consequence in this vision of a self-sustaining slave economy. Slaves, that is, to the whims of

[4]    'The Caracas Report on Alternative Development. 1989. Redefining Wealth and Progress: New Ways to Measure Economic, Social and Environmental Change', The Bootstrap Press, 1990
[5]    Susan George, 'Another World Possible if …' Verso, 2004, p49
[6]    News release, 'Brightening the Night in Africa', 5 September 2007, World Bank
[7]    Meg Carter, 'Man power: a great alternative', The Independent, 26 October 2006
[8]    Jonathon Porritt, 'An audience with Jonathon Porritt,' The Lowry, Salford Quays, 7 October 2003

nature—and also to the intrusion of the sustainable development lobby.

For most Africans, as it happens, a centralised distribution network of energy supply would actually be the *start* of the new world. African film-maker De Roy Kwesi Andrew makes the simple observation: 'Scientific, technological and industrial developments have given our peers in the West enviable and unparalleled freedom, choices and opportunities in life. The labour-intensive work in Ghana is intolerable.'[9] But even those who appear to want the best for the Third World, who recognise that debt and primary production are severe problems to be addressed and who say that they want to lift people out of poverty, argue that they 'need decades of "policy space" in order to prepare themselves.'[10] Not the most inspiring message for the starving of the world. Those offering the treadle pump as a liberation from having to buy diesel for the inefficient generators that now power their irrigation systems, say that it is good for families because the need to have a human being operating these things for six hours a day tends 'to reduce significantly seasonal migration for the father ... creating a more stable family environment for the children.' In other words, where a father might otherwise travel to the city to find work, the treadle pump forces him to stay at home—maintaining the self-preserving nuclear family. A report notes that 'the operating hours for the pump (from 5 am) did not conflict with school hours.'[11] Forget the aspiration, forget the homework, just get pedalling.

Nowadays, any old reactionary policy can be presented as enlightened thinking. Speaking about non-Western societies, UK journalist David Cox says that 'it is the desire of these people to abandon globally benign lifestyles and to mimic our destructive ones that poses the real threat to our future. Asians and Africans do not just covet our cars and televisions; they want to travel the world as well. Perhaps even more dangerously, they are developing a taste for meat.'[12] Let them eat dirt, maybe?

[9]   De Roy Kwesi Andrew, 'You hate being affluent? Then swap with us', spiked-online, 29 August 2007

[10]  Cowan Coventry, 'Opening address: Reclaiming science for sustainable development,' Public Good or Private Gain? ITDG, 11 November 2004

[11]  Adrien Couton, 'A Fairy Tale For All?: A Rapid Assessment of IDEI's Treadle Pump Program in Uttar Pradesh and its Impact on Children's Welfare', Acumen Fund, June 2007

[12]  David Cox, 'The multiplication factor', Comment is Free, The Guardian, 12 February 2007

Rousseau's 'let them eat cake' quip is perfectly apposite for the latest sustainability fad for understanding progress. The 'happiness agenda,' developed by Lord Layard at the behest of the UK government, simply states that personal and societal development should be measured on the basis of 'happiness' and 'well-being' instead of GDP and personal income. It concentrates on 'quality of life' issues as opposed to increased lifespan realities, and dares to suggest that a person in the developing world might be richer in ethereal contentment than his or her counterpart in the West. Tell that to the 58 million children worldwide suffering from acute malnutrition.[13] Even if you accept this relativistic tosh, the reality still remains that, in general, the person in the developing world is still poorer. The adoption of the happiness agenda in policy circles is transforming the developing world into a palace of imaginary riches without having to do anything. By a simple definitional sleight of hand, underdevelopment can be turned on its head.

The ex-mayor of Bogota, Columbia says 'I realised that we in the Third World are not going to catch up to the developed countries for two or three hundred years ... If we defined our success just in terms of income per capita, we would have to accept ourselves as second- or third-rate societies—as a bunch of losers—which is not exactly enticing for our young people. So we are forced to find another measure of success. I think the only real obvious measure of success is happiness.'[14] This kind of self-deception for domestic consumption in the underdeveloped world is one thing, but the fact that the developed world also chooses to celebrate it creates a wistful sense of Rousseau's 'noble savage', where undeveloped countries can be described as 'poor but happy.'[15] This type of approach—making a virtue of poverty—is summed up in the New Economics Foundation's (nef) 'Happy Planet Index' which shows that 'happiness doesn't have to cost the earth'. By their standards it doesn't have to cost anything. They assert that the South Pacific island nation of Vanuatu is the happiest country in the world: it is also one of the poorest in the world, but hey, you can't have everything. For nef they are at least, sustainably poor ... and happy, to boot. In 'The Future of Life', Harvard ecologist EO Wilson even makes the serious suggestion that the

[13]  Save The Children, 'Hunger', www.savethechildren.org.uk
[14]  Charles Montgomery, 'Bogota's urban happiness movement', Globe and Mail, 25 June 2007
[15]  Ruut Veenhoven, 'Sustainable Consumption And Happiness', Paper presented at the international workshop 'Driving forces and barriers to sustainable consumption' University of Leeds, UK, March 5-6, 2004

poor should be paid *not* to develop, on the contractual understanding that they steward the reserves of wilderness. I know that they
think that this hands-off response is not exploitative, but it is. It is the
moral equivalent of having the natives dance for the boss-man.

At least when old Nazi filmmaker, Leni Riefenstahl posed with
the Nubians in the 1970s ('a primitivist ... portrait of a people sub-
sisting in a pure harmony with their environment, untouched by
"civilization."'[16]) there was considerable critical debate about it. At
the time, it was an uncomfortable reminder of the West's close colonial past. In the contemporary period, the insidiousness inversion of
the reality of underdevelopment has been allowed to go unchal-
lenged. As long as poverty is seen as virtuous, attempts to improve
the lot of the poor can be interpreted as an act of defilement.
Vandana Shiva, the environmental campaigner feted in the West,
suggests that the problem with current policy initiatives is that they
focus on the belief that 'people are poor at a dollar a day. I've grown
up in the Himalayas,' she says, 'there's no cash economy there. People are wealthy at zero dollars a day. The point is that you need to
have a clean stream. If your forest is intact and your stream is flow-
ing and your knowledge is with you, and you can grow your food
and you recognise the herbs that can cure you and you have mutual-
ity of labour exchange, so that you come and work on my farm, and I
come and work at your farm, why on earth would you need either
dollars or rupees?'[17] Er ... to buy things?

Now, the World Bank's initiatives can mirror these pitiful examples of maintaining the poorest people in the world in conditions
that are deemed sustainable. Sheela Patel, founder of the Society for
the Promotion of Area Resources which campaigns on behalf of
pavement dwellers says that there are three typical responses when
it comes to demands for development investment for the urban
poor. 'First,' she says, 'the belief is that economic problems should be
sorted out in rural areas so that people stay there and don't move
into cities. Second, people who have abandoned the countryside
should move back, though they can't survive there anymore when
the whole global economic order is going toward more efficient agriculture and non-agricultural products. Finally, some urban planners

[16] Susan Sontag reviewing The Last of the Nuba by Leni Riefenstahl (1974)
'Fascinating Fascism', New York Review of Books, 6 February 1975, republished
in: Under the Sign of Saturn (New York) 1980, pp. 73-105
[17] Vandana Shiva, 'An Hour With Vandana Shiva, Indian Scientist and Leading
Critic of Corporate Globalization', Interview with Amy Goodman, Democracy
Now, 27 November 2003, www.democracynow.org

believe that poor migrants have "spoiled our city" and they want gated cities modelled on Singapore. In the meantime, the poor keep moving into the cities.'[18]

In Sierra Leone, officially designated, at the time of writing as the poorest country in the world, a Canadian International Development Agency is teaching the meaning of self-reliance by organising children to clean up pollution on the beach at Lakka. In one of its poster campaigns it flaunts its exploitative kernel: 'No pay. No Perks. Just hard work and a clean, healthy beach when they were done.' One of the children, Isaac, a child of around nine years old says, 'sometimes tourists give us money when they see what a great job we're doing. Then we can buy some food and fill our stomachs. I like that.'[19] As part of the UK's school curriculum, children are twinned with those in Sierra Leone where the latter clean up the sea, and are asked whether they found 'any treasures in your trash? Were there items that could be recycled? Composted?'[20] Presumably this is what Hilary Benn MP meant when he said that we have to work 'with the grain of local culture, not against it.'[21] In translation, it means maintaining the iniquitous standards of development in order to prop up extant social structures. But social structures are, or should be, in a state of flux: the meddling of aid organisations simply congeals these relations and refuses to accept that people want significantly more.

Charity Practical Action is providing help in flood prone Bangladesh where people's crops and livelihoods are regularly threatened by flood tides, by training them in 'aquaculture'; this means that instead of protecting them from the floods, they are encouraged to accommodate to it. They are trained to become fishermen — even though 11 million Bangladeshis are already fishermen of one sort or another — and to grow water resistant crops. This is not progress, this is a coping strategy and is the new way of squaring the sustainable development circle.

UK's Guardian newspaper ran a Christmas appeal with the charity Positive Action (established by Dr E F 'Small is beautiful'

[18]   Sheela Patel, 'Empowering Slum Dwellers: Bombay's Pavement Dwellers Live in Extreme Poverty — But With Hope', Development Gateway Communities, http://home.developmentgateway.org, 7 September 2004

[19]   OwlKids, 'Trash Busters,' Canadian International Development Agency

[20]   Natalie Charlton and Janet Sondresen, 'A Day in the Life of a Child in Sierra Leone', Grade 6 Social Studies Unit, BC/Sask

[21]   Hilary Benn, 'SERA Annual Lecture: "Can Development be Sustainable?"' 24 November 2004

Schumacher) focussing on Bangladesh, where, with their encouragement, locals were encouraged to be inventive with their only staple crop: lettuce. No questions asked about the dire nutritional situation the locals existed in; for them it was simply good enough to see that one woman had the wherewithal to have 'created a much talked about delicacy: lettuce fish curry.' [22] Yum!

Sustainability implies that progress to a high-input conventional agriculture is not a viable alternative. After all, the Millennium Development Goals are explicit in their insistence that 'no effort must be spared to free all of humanity... from the threat of living on a planet irredeemably spoilt by human activities'[23] and back-breaking labour is as environmentally-friendly as it gets. In the Kagera River Basin around Rwanda and Uganda there is a scheme proposed to encourage youth to remain in rural areas through improved livelihood opportunities arising out of 'sustainable intensification.'[24] High tech, energy-intensive rapid development is almost, by definition, impermissible. Instead, progress is reinterpreted to imply that the situation demands 'a shift toward a more sustainable farming system utilising local resources.'[25]

And so, what is really on offer to the Developing World is counselling advice about how to live sustainably — *within the limits of their social circumstances* — rather than providing any real assistance to lift themselves out of it. When it comes to global warming, the Big Idea is called 'mainstreaming adaptation.'[26] This means that 'developing countries should curb their rising greenhouse-gas emissions, even at the cost of slowing down development'.[27] The hypothesis (discussed in the Stern Review Report on the Economics of Climate Change) is that meliorating the effects of global warming is not really a viable option for poor countries, but altering their behaviour in line with the current low growth/ low carbon orthodoxy is eminently achiev-

[22] Randeep Ramesh, 'New hope for Bangladesh's climate change refugees', The Guardian, 6 January 2007
[23] Millennium Development Goals, Environment and Sustainable Development', United Nations Development Programme, www.undp.org
[24] United Nations Environment Programme: Global Environment Facility, 'Transboundary Agro-Ecosystem Management Programme For The Kagera River Basin (Kagera Tamp)', Full Project Brief, 2006, p25
[25] Tariq Banuri, Adil Najam, Nancy Odeh, ed, 'CIVIC Entrepreneurship: A Civil Society Perspective on Sustainable Development', Volume 5, South East Asia Report, Gandhara Academy Press, 2002, p84
[26] Stern Review Workshop, 'The Economics of Adaptation', HM Treasury, London, UK, 9 May 2006
[27] Chandrashekhar Dasgupta, 'Climate-Change Challenge for the Poor — Part I', YaleGlobal, Yale Center for the Study of Globalization, 26 September 2007

able. In Mali, for example, official suggestions to avoid the effects of climate change include using 'locally manufactured energy saving technologies (ovens, charcoal cookers and stoves ... using charcoal from agricultural wastes)'.[28] Anything vaguely modern will exacerbate climate change apparently, and so there is only advice on how to be more prudent and less ambitious. 'Rural communities (should) adopt more efficient alternative solutions,' one influential report says, 'without leaving their local environment, based on their own life experiences and on ancient traditions and practices.'[29] Thus sustainable development puts real development back fifty years.

## Natural states

As we have seen, an increasing number of commentators portray poverty as more rewarding than material development; and suggest that living in 'harmony with nature' is more honourable than modernity. One designer writes of a squatter settlement in Kenya: 'their dynamic attitude to shelter ... to those used to a more product-oriented building industry, can seem quite refreshing.'[30] Partly, this is about romanticising the simple life. French president Nicholas Sarkozy thus believes that 'the modern man who feels a need to reconcile himself with nature has a lot to learn from the African man who has lived in harmony with nature for millennia.'[31] In the guise of protecting the simple life, there is a dangerous rejection of progress (which is seen as unsustainable) and of development (which is viewed as unnecessary). But there is also a shift away from understanding poverty as a result of real, social and political forces, and towards blaming the forces of nature. The Department for International Development states that the 'degradation of ecosystem services is harming many of the world's poorest people and is sometimes the principal factor causing poverty.' It concludes that: 'Environmental objectives should therefore be integrated into development policy to avoid environmental risks and promote environmental opportunities for enhancing development.'[32]

[28]  Saleemul Huq, Atiq Rahman, Mama Konate, Youba Sokona and Hannah Reid, 'Mainstreaming Adaptation to Climate Change', IIED, 2003
[29]  Saleemul Huq, Atiq Rahman, Mama Konate, Youba Sokona and Hannah Reid, 'Mainstreaming Adaptation to Climate Change', IIED, 2003
[30]  Martin Valatin, 'Building Design', ArcPeace, 11 August 1995
[31]  President Nicholas Sarkozy, 'Excerpts from the speech by Nicholas Sarkozy', in Dakar, Senegal on 26 July 2007, Translation for the Royal African Society
[32]  Department for International Development, 'Environmental Sustainability Factsheet', November 2006

To put it starkly, Friends of the Earth believe that ecological damage is a 'principal factor causing poverty.'[33] But this isn't the way that the relationship between society and nature has always been seen. Back in 1972, the United Nations Stockholm Conference on the Human Environment noted that: 'In the developing countries most of the environmental problems are caused by under-development.'[34] The solution, at least notionally, was for more development. As we have seen, more development in today's context, is seen as potentially harmful and so, just 30 years later, the belief in human agency has been turned on its head and natural factors are cited as the cause of social ills.

Researcher David Satterthwaite notes that poverty and a poor environment need to be addressed simultaneously precisely because 'the poor suffer disproportionately from the ill effects of environmental decline'. His observation that poor people live in poor conditions might be blindingly obvious to some, but his remedy has less to do with the desire to lift people out of poverty and instead to insist on more environmental regulation. If the contemporary assumption is that poor environmental conditions actually *generate* poverty, then the primary focus is to alleviate environmental harm. Hey presto, protecting the environment becomes an anti-poverty measure. Conversely, the lives of the poor can be improved by objecting to any of their activities that might cause environmental harm. As an example, international agencies can argue that 'renewable energy' — which is implicitly benign — 'has a major role to play in reducing poverty while protecting the environment.'[35]

Campaigning authors, Frances Christie and Joseph Hanlon's work on Mozambique and the great floods of 2000 outlines their belief that 'the existence of dams did not ameliorate the floods ...' and in fact human activity made them worse. Increasingly, the people of the underdeveloped world are not only not being offered development, but there is a creeping self-justification that to provide development will be bad for them. WorldWrite, one of the rare pro-development charitable organisations, counters this correctly

[33] Roger Higman, Press Release, 'Millennium Ecosystem Assessment', 31 March 2005

[34] United Nations Development Programme, 'Declaration of the United Nations Conference on the Human Environment,' Proclamation 4, 16 June 1972

[35] World Bank, 'Improving Lives: World Bank Progress on Renewable Energy and Energy Efficiency in Fiscal Year 2006', 23 January 2007 reported in Kathryn McConnell, 'Energy Projects Can Play Key Role in Reducing Poverty', America.gov, 24 January 2007

by asking: 'Where is the risk of flooding worse: in Mozambique or in Holland; a country at or below sea level? In Mozambique obviously, and yet Western countries are far more developed and have many times more dams than Mozambique. It is not dams and irrigation schemes, but too few dams and too little irrigation that are the cause of Mozambique's problems.'[36]

After the recent cyclone devastation in Bangladesh, hardly any voices were raised to argue for flood barriers, major roads and a Bangladeshi national economy that goes beyond subsistence. In fact the World Bank said that preparing 'elaborate action plans is not the way to go' preferring to implement early warning systems and after-the- event disaster mitigation programmes.[37] The brute forces of nature, you see, are apparently brought on by too much, not too little, development.

Instead of recognising the need to tackle the iniquities of the system, organisations like The Food and Agriculture Organisation of the United Nations (FAO) are promoting a retreat into parochial social relations. It defines Sustainable Agriculture and Rural Development (SARD) as a process which provides 'basic nutritional requirements' avoiding 'disrupting the functioning of basic ecological cycles and natural balances' while 'strengthen(ing) self-reliance'.[38] This official focus on natural and local causality means that few sustainability advocates ever really protest about the geo-political reality of under-development. The reality for developing countries is that they still have to produce cash crops for export in order to pay mounting debt levels. This political (and note: *not* an environmental problem) is swept under the carpet by a promotion of the idea that inequalities are a function of climate fluctuations, natural occurrences and suchlike.

Sustainability has now become the catch-all position and explanation for almost all complicated geo-political and economic global problems. For example, a Palestinian National Authority spokesman argues that the 'Israeli occupation has destroyed (infrastructural) projects in order to devastate the Palestinian economy and to prevent

[36]  WORLDwrite, 'WSSD World Summit on Sustainable Development: A critical Memorandum', 2002, p10
[37]  Xian Zhu, Country Director, World Bank, 'Floods in Bangladesh: The Way Forward,' 6 November 2007
[38]  From FAO Trainer's Manual, Vol. 1, 'Sustainability issues in agricultural and rural development policies,' Food and Agricultural Organisation, 1995

the Palestinians from achieving sustainable development.'[39] After fifty years of geo-politics, 'sustainability' must surely be one of the dumbest critiques of the motivations of the Arab-Israeli conflict. But there's worse. After a century of colonialism and civil war the Rwandan Minister of State for Lands and Environment can say that 'climate change has a very high negative impact on Rwanda's economy, our food security, and the health and well being of our people'.[40] Nothing, it seems, destroys perspective like environmentalism.

## Intervention

For some time, pro-Third World campaigners have insisted that the West had a penitential duty to intervene to right its prior wrongs. This served to legitimise the notion that intervention, of the right sort, was desirable as a way of compensating for the 'consequence(s) of our colonial past'.[41] Under the sustainability mandate, this takes on a more urgent focus. Given that it is no longer seen as illegitimate to intervene to protect the environment, the only questions remaining are: what are the criteria for intervention? — and which are the unfortunate countries to receive colonial largesse? The Department for International Development (DfID) White Paper 'Making governance work for poor people' aims to '(build) states that are capable, responsive and accountable to their citizens.'[42] In other words, this is about intervention in the affairs of sovereign states. The influential Commission for Africa states that they must carry out its bidding and are told that they must include sustainable development in their policymaking bodies: 'If Africa fails to do all this, the international community will find it far more difficult to discharge its responsibilities'.[43]

Not so long ago, activists used to protest about the International Monetary Fund (IMF) and World Bank's intrusion into the Third World and rightly expose the brutal nature of its 'structural adjust-

[39] 'Statement by State of Palestine at the World Summit on Sustainable Development', Johannesburg, South Africa, 4 September 2002
[40] Patricia Hajabakiga, Rwanda's Minister of State in Charge of Lands and Environment, 'Rwanda: Coping with Global Warming in Africa', Development Gateway Special Collection, May 2007
[41] Anton La Guardia, 'Straw blames crises on Britain's colonial past,' Daily Telegraph, 15 November 2002
[42] The Department for International Development, 'Making governance work for poor people: Eliminating world poverty', White Paper, DfID
[43] 'Our Common Interest: Report of the Commission for Africa', Part 2, Analysis and Evidence, Item 33, 11 March 2005, p89

ment programmes' which imposed duties on the government and businesses within the donee country to liberalise trade relations at the expense of sovereign authority. Now a main criticism seems to be that the intervention in the affairs of another nation state is not being carried out sufficiently stringently. As Oxfam put it in their report on the causes of hunger in Africa, 'donor institutions such as the World Bank are rightly accused of ... failing to enforce conditions that would ensure proper use and full accountability of loans and aid.'[44] The New Economic Foundation calls them 'sustainable adjustment programmes'.[45] Same intervention; different language. Instead of debt repayments, sustainable aid campaigners demand 'transparency' and environmental accountability. One agency clarifies colonial opportunities on offer: 'Aid for Africa is just great value for money ... the investment reaps huge returns.'[46] That wasn't the International Monetary Fund speaking, circa 1975; that was Africa's eco-saviour, Bono, speaking his mind in 2005.

The new interventions are legitimated on the basis of sustainability. 'Good governance' incorporates the notion of responsible, sustainable development. In this way sustainability is a vehicle for Western intervention into sovereign states and forms the backbone of sustainable development as far as international agencies such as the United Nations and World Bank are concerned. With particular reference to Africa, governance describes 'the general manner in which a people are governed'[47] and these global institutions set out to influence that process. It's what author Paul Driessen calls 'eco-imperialism' or 'a virulent kind of neo-colonialism'.[48] The United Nations Millennium Declaration 2000 seeks to intervene even more explicitly in the business of errant countries to ensure that their debt is 'sustainable' and it empowers member States to 'spare no effort to promote democracy and strengthen the rule of law, as

[44]  Oxfam Briefing Paper, 'Causing Hunger an overview of the food crisis in Africa', OXFAM, 24 July 2006

[45]  Andrew Simms, 'An Environmental War Economy The lessons of ecological debt and global warming', New Economics Foundation, 2001, p22

[46]  Bono, TED Talks, 'TED Prize Wish: Join my call to action on Africa', www.ted.com, Feb 2005 (Posted Oct 2006)

[47]  Patricia McCarney, Mohamed Halfani and Alfredo Rodriguez, 'Towards an Understanding of Governance' quoted in Richard Stren and Judith Bell, ed., 'Urban Research in the Developing World. Vol. 4. Perspectives on the City'. Toronto: Centre for Urban and Community Studies, University of Toronto) 1995, p94

[48]  Paul Driessen, 'Eco-Imperialism: Green Power - Black Death', Free Enterprise Press. 2003

well as respect for all internationally recognised human rights and fundamental freedoms.'[49] Nothing wrong with the words, you understand, it's just that it is faintly reminiscent of past interventions by agencies helping to improve the stability and alleviate the injustices of their own making. In 1944, the Venerable Archdeacon A. P. Gower-Rees described the benefits of Empire as having:

> established peace, order and justice ... It guarantees to every individual of whatever race or colour, an equal liberty ... It protects them from devastation from without and from disorder within. It bridges, in its laws and institutions, the gulf between East and West, between white and black, between race and race ... To all it promises not good government only, but eventual self-government. Its whole purpose is to ensure that every citizen may lead the fullest and freest life, consistent with the acknowledgement and discharge of his duties.[50]

Today, the ambitions for 'sustainability' could easily be substituted for 'Empire' as once again, a social and economic project manifests itself as a means of social solidarity at home via its moral mission to save 'Johnny Foreigner' from himself. And they are starting them young. As part of the UK's education system, the Qualifications and Standards Authority (the body that sets the citizenship agenda as a key aspect of every lesson in the curriculum), says 'Empire paternalism has given way to relationships with the European Union, Commonwealth and United Nations, and broader issues of global interdependence and sustainable development.'[51] In this framing, sustainability is simply the latest in a long historical continuum of interventions.

So argues the UK-based charity WorldWrite in their film 'Damned by Debt Relief'. Under the more allegedly benign interventions, like the fight against poverty for example: 'Poverty reduction strategies have created a new regulatory framework, one which gives western donors the authority to police every aspect of life in the poorest countries ... This level of western interference and prescription out-

[49] United Nations, 'United Nations Millennium Declaration', General Assembly resolution 55/2, 8 September 2000

[50] A. P. Gower-Rees, 'Sharing The Responsibilities Of Empire', An Address By The Venerable Archdeacon A. P. Gower-Rees, Archdeacon of Montreal, The Empire Club of Canada, 13 January 1944

[51] Ofsted, 'Towards consensus? Citizenship in secondary schools', September 2006, p8

strips colonial rule in its capacity to seep into every facet of life unopposed.'[52]

Robert H. Nelson, professor at the School of Public Affairs of Maryland says that environmentalists display a 'colonial- style paternalism toward people they regard as the benighted peasants of the Third World, and (are motivated) by guilt for the perceived wrongdoing of their colonial antecedents. This pursuit of a mixture of material and socio-political aims has become endemic in Third World conservation projects initiated by Westerners.'[53] Once the legitimacy for intervening in sovereign states is drawn, some people feel relaxed enough to flex their previously dormant colonial rhetoric. Enter, environmental activist, Jonathon Porritt (son of Lord Porritt, who held the ex-imperial position of Governor-General and Commander-in-Chief in and over New Zealand) who is quick to show his quasi-colonial colours: 'It's blindingly obvious,' he says, 'completely unsustainable population growth in most of Africa will keep it permanently, hopelessly stuck in deepest, darkest poverty.'[54] What is blindingly obvious is Lord Porritt's recipe for disaster in his Dark Continent. His refusal to countenance progressing underdeveloped countries so that they can cast off the uncertain, insanitary conditions that many have to put up with, is precisely because that would necessitate their growing use of energy and resources. It is inconceivable to him that they be allowed to increase their carbon footprint.

## Speaking for the disenfranchised

Non-experts, such as Porritt, Friends of the Earth, New Economics Foundation, et al are just as dangerous as any governmental or World Bank interference. They describe how, from 2008, at a stroke, the World Bank has been advised to stop financing oil and coal extractive industries especially in countries with 'weak governance'.[55] The repercussions are undocumented as yet, but such a devastating withdrawal has been justified on the basis of averting climate change, from which the poor will be the most susceptible. So,

[52] WorldWrite, 'Damned by Debt Relief: Pricking the Missionary Position', www.worldwrite.org.uk
[53] Robert H. Nelson, 'Environmental Colonialism "Saving" Africa from Africans,' The Independent Review, vol. VIII, n.1, Summer 2003
[54] Jonathon Porritt, 'If I was in government ... Jonathon Porritt makes population his number one issue', Ecologist Online, April 2007, www.optimumpopulation.org
[55] Friends of the Earth, 'Extracting the World Bank from fossil fuels', quoted in Andrew Simms, John Magrath and Hannah Reid 'Up in smoke? Threats from, and responses to, the impact of global warming on human development', nef, 2004

with the magic bullet of environmentalism, even throwing people out of jobs can be re-defined as a positive pro-poor policy.

The influential International Institute for Environment and Development (IIED) says that 'As a subsistence activity, then, farming forms a direct link between the production of food and the health and well-being of the small producer – a link that is far more immediate than in those countries where farming is simply a means of earning money.'[56] For them, subsistence farming is a cultural activity. Andrew Simms of the New Economics Foundation says that '"sustainable agriculture" – a mixture of environmental and pro-poor approaches to growing food – brings massively higher increases in overall productivity than anything achieved through genetic modification'.[57] He means, of course, 'resource productivity' not 'human productivity'. In Simms' world, expending human labour time on the mundane is of no consequence if it can be shown that fewer natural materials are used.

Criticising the 'corporates' for seeking profit over poverty reduction – which is hardly an earth-shattering revelation about the global market – he presumes to speak for the poor and disenfranchised. Disenfranchisement is a boon for those organisations that then seek to act as their spokespersons, even though these unelected 'representatives' don't seem to recognise the irony of speaking on their behalf. Their position guarantees that the people for whom they deign to speak remain in disempowered penury for a while longer; for at least as long as hard-labour (or ... 'sustainable agriculture') remains their only agricultural choice. For anti-corporate activists, as long as it is nation states (and NGOs) rather than corporates that legitimate the unending drudgery suffered by subsistence farmers, forcing them to eke a miserable living, then, it seems, it's OK. And as long as subsistence farmers scratch their living using traditional, sustainable implements, sustainability advocates can rest contented in their beds. The dominance of this rhetoric means that even those who wish to improve the lot of the poor of the world have to tread carefully. For all their hype, most countries in the Third World – even the more rapidly developing world – find it

[56] Michel Pimbert, Khanh Tran-Thanh, Estelle Deléage, Magali Reinert, Christophe Trehet and Elizabeth Bennett, (eds), 'Farmers' Views on the Future of Food and Small-Scale Producers', Summary of an Electronic Conference, 14 April to 1 July, 2005, p20

[57] Andrew Simms, 'World hunger needs a simple solution rather than hi-tech GM food', The Guardian, 4 August 2003

impossible to opt out of the moral framework of geopolitical relations today, i.e. sustainability. Here's a few examples:

Zimbabwe, a country suffering from acute food shortages and rampant inflation, now leads the UN Commission on Sustainable Development. The United Nations is currently prioritising sustainable development principles in the industrial sector in Baghdad and assuring the involvement of 'civil society and NGO (*sic*) in the environmental and social problems.'[58] Villagers in rural Guatemala, a country with the highest malnutrition rate in Latin America[59] are encouraged to 'promote sustainable agriculture' by selling sacks of chicken manure to be used as organic fertilizer. Commenting on Ethiopia's export of flowers, Hilary Benn, UK's previous secretary of state for international development insisted that a country with between 6 and 13 million people at risk of starvation, should show that there is 'room for improvement … in their environmental practice'.[60] Sudan, wracked by civil war, is proud to announce that it has been using unleaded fuel since 2002.[61] WaterAid is working with Malawi, the poorest country on earth, to provide sustainable sanitation stating that: 'Many cultures have understood the value of urine and faeces for agricultural purposes for centuries.'[62] These are just some of the weird and not-so-wonderful examples of the inexorable spread of sustainability into the developing world.

Watching the developing world's dynamic potential being restrained, some in the West are frustrated at the wasted opportunities, but are tied up in their own battles with sustainability. Sir Richard Branson wants further ties with Kenya but his Virgin flights to Nairobi have been criticised by those who want to reduce the amount of 'carbon miles' of food produce, threatening to cut off the trade benefits to more than a million people opening up to the world

[58]   'The Environmental and Social Assessment of the Industrial Sector in Baghdad', UN Department for Economic and Social Affairs, Division of Sustainable Development, http://webapps01.un.org

[59]   UNICEF, 'Progress For Children: A Report Card on Nutrition', Number 4, May 2006, The United Nations Children's Fund and www.unicef.org

[60]   Hilary Benn, MP, in 'Commons Hansard', House of Commons, 23 March 2007, Column 1155W

[61]   Saadeldin Ibrahim, Secretary-General For The High Council On Environment And Natural Resources Of The Sudan, 'Sustainable Development Commission Concludes Fifteenth Session Without Policy Decisions On Energy, Industrial Development, Air Pollution, Climate Change', Commission On Sustainable Development, Fifteenth Session, 11th & 12th Meetings, Economic And Social Council, Env/Dev/938, 11 May 2007

[62]   Steven Sugden, 'One step closer to sustainable sanitation: Experiences of an ecological sanitation project in Malawi', WaterAid, Malawi, August 2003

market. To his credit, Branson pointed out that whatever you might think about the global environment — and he has a record of pontificating about climate change himself — stopping trade in this way with Africa 'was a step too far'. He said, 'Let the Africans have a chance to have some dignity and have a life.'[63] Unfortunately, the logic of sustainability denies them that.

## Turning East

One player less restricted than most, is China. China is a major development force in countries as far afield as Sudan to Brazil and has altered the perception of morally-charged aid packages. China, it seems, is primarily interested in business relationships. In many respects, its friendship is pragmatic, built as it is on the desire to benefit from purely profitable market relations as opposed to developing the relations of social capital. While the poor countries benefit, this is definitely still a profit-driven relationship. But lets not get carried away. Professor Robert L Paarlberg, in response to Lester Brown's Worldwatch Institute argued that while China (and the West) has good standards of living, it is Africa, not China that faces the food crisis.[64] Excluding South Africa, the continent (of Africa) produces only as much as Belgium ... by 2000, the typical African economy had an income no larger than the suburb of a major American city.'[65]

Even so, remote towns in like Novo Progresso (appositely translated as New Progress) in faraway Brazil, are providing top class timber for China's massive construction boom. Nearer to home, China has signed an aid package[66] worth £400 million with Cambodia and is lending £300 million to the Philippines for a railway project. Chinese president Hu Jintao recently pledged increased funding for Africa including £2 billion in loans, £1.5 billion in export credits and a £3 billion fund to encourage even more investment in Africa. His claim that China follows 'a policy of non-interference in other countries' internal affairs' is somewhat ironic, but International Relations expert Chris Alden does concede that 'the ideology of a "civilising mission", the accompanying territorial imperative

[63]   Hugo Duncan, 'Branson slams M&S on Africa import cuts', Thisismoney.co.uk, 4 June 2007
[64]   Robert L Paarlberg, 'Rice Bowls and Dust Bowls: Africa, Not China, Faces a Food Crisis', Foreign Affairs, May/June 1996
[65]   Robert Calderisi, 'The Trouble with Africa: Why Foreign Aid Isn't Working', Yale University Press, 2006, p43
[66]   Chris Alden, 'China in Africa', African Arguments, Zed Books, 2007, p127

and forging of exclusionary trade relations — are distinctly lacking in China's foreign policy'. However, this has to be weighed up against the fact that during the period between 2000 and 2005 when China quadrupled its investment in Africa from £7.5 billion to £30 billion, growth in GDP in sub-Saharan Africa has doubled from 3 to 6 per cent over the same period, with productivity reaching 3 per cent in 2006.[67] Surely no coincidence? A hydroelectric plant at the Inga Rapids, near the mouth of the River Congo in the western Democratic Republic of Congo, costs over £35 billion but will generate around 40,000 megawatts, twice the power of China's Three Gorges dam, becoming the world's largest power project.

One leading US environmental networking site describes sustainability as 'both a revolution and an inevitable next stage for humanity — akin to the industrial revolution,' adding that it is also, in many ways, 'that period's polar opposite.'[68] Actually, it is simply its opposite: it is low growth and slow industrialisation. In many regards, it is as a revolt against this stasis that the underdeveloped world is tiring of Western intervention. As the reinvigorated Pan-African Movement say: 'Africans must stop looking outside for our progress. Our salvation is within us. We are our own liberators.'[69] They want more than passive happiness, they want the real world — or at least they want a damn sight more of what the rest of the world has. And good luck to them: they should have it. Nigerian president Olusegun Obasanjo is quoted a saying that 'the 21st century is the century for China to lead the world. And when you are leading the world, we want to be close behind you. When you are going to the moon, we don't want to be left behind.'[70]

[67]   International Monetary Fund, 'World Economic and Financial Surveys, 'Regional Economic Outlook: Sub-Saharan Africa', April 2007
[68]   www.lime.com
[69]   Dr Tajudeen Abdul-Raheem, General-Secretary of the Pan African Movement, 'Nothing about us without us', Pambazuka News, News from Africa, 10 June 2005
[70]   Chris Alden, 'China in Africa', African Arguments, Zed Books, 2007, p68-69

# CHAPTER 7

# THE MISANTHROPISTS

*America's unease with Modernity*

A spectre is haunting America — the spectre of sustainability. However, such is the softly-softly approach to this incursion that few American political pundits will recognise the extent of the incendiary influence it already plays in the US. Meanwhile, across the Atlantic in Great Britain, the assertion that sustainability plays any significant part at all in American society will be greeted with incredulity, especially by the environmental hardcore in Britain who consider 'anti-environmentalism' synonymous with 'corporate America'. As UK journalist, and the ex-Washington correspondent of The Guardian newspaper, Matthew Engel said: 'the US is a world leader in hastening each of these five crises ... lack of fresh water; destruction of forest and crop land; global warming; overuse of natural resources; and the continuing rise in the population ... bringing its gargantuan appetite to the business of ravaging the planet.'[1]

The anti-American sentiment inherent the environmental cause and regularly displayed by some sections of the UK's media establishment seems to have reinvigorated a tired British political scene. Two renowned British cultural commentators observe that a 'loathing for America is about as close as we can get to a universal sentiment.'[2] A desire not to be seen as America's poodle frequently lurks under the surface of the debate, and is something of a stick to beat the Americans with. From the Special Relationship to the Gulf War, par-

[1]  Road to ruin', Matthew Engel, Guardian Weekly, 24 October 2003
[2]  Ziauddin Sardar and Merryl Wyn Davies, 'Why Do People Hate America', Icon Books, 2002, p195

odies of Britain's subservience to successive American presidents
have focussed years of resentment, which is now finding expression
in the coded displays of British anti-Americanism around the issue
of sustainability.

Over in the States, born-again environmentalists like Robert F
Kennedy Jnr gleefully state that if you ask anyone to name 'the greatest threat to the global environment, the answer wouldn't be over-
population or global warming or sprawl. The nearly unanimous
response would be George W Bush.'[3] Leave aside, for now, the
casual way that overpopulation is now posed as a global threat—on
both sides of the Atlantic—it is clear that some people are hiding
behind the mantle of an ecological consensus as an easier way of
dealing specifically with tough questions of Bush's presidency.
More importantly, it sounds like an alternative political vision without having any real need for substance. An environmental assault is
the easy, non-political option. As the presidential election indicates,
we may well be witnessing the rise of the anti-political politician,[4]
but we are also seeing the disappearance of political opposition. As
academic, Matthew Humphrey explains, there is a 'slightly ... worrying trend in some green political thought, the attempt to eliminate
contingency.'[5] The moral highground of sustainability and environmentalism brooks no challenge.

Admittedly, US sustainability is often honoured more in the
breach than in the observance. Californian governor, Arnold
Schwarzenegger has developed a peculiar way of popularising environmental concerns that don't seem to fit in with the classic European model. He is keen 'to show leadership in protecting our
environment'[6] even pimping his Hummer with a biodiesel conversion on prime-time TV. He boasts that now 'you can have an engine
that's fast and furious and still reduce greenhouse-gas emissions by
30 to 40 percent.'[7] For British audiences, this might seem ironic. For
contemptuous anti-Americans, it might reinforce deeply held preju-
dices. As one commentator sees it: 'in this energy-conscious culture,

[3]    Robert F Kennedy Jnr, 'Crimes Against Nature: Standing up to Bush and the
       Kyoto killers who are cashing in on our world', Penguin, 2004, p2
[4]    Mick Hume, 'What Hope for real Change in America?' 9 January 2008,
       www.spiked-online.com
[5]    Matthew Humphrey, 'Ecology, democracy and autonomy' in Marcel
       Wissenburg, Yoram Levy (eds), 'Liberal Democracy and Environmental-ism:
       The End of Environmentalism', Routledge, 2004, p125
[6]    Arnold Schwarzenegger, 'Meet the Press' NBC, 25th November, 2006
[7]    Karen Breslau, 'The Green Giant', Newsweek, April 16, 2007

driving a hybrid is noble, responsible. Drive an SUV, and you risk being seen as a villain.'[8] It is worth noting that in the same year that Schwarzenegger was customising his one-mile-a-gallon monster truck, there were six bills in the Senate addressing global warming, 'with all but one of them including a mandatory "cap and trade" system to limit carbon emissions.'[9] However you look at it, even in America, green is definitely the new black. All hail, Arnold Grünenegger. Since the start of Bush's presidency, the federal government has invested $12 billion to develop cleaner, cheaper, and more reliable energy sources[10] and launched the Advanced Energy Initiative promoting ethanol, hybrids, fuel cells and much else besides.[11] It is also reported to be 'investing more than the EU (European Union) in technologies such as carbon capture.'[12] Tell that to a British environmentalist and they won't believe you.

There is indeed a spectre haunting America—the spectre of sustainability. Sustainability dominates the European scene and is one invader that the US is powerless to prevent: to paraphrase Frederick Engels, it seems as if all the powers of old Europe have entered into an unholy alliance to promote it. In March 2007, a spokesperson for Tony Blair noted that, on the framework for a post-Kyoto agreement, the European Union was 'taking a very serious step on energy and climate change (which) in turn will give Europe the right to claim leadership in the run-up to the G8-plus-5.'[13] The purpose of this leadership is to push the rest of the developed and developing world into accepting an environmental agenda that will gradually constrain their material ambition. Sustainability is a key agenda for those states that relate to America and, as such, America is being asked to learn a new European language of restraint. As José Manuel Barroso, President of the European Commission says 'Europe must lead the world into a new, or maybe one should say post-industrial

[8]   Jason Newell, Stop Global Warming, 18 August 2006
      www.stopglobalwarming.org/
[9]   Phil Mckenna, 'The Climate Changes On Capitol Hill', New Scientist, 29 March 2007
[10]  Office of the Press Secretary, US Department of State, 'Twenty In Ten: Strengthening Energy Security And Addressing Climate Change', The White House, Washington, DC, 14 May 2007
[11]  'Advanced Energy Initiative', The White House, National Economic Council, February 2006
[12]  Stephen Castle, 'Divisions over global warming threaten EU-US climate meeting', The Independent, 27 April 2007
[13]  David Charter and Rory Watson, 'EU split over the green road ahead', The Times, March 9, 2007

revolution.'[14] Vigorously pushed by the UK — the previous foreign secretary, Margaret Becket, considered that 'dealing with climate change was no longer a choice but an imperative'[15] — this is one of the few major export markets that has successfully infiltrated the American market.

But it is now firmly established in America on its own terms. In essence, Al Gore's 1992 prediction that 'we must make the rescue of the environment the central organising principle for the world'[16] has effectively come to pass. Nowadays, if you aren't on the Gore-style environmental bandwagon, you had better, at least, be pedalling alongside if you want to be part of the global club. The classic partisan approach to political grandstanding, and one that plays well in old-style Democratic circles is that the current administration is coterminous with environmental degradation. Such is Kennedy Jnr's cheap, but stinging criticism of 'the anti-environmentalist agenda of today's White House'[17] or director of Greenpeace, Stephen Tyndall's accusation of its 'selfish, lethal, immoral' pandering to the oil industry.[18] But this is becoming more difficult to substantiate. To engage in environmental discourse will be a difficult *volte face* for the Republican Grand Old Party given its historical and rhetorical foundations and it's true that President Bush's criticism that America is 'addicted to oil'[19] rings a little hollow given the background to his families' fortunes. But the oil tanker is turning.

Back in 1997, only five years after Gore's Messianic call to arms, Senator John McCain criticised his own party by pointing out that 'the electorate (is) gravely concerned about the Republican party's commitment to the environment. In fact, it is their greatest concern ... by a margin of two to one over the next issue.' A decade further on, and Barack Obama has recognised environmentalism as the audacious consensus-forming issue he had hoped for: as far as he's concerned, it's not 'an upper-income issue, it's not a white issue, it's not a black issue, it's not a South or a North or an East or a West issue.

[14]  José Manuel Barroso, President of the European Commission, 'Energy for a Changing World', Speaking points, press conference, 10 January 2007

[15]  'Halting Climate Change No Longer Choice but Imperative; Failure to Do So Risks Undermining Prosperity, Security Worldwide, General Assembly Told' United Nations Information Service, GA/10506, 25 September 2006

[16]  Al Gore, 'Earth in the Balance — Forging a New Common Purpose', Earthscan: London, 1992

[17]  Robert F Kennedy, 'Crimes Against Nature', Penguin Books, 2004, p13

[18]  Jamie Wilson and Hugh Muir, 'Fortress London braced for anti-Bush demos', The Guardian, 19 November 2003

[19]  President Bush, State of the Union address, January 31st 2006.

It's an issue that all of us have a stake in.'[20] Prior to his competitive race to the White House, he joined forces with McCain to push for a significant carbon reduction scheme. Democratic candidate Hilary Clinton cites the Supreme Court's 'reject(ion of) the Bush Administration's "do-nothing" approach to the problem (of global warming)'[21] and begs Al Gore's blessing. The mayors of more than 300 cities across the US have come together to sign a Climate Protection Agreement 'in which they have pledged to meet the emissions-cutting timetable laid down by the Kyoto Protocol — regardless of what the Bush administration decides.'[22] Since the early 90s, the Office of International Affairs now estimates that 'there are between 850–1000 environmental NGOs (in America) and the total membership of US environmental groups (is) over 14 million people.' Since 2000, membership of the Sierra Club, America's oldest environmental organisation went up by about a third, to 800,000, in four years. This is a big, cross party issue.

It might sound as if it is a good thing that people are joining groups and that politics is being rejuvenated around an environmental consensus. After all, the decline of social capital identified by Robert Putnam[23] is a very real problem, whereby the public seems to have become estranged from collective activity and the social trust networks that they embody, and so the collective mobilisation of society to address the climate change issue might be seen positively as a creative imperative. But environmentalism, by its very nature, is founded on the notion that humans are responsible for harming the planet (regardless of the counterclaim that humans can repair it). If humans are the problem — as environmentalism argues — then human solutions can only, at best, be viewed with suspicion, and at worst, with a sneering contempt. Al Gore doesn't appreciate contrary viewpoints, pointing out that, 'part of the challenge the news media has had in covering this story is the old habit of taking the "on the one hand, on the other hand"

[20]  Amanda Griscom, 'Barack Star: Illinois Senate candidate Barack Obama's got green cred', Grist, 4 Aug 2004
[21]  Statement of Senator Hillary Rodham Clinton on the Supreme Court's Global Warming Decision, April 2, 2007
[22]  'US direct action: How American cities have bypassed Bush on Kyoto' Andrew Gumbel, 'The Independent', 1 September 2006
[23]  Robert Putnam, 'Bowling Alone: The Collapse and Revival of American Community', Simon & Schuster, 2001

approach'.[24] He would prefer that the environmental agenda had a clear run. Robert F Kennedy is less liberal, exasperatedly calling the author of a book denying the dangers of global warming, a 'fascism advocate'[25] or Boston Globe correspondent Ellen Goodman can suggest that 'we're at a point where global warming is impossible to deny. Let's just say that global warming deniers are now on a par with Holocaust deniers, though one denies the past and the other denies the present and future.'[26] Denying the future?

The absence of a critically engaged public discourse on environmental issues — and political issues more generally — caused by the closing down of public debate around environmental concerns, means that 'green' issues have entered the public domain as mantras rather than propositions to be debated, fine-tuned and rejected or accepted according to their own merits. In truth, their elevated status has been given to them, rather than won. The collapse of mainstream politics has simply left the stage open for environmentalism to dominate without them having had to win any substantial political arguments.

Undoubtedly, the flimsy nature of environmentalists' social standing is certainly something that humanists (in critical distinction to environmentalists) can capitalise on, but the cynicism about human motives that environmentalists have generated over the last two decades means that it will still be difficult even for humanists to create a political dynamic for human-centred change. There is now some trouble in the environmental camp, but before we get too enthusiastic about the greens eating themselves, we should realise that, left to its own devices, this could create an even greater, misanthropic void in political life. Even though environmentalists are not solely to blame for today's political malaise, their cynicism about human-centred actions has been, and continues to be, corrosive. Because of their influence, the progressive humanist project in which the environment can be thought of as something to be manipulated to our own ends is evaporating.

[24]   Al Gore interview with Meredith Viera on 'NBC's Today Show' quoted in Chris Mooney 'Defining Science: Out of Balance', Science Progress, 14 November 2007

[25]   Robert F Kennedy video clip shown/ quoted in CNN Transcripts of 'Glenn Beck' Aired July 12, 2007, http://transcripts.cnn.com; also Robert F. Kennedy Jr, 'For the Last, Stubborn Holdouts on Global Warming', Huffington Post, 16 January 2007

[26]   Ellen Goodman, 'No change in political climate', Boston Globe, 9 February 2007

Gone is the notion of progress defined as the exercise of human-kind's ability to overcome natural barriers. Wallowing in the contemporary acceptance of humanity's subservient — and inherently harmful — relationship with nature, has undoubtedly done psychological damage to the belief in our ability to act positively to change the world for the better. If man's actions are harmful, what good can come out of man's further intervention? When Schumacher described the desire to control nature as 'human wickedness', then it is inevitable that over the intervening years, motivations to transform the world immediately became suspect.

Being fearful of the future, and suspicious of our own motivations for wanting to get there, is not the best starting point to be able to change things for the better. Transforming the future cannot come about by kow-towing to the present or by a subservient approach to nature, but it seems that there is little intellectual opposition to the sanctification of nature and the penitential reproach to human creativity. Some commentators are embarrassed that 'America is guilty of excess consumption.'[27] Where once America was feted for its adventurism, after Hurricane Katrina some appeared to be ashamed at its recklessness, with economist Jeremy Rifkin suggesting that 'we Americans created these monster storms.'[28] Gone are the days, it seems, when Americans knew that 'Chaos was the law of nature; Order was the dream of man.'[29] In August 2006, over ninety years after his death, John Muir, the founder of America's conservation movement, the man who argued that 'that humans had no right to assert their own laws over the laws of nature'[30] and condemned the 'galling harness of civilisation',[31] was inducted in the California Hall of Fame.

Currently, in Europe, the traditional desire for what used to be called 'social betterment' is now re-interpreted as an irresponsible, excessive, wanton profligacy giving rise to 'unsustainable' levels of

[27] Stephen S. Roach, 'When Weakness Is a Strength', New York Times, 26 November 2004

[28] Jeremy Rifkin, 'Sorry, Mr President, homilies won't stop the hurricanes', The Guardian, 23 September 2005

[29] Henry Adams, 'The Education of Henry Adams', Modern Library, 1931, p451, cited in David E Nye, 'America as Second Creation: Technology and Narratives of New Beginnings', MIT Press, 2003, p281

[30] Apple Gifford, 'Learning From the Laws of Nature: Nature as Salvation in the Early Works of John Muir', Sierra Club, originally published as 'Wilderness and the American Imagination', Yale American Studies Seminar, Fall, 1995

[31] John Muir, 'John Of The Mountains', ed Linnie Marsh Wolfe, University of Wisconsin Press, 1938, p. 317

energy use, consumption and waste. 'Economic growth cannot continue to be pursued as if there were no limits,'[32] announces one of UK's leading environmental hardliners. Once consumerism, development and modernity are viewed through this misanthropic prism, America — the one country that best exemplifies all these cultural-material aspirations — can only be seen as a problem. As such, anti-Americanism is catching on in America too. Influential architect Andres Duany suggests that 'What is causing global warming is the American middle class.'[33] The logic is simple: once 'the environment' becomes the sole framework for debate, every previously acknowledged progressive development (especially if it is shown to be carbon-intensive) is up for grabs. As far as America's car culture goes, for example, commentators can now point out that 'rebuilding freeways in an age of global warming is like rebuilding deck-chairs on the Titanic.'[34] As far as American industrial production goes, Harvard economist Benjamin Friedman says that, 'if we're going to cope with global warming, we may also have to cope with the end of infinite, unrestrained economic expansion.'

## The end of Captain America

One of the last bastions of unrestrained, unsustainable opinion is reviled shock jock, Rush Limbaugh. He may be over the top, but has been known to hit the nail on the head once in a while. Ranting about how environmentalists blame America's industrial output for climate change, he said:

> If we say there's global warming and blame humanity for it, who do we actually blame? Who — who's doing all this inventing? Who's doing all this technological advancement? It's the United States ... It's an attack on us. It's an attack on our exceptionalism. It's an attack on our abundance, an attack on our prosperity, an attack on our freedom.[35]

Unfortunately, Limbaugh's aggrieved victimhood undermines his argument somewhat. His faux-hawkish belief that the rest of the world is against him, doesn't address the fact that there are powerful

[32]  Mayer Hillman, 'How We Can Save The Planet', Penguin, 2004, p30
[33]  Andres Duany quoted in Bryan Walsh, 'How Green is Your Neighborhood?', Time, 19 December 2007
[34]  Charles Siegel, (author of The End of Economic Growth), Planetizen, 19 March 2007
[35]  'The Rush Limbaugh Show', broadcast 19 July 2004 cited in 'Limbaugh distorted and misconstrued Kyoto Protocol', Media Matters for America, 20 July 2004, www.mediamatters.org

*internal* forces decrying what they see as America's unsustainable growth, greed and over-consumption. As one journal admitted, 'taking responsibility for changing wasteful habits means saying "mea culpa".'[36] As Nils Gilman argues in *Mandarins of the Future*, 'all the celebration of America's wonderful modernity was, in fact, a thin cover for a deep-seated anxiety about the state of the world and about America's role in it.'[37]

All-American Brad Pitt accepts that 'we can't keep consuming ourselves into extinction.'[38] Others suggest 'a much-needed antidote to … the oxymoronic idea of continuous (economic) improvement' suggesting instead 'the idea of "enough".'[39] Limbaugh is happy to believe that the sustainable development mantra is a left-liberal conspiracy by 'environmentalist wackos, and Communists.'[40] In the UK, leading environmental sceptic, Nigel Lawson is similarly worried at the damaging effect that environmentalism will have on the planet if we carry on with our obsession with carbon rationing and limits to growth theorising. He too underestimates the dominance of the sustainability agenda and thinks that 'people will come to their senses, but it'll take a bit of time.'[41] If they are so 'wacko' or senseless, why have they not been intellectually challenged or defeated? If it is such an aberrant ideology, why is environmentalism the default condition for much of the debate in America and Europe?

Take for example, General Michael E. Ryan, 110 Air Force Chief of Staff saying that the US Air Force is a 'national leader in environmental stewardship' because its vision is to 'act routinely in ways that either improve the environment or have the least impact on it while enhancing mission readiness … in harmony with the environment, sustaining a healthy planet, and conserving natural resources for future generations.'[42] One of the mechanisms for fulfilling this

[36] Phil Bailey, 'The Environment, 2008 Sleeper Issue?' 19 February 2007, AOL News
[37] Nils Gilman, 'Mandarins of the Future: Modernisation Theory in Cold War America', JHU Press, 2003, pix
[38] Brad Pitt quoted in Joshua W. Jackson, 'Brad Pitt Ponders a Better Life', The Green Room, www.lime.com, 24 August 2007
[39] Amanda Ball and Markus J. Milne, 'Sustainability and management control', in AJ Berry, J Broadbent and DT Otley (eds) 'Management Control Systems; Theories, Issues and Performance', Palgrave: London, 2005, pp.314-337
[40] Rush Limbaugh, 'Rush Limbaugh: Radical Environmentalism Attacks American Values,' RushLimbaugh.com, 15 December 2004
[41] Dan Stewart, 'Conversation with a heretic', Building Magazine, 1 June 2007, p40
[42] General Michael E. Ryan, 'Guidance for Greening Military Installations', Air Force Center for Environmental Excellence (AFCEE) for the Texas Pollution Prevention Partnership, 25 April 2000

pledge of war-ecology is to ensure that bullets have a low lead content, so that the soil on which the dead fall does not become contaminated over the long term. Take for example, the fact that Theodore Roosevelt IV, managing director of Lehman Brothers, Sherwood Boehlert a member of the House Intelligence Committee and Lieutenant General Brent Scowcroft, ex-National Security Affairs assistant to ex-president George Bush Snr are all on the board of the Alliance for Climate Protection—the unlikely wacko, Communist, hip-hopsters who organised Live Earth. Or the fact that Ron Bailey, writer for the erstwhile libertarian American magazine Reason now states that 'I now believe that Gore has got it basically right.'[43] Environmentalism, I'm afraid, is mainstream. What Limbaugh *et al* can't understand is that the prevalence of environmental reference points reflects a collapse of nerve amongst the establishment.

In the classic 'La democratie en Amerique,' written in 1831, Alexis de Tocqueville presented what he observed as America's credo of modernity: democratic government, the market mechanism and freedom of thought. He concluded of America that 'it is only when one comes around to consider the role of free thinking that one truly perceives to what extent the power of the majority surpasses all powers that we recognise in Europe.'[44] Barely six generations later, political commentator, Robert Kagan believes that Europeans have 'greater nuance and sophistication' as opposed to America's 'culture of death.'[45] And one sociologist has noted, that at present 'American writers currently indulge in self-flagellation'[46] of terminal decline. This has less to do with the subsequent success of Europe than with a collective loss of nerve in America's ability to defend the very modernity at which de Tocqueville marvelled. In fact, Marvel Comics have even killed off Captain America, an act that symbolised 'the death of the American dream.'[47] While James Truslow Adams, who coined the idea of the American Dream in the 1930s, said it was 'that dream of a land in which life should be better and richer and fuller for everyone, with opportunity for each according to ability or

[43]  Ronald Bailey, 'Congratulations to Al Gore: But be wary of the man's proposed solutions for global warming', 12 October 2007
[44]  Alexis de Tocqueville, Vol 1 'Democracy in America', in Alexis de Tocqueville, Olivier Zunz, Alan S Kahan, Blackwell Publishing, 2002, p104
[45]  Robert Kagan, 'Of Paradise and Power: America and Europe in the New World Order', Alfred A Knopf, 2003, p4-5
[46]  P Sztompka, 'Europe strikes back', editorial, European Review, Volume 13, Issue 02, May 2005, 13: 165-168 Cambridge University Press
[47]  Jacob Heilbrunn, 'Captain America, RIP', Los Angeles Times, 9 March 2007

achievement.' Take a look at the modern New American Dream — it is an organisation that has been set up to help 'Americans consume responsibly to protect the environment'.[48] God Help America.

Limbaugh can't bring himself to recognise the extent of this environmental incursion, because it would mean that he would have to stop his dialogue of the deaf and engage in a meaningful critique.

## Closing the American mind

The United States Constitution, Bill of Rights Amendment 1 states that: 'Congress shall make no law ... abridging the freedom of speech.' Admittedly, America may not have been as diligent in its observance of such liberal ambitions as it could have been, but it is shocking to see the underlying values represented in this foundation document so readily and unquestioningly thrown to the wind, under the censorious climate of climate change. In its acceptance of the global warming orthodoxy, this rhetorical bastion of American values is under threat. Once it has been established that individuals should be blamed for environmental harm — merely through their everyday actions — then small-scale and not-so-small scale cuts in individual liberty and invasions into our private lives, can easily be justified. Environmental author Sir Crispin Tickell says: 'George Bush senior tried to reassure the American people by saying that no-one was going to change the American way of life. Apparently George Bush junior thinks the same. They are both dead wrong. North Americans must change their way of life, as we in Europe must change ours.'[49] Those changes may not be painless and they may not be democratically mandated by the next elected president, because it is the moral environmental majority who will decide who can expect to be ostracised. In this there is no room for debate (after all, as they say, 'the debate is over').[50]

As a result of closing down debate on this subject, real politics — meaningful decisions, disagreements and arguments about core issues (like, for instance, civil liberties, freedom of expression, poverty, development, even military intervention) — are all too often put on the back burner or recast as issues to be determined from an 'environ-

[48]  Mission Statement, The New American Dream, www.newdream.org

[49]  Sir Crispin Tickell, 'Sustainability: The Way Forward', Lecture: Scottish Council Foundation, Ramsay Garden Seminar Series, Edinburgh, 15 January 2004

[50]  Bill McKibben, 'The Debate is Over: No serious scientist doubts that humans are warming up the planet', Rolling Stone, 3 November 2003 and quoted in Al Gore, 'The Time to Act Is Now: The climate crisis and the need for leadership', Rolling Stone, 3 November 2005

mental perspective'. Barack Obama observes in his attack on the impositions of constraints on free and open debate post 9/11, 'the irony, of course, was that ... disregard of the rules and the manipulation of language to achieve a particular outcome (was) precisely what conservatives had long accused liberals of doing.'[51] Much of this is far too reminiscent of McCarthyism to be comfortable.

The UN Framework Convention on Climate Change effectively equates human existence and its affect upon the planet as 'dangerous anthropogenic interference'[52] and there is swift retributive justice for anyone who says differently. A US environmental magazine can argue for 'war crimes trials for these bastards', referring, of course, to the 'global warming deniers.'[53] One Australian columnist has proposed outlawing 'climate change denial' suggesting that 'there is a case for making climate change denial an offence. It is a crime against humanity, after all.'[54] While this censorious rhetoric festers in hyperspace, on the ground Washington State's associate state climatologist has been stripped of his title because he challenged the guardians of the climate change establishment.[55] Oregon's state climatologist (actually, a meteorologist) is similarly under threat. The same can be said in Delaware, Seattle, and Virginia. The position of 'state climatologist' is something of an honorary title, but still they risk being 'stripped of (their) title for overstating the case against global warming.'[56] This is terrible symbolic assault on scientific enquiry. It is a fundamental assault on free speech. And all done under the caring hand of environmental protection.

And it's not just an assault of free speech — there is an increasingly regimented intrusion into personal and private activities that would have been rejected out of hand a few years ago. Now, given that such intrusion is promoted as being for the best, more people are accepting the corrective hand of the state in personal affairs.

[51]  'The Audacity of Hope: Thoughts on reclaiming the American Dream', Barack Obama, Crown Publishers New York, 2006, p78
[52]  United Nations, 'UN Framework Convention on Climate Change', 1992, Article 2, p4
[53]  David Roberts, 'The Denial Industry', Grist Magazine, 11:40 am, 19 September 2006, http://gristmill.grist.org
[54]  Margo Kingston, `Himalayan lakes disaster', DailyBriefing, 21 November 2005
[55]  Warren Cornwall, 'How one number touched off big climate change fight at UW', Seattle Times, 15 March 2007
[56]  Lee Hochberg, 'Oregon Global Warming Skeptic Finds Controversy', PBS Online News Hour, Transcript, 21 June 2007

New York's Sanitation Dept issue Violations for 'failure to flatten and tie corrugated cardboard' or a 'failure to rinse foil clean of food and residue.' They also offer moronic lifestyle guidance: 'Mop heads can be laundered, sponges can be cleaned and reused' ... 'Reuse margarine tubs, glass jars, and other containers for storing toys, nails and screws, or sewing accessories' ... 'Pantyhose make perfect plant ties to secure stems to stakes, since they are weather-resistant and don't harm the stalk.'[57] This is more 'war-economy', than 'dynamic economy' and indicates the level of petty, intrusive, time-wasting, labour-intensive, mundane and dirty jobs that a reversion to environmentally-friendly ways might create. Fortunately, even in Britain, this level of nanny-statism is beginning to be received with some horror by erstwhile supporters of the eco-agenda. Tabloid hack and breakfast TV presenter Fiona Phillips is at breaking point, promising a very British protest over the issue: 'I am so fed up of being told what to do by opportunists hanging on to the environmentally-friendly bandwagon that I'm thinking of abandoning my rigorous recycling and leaving everything on stand-by all night.'[58]

The 'belt-tightening' rhetoric plays far better in America where demands such as these often manifests themselves in the patriotic colours of 'Keep America Beautiful', whereas in Britain (where national identity is in even greater crisis) there is a slightly less ambitious goal to 'Keep Britain Tidy' (now called 'Environmental Campaigns'). But rummaging in bins to wash, sort, and place erstwhile pieces of garbage in specific containers is not the most community-friendly activity. There is nothing progressive about it at all. Fundamentally, it actually sets up mechanisms of mistrust against those who are seen, or are believed not to be doing it. The notion of independent, political decision-making and personal political choices are being undermined in a moral climate of observation, suspicion and condemnation. This is the real meaning of Gore's 'Inconvenient Truth'... that personal inconvenience and societal fracturing will become greater the more that we sacrifice the gains of modernity on the altar of carbon efficiency. As Philip Pullman, author of *The Golden Compass* says, 'We should have a fixed limit (of carbon) and if you

[57]  NYC  WasteLe$$,  New  York  Sanitation  Department,www.nyc.gov/nyc wasteless
[58]  Fiona Philips, 'Going Green With Nausea', Daily Mirror, April 28th 2007

use it all up in October, then tough, you shiver for the rest of the year.'[59] So there.

Sorting out your own garbage—aside from the fact that it's unpleasant and that there should be a company to do it for you—is just one of a creeping list of regulations halting the historic drive to be liberated from menial, parochial, inconsequential, time-wasting tasks. How ironic when the US has led the way in time-saving consumer devices. We are throwing away the gains of modernity if we allow ourselves to indulge in activities that any self-respecting, aspirational Third World rag-picker would want to escape from.

But surely, in a world where political debate has become as debased as this—with pundits pontificating on the most trivial examples of personal behaviour patterns—it is about time that we reinstated more enlightened notions of development, progress, experimentation and ambition at the forefront of society's goals. The hyperbole and intolerance surrounding sustainability in general, and global warming in particular, is anathema to the commonly accepted notions of progress towards rebuilding a better society.

It is clear that 'progress', in common parlance, no longer means an improvement on what went before, but it is now simply a coded description of moral culpability in potential 'crimes against nature' (the title of Robert F Kennedy's latest book). Following through the logic, we are meant to live more mean, meagre and miserable lives as a consequence. Friends of the Earth are quoted as saying that 'there is a lot to learn from the developing world, where a scavenger mentality, grass roots recycling and sheer necessity can lead to imaginative leaps in redeploying waste.'[60]

To revel in the joylessness of 'scavenging' and 'sheer necessity' chastises 'frivolous' Western consumption, and advocates that we all learn how to live with less. The Harvard International Review says that 'only local communities, in effective collaboration with national governments and global environmental networks and institutions, can serve as guarantors of our fragile "island" Earth's well-being for future generations.'[61] Scarcely a day goes by without yet another intrusive un-mandated multi-agency encouraging us to use less, consume less and sanctify everyday objects.

[59]  Philip Pullman quoted in Andrew Simms, 'Philip Pullman: new brand of environmentalism', Daily Telegraph, 19 January 2008
[60]  Dan McDougall, 'Waste not, want not in the £700m slum', The Observer, March 4th 2007
[61]  Richard Grove. 'Colonialism and the History of Environmentalism', Harvard International Review, Vol. 23 (4), Winter 2002

It's one thing 'complying' as a matter of common sense or personal choice, but since when is it the business of an unelected lobby group to impose their vision of what we do in the privacy of our own home? It may sound innocuous, but this goes way beyond simple paternalism and veers into the realm of authoritarian condescension affecting 'what you eat, what you drive, how you build your home'.[62] Federal recycling regulations are commonplace, mandating hefty fines for non-compliance. As an aside, the US Fourth Amendment proclaims that 'the right of the people to be secure in their persons, houses, papers, and effects, against unreasonable searches and seizures, shall not be violated.' Some argue that it is 'imperative' that we 'adopt new modes of behaviour and avoid "frivolous" consumption or the destructive, self-centred, "egotistical", consumption.'[63] But by this gradual war of attrition, America — with its Statue of Liberty, with its Bill of Rights, with its mass consumption— is losing sight of what it represents in its confusion over the onslaught by environmental initiatives.

## Collapse

As we have seen, over-hyping global warming is a cohering issue for the establishment, and nominally for society. But the inherent blame culture that arises from it can only eventually erode public solidarity. When UN Secretary General Ban Ki-moon warns that climate change poses as much of a danger to the world as war, who is the enemy? Wangari Maatherai and Al Gore, two environmental campaigners, have won separate Nobel Peace prizes — allocated for the 'abolition or reduction of standing armies'[64] — as voices of reason in the ensuing battle? When David King, ex-chief scientific adviser to the UK government, announces that 'global warming is more of a threat than terrorism,' is he suggesting that we are all suspects? When ex-president Clinton said that climate change is 'the only thing we face that has the power to remove the preconditions of civilised society',[65] is it not more likely to engender a climate of fear and uncertainty, than decisive clarity?

[62]  'Take Action', www.stopglobalwarming.org, 24 January 2008
[63]  'What is at stake at the first International Consumption Symposium?' Toward Sustainable Consumption', First International Consumption Symposium, 1 December 2003
[64]  Excerpt from the Will of Alfred Nobel, nobelprize.org
[65]  'Clinton: "Get Off Our Butts" to Halt Global Warming', Environment News Service, May 2006

And this is the problem, Western—by which I mean developed, progressive, democratic—values have no purchase in the sustainable universe. Gone are the certainties of a society that feels confident in its humanity. Sustainability advocates that we should reassess the very notion of human-centredness contending instead that social advancement has resulted in global misery rather than global opportunity; environmental degradation rather than social, physical and economic improvements. If humanity is a blight then, logically, visions of the future will be constrained by a narrative of paranoia. If society has carried out a risk assessment on itself and found, as one leading managerial guru has, that 'the enemy is us,'[66] then the notion of freedom, democracy and the citizens' inalienable rights must be of secondary importance in the war against ourselves. Once we believe 'that the US may simply have postponed the day of reckoning. Major environmental problems remain, and some are getting worse—all of them in one way or another connected to US population growth',[67] we have more than an existential crisis on our hands. As one commentator puts it:

> All of mankind is in danger because of the global warming resulting to a large degree from the emissions of the factories of the major corporations, yet despite that, the representative of these corporations in the White House insists on not observing the Kyoto accord, with the knowledge that the statistic speaks of the death and displacement of millions of human beings because of that, especially in Africa.

Thus spake Osama Bin Laden from his eco-hideaway. It seems that environmentally-conscious Bin Laden spends his time plotting how to reduce the population in the West while minimising his carbon footprint by living the simple life. In a report by the environmental research organisation, the Worldwatch Institute entitled 'Climate Change Poses Greater Security Threat Than Terrorism', the authors report that climate change's 'parallels with terrorism are compelling.' It was so busy feeding the fear-machine to generate support for more environmental measures, that they didn't realise the ironic truth behind their claim. Environmentalism is the real terror network: a shadowy outfit of unconnected cells, plotting to undermine

[66] Charles Handy, 'Finding Sense in Uncertainty', in Rowan Gibson, 'Rethinking the Future', Nicholas Brealey Publishing, 1997, p28
[67] Brad Knickerbocker, 'The Environmental Load of 300 Million: How Heavy?', Christian Science Monitor, 26 September 2006

the democratically mandated, productive, liberated American way of life.

These similarities between Islamicism and Environmentalism are just coincidences, you understand, they don't really mean that environmentalism has become a religion, or that it has become the voice of a non-Western ideology. And similarly, Islamism has certainly not triumphed over the collapse of Western values. It is simply that environmentalism concurs with the insidious notion that modernity is not progressive (an Islamicist perception is that 'modernity is unsustainable'[68]) and that we need a more moral agenda of spiritual renewal. So environmentalism, like radical Islam, seems simultaneously to address, and reinforce, the pernicious sense of estrangement from society. The simplistic belief that untenable US involvement in Iraq, for example, is the cause of the 'unravelling American modernity'[69] is mistaken. The unravelling is caused by a domestic malaise.

From the West's ideological perspective, this is a serious case of throwing in the towel, and it is in this that there are parallels between the anti-humanism of environmentalism and the nihilism of radical Islamicists. For all its rhetorical nods towards 'the science', environmentalist's misanthropy is feeding the growing demoralisation with rational modernity, preferring instead to wallow in the metaphysics of 'Gaia'. Unfortunately, it is also true that Islam is tapping into the cultural vacuum in Western modernity, but not exactly from a sense of strength. It too, needs to justify itself by connection with the trump card of environmentalism. Such is the weakness of cogent belief systems — whether amongst politicos or religious faiths — that everyone from democrats to republicans, Catholics to Muslims are tapping into the automatic kudos granted by an association with sustainability. Everyone likes the warm consensual glow that emanates from the bosom of environmentalism. Whether it's evangelicals showing how best to 'Serve God, Save the Planet' to the environmentalist Worldwatch Institute's 'Inspiring Progress: Religions' Contributions to Sustainable Development' all the way to renowned scientist and secular humanist E O Wilson's 2006 book

[68]  Fazlun M. Khalid, 'Sustainable Development And Environmental Collapse: An Islamic Perspective,' Muslim Convention on Sustainable Development, World Summit on Sustainable Development parallel event, National Awqaf Foundation of South Africa, 1 September 2002, p6
[69]  Michael Vlahos, 'The Fall of Modernity: Has the American narrative authored its own undoing?' The American Conservative, 26 February 2007

*The Creation: An Appeal to Save Life on Earth*, each can't help finding succour in environmentalism's religiosity.

In an article entitled, 'Muslims go green', Dr. Richard Foltz, author of *Islam and Ecology*, points out that there is a rise in green Islamic consciousness because 'the Qur'an is said to prohibit over-consumption and waste.'[70] Hey presto, no need for all that difficult conversion-to-ones'-belief stuff, if you can simply convince people of your superior record on recycling. But when the old environmental commentator Helena Norberg-Hodge can seriously argue that 'To really understand the rise in religious fundamentalism and ethnic conflict we need to look at the deep impacts of what might be described as the jihad of the global consumer culture against the diversity of living cultures on the planet,'[71] we have truly lost our sense of direction.

[70]   Anayat Durrani, 'Muslims go green', Southern California InFocus, Vol. 3 Issue No. 8, September 2007

[71]   Helena Norberg-Hodge, 'Globalisation and Terror' International Society for Ecology and Culture, http://www.isec.org.uk/

CONCLUSION

# THE
# 'PROGRESSIVES'

*The need to reclaim the Future*

Environmentalists have painted a bleak picture of the world. Recognising that 'the most accomplished promoters of crisis are environmental groups'[1] many environmentalists are now concerned that they are being too negative. If they aren't frightening children into behaving in an environmentally sensitive way (what one professor of political science calls 'scaring children green'[2]), science writers are claiming that 'the world is approaching an abyss … (with) terrifying prospects.'[3] Added to that, the list of ills that we are told will befall the planet if we don't amend our ways, reads like the longest sick note in history: forests are 'damaged'; the soil is 'degraded'; fish are 'overexploited'; reservoirs are coping with water 'stress'; waste needs treatment and; even the ozone layer is suffering from lapses in concentration.[4]

It is all a bit too much for American environmentalist authors Nordhaus and Shellenberger, who are concerned by the 'doomsday discourse'; the way that environmentalism portrays nature as being in need of collective therapy, people as requiring restraint and the future as a bleak place to be. They worry about environmentalism's

[1]    Michael Sanera and Jane S Shaw, 'Facts not Fear: Teaching Children About the Environment', Regnery Publishing, 1999, p6-7
[2]    Jacqueline Vaughn Switzer, 'Green Backlash: The History and Politics of the Environmental Opposition', Lynne Rienner Publishers, 1997, p129
[3]    Fred Pearce, 'Memo to the G8', Open Democracy, 31 May 2005
[4]    European Environment Agency, 'Environmental assessment report, No 10: Europe's environment: the third assessment', Luxembourg: Office for Official Publications of the European Communities, 2003

'failure to articulate an inspiring and positive vision' and want to 'expand the frame of political environmentalism to encompass core American values'. They want something 'pro-growth, progressive, and internationalist.'[5]

Sir David King, author of *The Hot Topic* is a convert to this new green-spin. He too believes that environmentalists have gone too far, constantly wallowing in negative scenarios. Lest we forget, King regularly pontificates about the fantastical notion of a six to seven metre sea level rise[6] but at least he counters his scaremongering with the belief that there will be 'technological solutions to a technologically driven problem, so the last thing we must do is eschew technology'.[7] But, whatever techno-fixes are used to substantiate their claims to be the gatekeepers of the future, environmentalists have a singular problem, which is that their underlying message—the message identified in the chapters of this book—is an unequivocally miserable one. King, for example, urges the reader 'not to despair', 'cheer up' and 'be positive'.[8] This from a man who, in one single chapter of the same book includes '37 separate depictions of climatic fear, one for every 120 words. We have climate change that is "frightening" six times and "alarming" twice, four "disaster scenarios", four "tipping points", three "collapses", two "abrupt dramas", not to mention the "bleak outlooks", the "catastrophe" and the three "grave dangers to our civilisation".'[9] As we have seen, we must be on our guard against miserablists bearing happiness agendas.

As Richard Florida, author of *Rise of the Creative Class* puts it: 'The Industrial Age gave us an environmentalism of limits and a politics of "no." The Creative Age requires a politics and culture of "yes".' It is this purely presentational shift that I want to explore here in order that progressives might reclaim the future.

\*\*\*

The Brundtland definition of sustainability, or sustainable development, is that which 'ensure(s) it meets the needs of the present with-

[5]   Ronald Bailey, 'Techno-Optimistic Environmentalism', Reason Magazine, 27 November 2007

[6]   David King, 'Transcript of Sir David King speaking at the Greenpeace Business lecture on global warming', www.greenpeace.org.uk, published 13 October 2004

[7]   Sir David King quoted in Oliver Burkeman, 'The war on hot air', The Guardian, 12 January 2008

[8]   David King, Gabrielle Walker, 'The Hot Topic : How to Tackle Global Warming and Still Keep the Lights On', Bloomsbury, 2008

[9]   Mike Hulme, review, 'The Hot Topic, By Gabrielle Walker & David King: Overheated, underpowered', The Independent, 18 January 2008

out compromising the ability of future generations to meet their own needs.'[10] In this way, the sustainability industry seems automatically to have a claim on the future, and sets the benchmark of our relationship with it. Professor Robert Bruegmann from the University of Illinois at Chicago suggests that American 'progressives' have developed a 'widespread erosion of confidence in the future.'[11] He is right, but such an erosion is primarily the result of their inability to shift the frame of reference.

For as long as environmentalists and sustainability advocates can position themselves as the leading voices in the race for the future, their guiding principle will still reign supreme: 'When an activity raises threats of harm to the environment or human health, precautionary measures should be taken even if some cause and effect relationships are not fully established scientifically'.[12] So even if there is no causal relationship shown, if it simply believed (by whom?) that certain acts may cause harm (to future generations), then those acts will be restricted until proven otherwise. It is one thing exercising sensible scientific caution in relation to, say, drugs' testing; quite another when it becomes a principle to be attached to irrational fears; from mobile phones to GM crops. This definition of the precautionary principle exemplifies both sustainability's *collapse* of imagination and its *reliance* on imagination. That is to say, an imagination imprisoned within a rigid framework tends to survive on feel-good wishful-thinking. And so we are beginning to see more 'imaginative' presentations of the sustainability orthodoxy. Al Gore, for instance, is a traditionalist and somehow wishes to 'preserve' the future.[13] Andrew Simms, in his pamphlet, 'An Environmental War Economy' goes for the purely depressing viewpoint that 'the smallest possibility of irreversible change makes the risk of inadequate action too great.'[14] Whereas Nordhaus and Shellenberger prefer the feel-good route. In the war economy scenario, they are the Busby Berkeleys of sustainability.

[10]  The Report of the Brundtland Commission, 'Our Common Future', Oxford University Press, 1987, p8
[11]  Robert Bruegmann, 'Sprawl: A Compact History', University of Chicago Press, 2005, p163
[12]  Wingspread Statement on the Precautionary Principle, Wingspread Conference Center, Racine, Wisconsin, 23-25 January 1998
[13]  Al Gore, 'Earth in the Balance: Forging a New Common Purpose', Earthscan, 2007, p368
[14]  Andrew Simms, 'An Environmental War Economy: The lessons of ecological debt and global warming', New Economics Foundation, 2001, p12

The first thing to note, then, is that while it might appear that sustainability is taking on a positive, progressive direction, when you scratch the surface it's business as usual. It was Lyndon Johnson who said: 'Beware of those who fear and doubt and those who rave and rant about the dangers of progress.'[15] But we should beware more those who fear and doubt while raving and ranting about the *benefits* of progress. James Martin, in his popular book 'The meaning of the 21st century' for example, is excited by the creative prospects for the future, but only in terms of a 'catastrophe-first' set of scenarios. Essentially, even though the new talk is about progress, technology and 'the future', sustainability is still confined by the same misanthropic environmental parameters that empties the aforementioned talk of 'progress' of meaningful content.

Admittedly, things are changing, with sustainability regularly lauded for introducing 'innovative technologies'[16] — innovations which are generally thin on the ground in every other sector of the market and which are also deemed to have had other knock-on effects on the way that environmentalists view society. For instance, who would have thought that nowadays, environmentalists would frequently be seen to be the biggest advocates of high-rise buildings? Herbert Girardet, president of the 'Small is Beautiful' Schumacher Society (and the man who describes 'the city as parasite'[17]) is actually now lead adviser to the construction of a new mega-city in China? Scratch the surface and unsurprisingly all is not what it seems. Environmentalists actually praise tall buildings because they have the smallest 'footprint', and Girardet's city is Dongtan is proposed as the model of environmental restraint. The end result may be a large city, but the political argument in which it is wrapped, is decidedly small-town.

We really have to listen not just to the warm words, but we have to unpick the underlying message. Steward Brand, founder member of the Global Business Network calls himself an 'eco-pragmatist' and represents the growth of a *scientific* environmentalism as opposed to *romantic* environmentalism. He too, defends large-scale urban developments. It all sounds so progressive, until you realise that he wants to minimise (what sustainability advocates perceive as) the

[15]   Lyndon Johnson quoted in 'Promises & Punches', Time magazine, 2 October 1964
[16]   Ira Ehrenpreis, introductory presentation, 'The Green Rush: Prospects, Perils, and Opportunities', Churchill Club, Menlo Park, California, 29 Jan 2008
[17]   Herbert Girardet, Chapter heading, ''The city as parasite', in 'The Gaia Atlas of Cities', Gaia Books, 1992

inherently detrimental impact of humanity by collecting them in cities and turning their towns over to nature. He also applauds cities for the 'great news' that population rates in urban habitats are usually less than in rural areas. He says, 'Although more children are an asset in the countryside, they're a liability in the city.'[18] How mean spirited can you get? So much for the new enlightened environmentalist; this is simply a reworking of Paul Erhlich's 'Population Bomb' (Brand's old teacher) and merely represents the new environmental spin machine at work.

The second problem is that rather than recognising humanity as the source of creativity, the new breed of environmentalist still sees it as destructive and in need of reduction. If that can be portrayed in a positive way, then for them, it doesn't matter how cynically 'positive' the message device, provided that the out-turn results are the same. For progressive humanists on the other hand, more people is a good thing; as a source of innovation, creativity, imagination and socialisation.

Given that the population question is constantly lurking under the surface of all these debates, it appears that scientific environmentalism is as crude in its view of humanity (viewing them as no more than a collection of indicators and statistics) as those very faceless corporations that the environmentalists berate for their lack of morality. But this should hardly be surprising, given that environmentalism is not an attack on the social organisation of society, but is simply a method of removing some of its rougher edges. When Climate Exchange, a London-based carbon trading company has cornered 80 per cent of the market, and is now worth more than £160 million and its co-founder, Neil Eckert has a 5 per cent share worth £8 million,[19] its no wonder that some of them are keen to drop their rhetorical opposition to economic growth per se.

In some ways, sustainability does seem to provide a way of giving Western economies a much-needed economic boost. Many companies, after all, are developing an environmental portfolio, from solar panel manufacturers to carbon offset enterprises. The old arguments that environmentalists are hair-shirts won't wash, and a new breed of enterprise-environmentalist is emerging. Newsweek revels in these 'thrilling times' which it describes as 'the beginning of a technological and social revolution that could vault our society into a

[18] Steward Brand, 'Environmental Heresies', MIT Technology Review, 8 April 2005
[19] Anthony Browne, 'The green goldrush that is creating multimillionaires', The Times, 4 November 2006

post-post-industrial future.'[20] Corporate leaders in the UK say that 'domestic climate change policy has the potential to deliver significant economic benefits to the UK. These include improvements in economic performance through increasing energy efficiency, improved growth as a result of technological innovation, greater energy security and access to significant global export markets for low-carbon technologies.'[21]

The influential American director of the Rocky Mountain Institute, Amory Lovins has made a healthy career of his own identifying examples of how the environmental future needn't be constraining. His book *Factor Four* explicitly offered several examples of resource-efficient products that could be deemed both environmentally-friendly and innovative. He suggested that the profit opportunities would be like 'picking up £20 notes in the street.'[22]

But before we get too carried away, Lovins still notes that the developed world will have 'to learn to live with far smaller per capita rates of resource consumption.' Whatever the positive rhetoric, it can't mask the fact that the 'sustainable growth' that these commentators refer to, is not the same thing as growth: in the same way that sustainable development is not the same thing as development. The environmentalists' version of growth (and let's be clear here that welcoming *any* growth is still a marginal activity for environmental commentators) means growth with limits; it means growth with parameters; it means, 'growth scepticism'. Financial journalist Daniel Ben-Ami notes that 'in the past, there was almost universal agreement in the need to strive to make society wealthier. Nowadays this objective is viewed with suspicion if not outright hostility, with the new emphasis on restraining consumption and promoting sustainability.'[23] Growth, with hidden caveats, is worthless, especially if those caveats suggest that growth should not be a universal aspiration. It is easy to point out that the developing world needs development; but the corresponding notion that we, in the developed world should slow down, is anathema to anyone who has noticed the continuance of poor living standards in the UK alone.

Environmental campaigner, Jonathon Porritt says that 'many of us in the west wrestle with our conscience over our lifestyle, what we

[20]  Jerry Adler, 'The Greening of America', Newsweek, 15 Oct 2007
[21]  Corporate Leaders Group on Climate Change, Open letter to Tony Blair, 6 June 2006
[22]  Ernst von Weizecker, Amory B Lovins and L Hunter Lovins, 'Factor Four: Doubling Wealth, Halving Resource Use', Earthscan, 1997, p249
[23]  Daniel Ben-Ami, 'Why Globalisation Works', spiked-online, 15 October 2004

eat, how we get around.' Undoubtedly Porritt *et al* agonise deeply about whether to eat the organically-farmed salmon or the ethically-produced foie gras; whether to dump the Bentley and replace it with a Prius, but such painful dilemmas will probably not be shared by those in the West who are confronted by fewer smug choices. Most of us haven't got enough and want more. While sustainable growth proponents want society to develop to provide environmentally-benign products, by definition they want to restrain our demands for them. I believe that society needs to develop to provide for all needs and desires.

The third problem is that by restricting our scientific and techno-logical imaginations to whatever can be fitted into the sustainability rubric, we are, by definition, restricting the terms of open inquiry. Scientific research must be allowed to explore, experiment and even make mistakes. 'Science' which is directed towards an 'agenda' is not science; it is policy, and pigeon-holing progress in this way is truly unsustainable. It is also dangerous given that scientists will be liable to serious influence by governments or pressure groups to behave in the aforesaid 'environmentally responsible manner.' The American Union of Concerned Scientists (UCS) are campaigning to 'end political interference in science' and rightly so. However, the UCS need to be reminded that this interference extends to the creep-ing nature of environmentally-friendly research, as well as to the usual pro-business suspects. For example, the UCS advocates reduc-tions in 'human over-population' and that 'developing nations (need to) create environmental policies.'[24] They obviously have a slender grasp of the notion of 'political interference' but I would advise that they get on with their research and mind their own busi-ness, lest it colour their scientific independence. After all, their suggestion that 'human beings and the natural world are on a collision course' is not the most open-minded starting point for human-centric scientific exploration.

Fourthly, this dim view of humanity has serious repercussions for the future. The environmentalist Jeffrey Sach's Reith Lecture series concluded with an ambition for us to aim for a 'sustainable civilisa-tion consilient with natural ecosystems.'[25] No thanks, Jeff. The very

[24]  Union of Concerned Scientists, 'World Scientists' Warning to Humanity', November 1992

[25]  Marty Hoffert, 'The Cold Equations of Global Warming', paper presented at 'The Human Footprint – Has Civilisation Gone Too Far?' New York Salon, 13 February 2007

nature of progress is overcoming — or striving to overcome — natural barriers. The key to human progress is the drive to minimise human effort in the creation of a given resource: to do that we have to increase external energy sources in order to free up our time so that humans can do other things. None of that is 'natural'.

***

What does ambition mean if we allow humanity to be represented as the biggest problem on the planet, rather than as the creators of a better future? Even those environmentalists who purport to want a better future, actually want that future dictated by our response to nature. If our ambition is to put nature first, humans come second. Period. This is exemplified in the contemporary Apollo Programme. Not for environmentalists the audacious, progressive, explorative, human endeavour of old; instead the new Apollo Project is a miserable, defensive, safe and sanctimonious cry for reduced consumption.

The Apollo Alliance is an affiliation of protectionists attempting to break America's reliance on foreign oil and is a far cry from Kennedy's original Apollo speech heralding the onset of the space race as a search for knowledge, progress and strength. Advocates of a new Apollo Project aim to save the planet 'from the ravages of climate change'.[26] Hilary Clinton stated that 'energy independence 'should be our Apollo moonshot'[27] while New York's Apollo Alliance 'promotes waste prevention as well as recycling, reusing, and remanufacturing existing materials'.[28] Some people may seriously believe today that a rocket can be refashioned out of recycled oil cans, but if this really is the new Big Idea — concerned as it is, with altering personal habits and depressing material ambitions — then the petty-mindedness of the European spectre of sustainability has well and truly floated into America. Space expert Greg Klerkx bemoans the fact that 'at the beginning of the twenty- first century, we look back wistfully, sometimes with mild shock, at an era of human space exploration whose promise sees to have evaporated'.[29] We need to reclaim it.

[26]  Lord Rees quoted press release, 'Lord Rees' call for a new "Apollo project" to fight climate change — Greenpeace reaction', Greenpeace, 4 August 2006

[27]  Press release, 'Presidential Debate Showcases Apollo Energy Agenda', Apollo Alliance, 16 January 2008, www.apolloalliance.org

[28]  NYC Apollo Alliance, 'Good Jobs and Energy Independence: NYC Apollo Ten-Point Plan for the 21st Century', 2007

[29]  Greg Klerkx, 'Lost in Space: The fall of NASA and the dream of a new Space Age', Secker & Warburg, 2004, p9

John F Kennedy's speech, which effectively launched the Apollo Program way back in 1962, and which is widely acclaimed as heralding the space age, still has the power to inspire. 'We choose to go to the moon,' he said (note, not we *need* to go to the moon) '... We choose to go to the moon in this decade and do the other things, not because they are easy, but because they are hard.'[30]

In the light of the modern miserablist malaise, many modern commentators are trying to reclaim Kennedy's enthusiastic aura. They utter the warm words, they proffer the rhetorical flourishes, and they repeat the phrases verbatim. However, the content is missing. Riding on the coat-tails and co-opting the spirit of the Space Age (or the Victorian Age in Britain) is easier than building a real, dynamic, ambitious, forward-thinking, experimental society, but build it we must; not because it is easy, but because it is essential. It's about time that we recaptured more than the rhetoric and exposed those that hide behind it.

To create the conditions for a really progressive future, we need a truly human-centred politics that puts people first; that challenges the shallow parameters of environmental discourse; that argues for development without prefixes; that raises our aspirations beyond the local; that encourages robust debate; that increases emancipation and encourages socialisation; that sees humans as creative agents of change; and that is bold enough to aim for the stars. This book is intended as a contribution to that enlightenment project and I look forward to continuing an open-minded debate.

[30]  President John F. Kennedy, 'Address at Rice University on the Nation's Space Effort', Houston, Texas, 12 September 1962

# Index

Frankfurt School 3
Franklin D Roosevelt 1, 136
Free speech 138
Friends of the Earth 5, 24, 117, 122, 140

G8 129
Gandhi 91, 103
Gardening 78
George Bush
   junior 128, 137
   senior 136-137
Ghana 111
Global Business Network 148
GM crops 103, 147
Greenhouse gases 23, 32, 115, 128
Greenland 24
Greenpeace 43, 76, 89, 130
Greenwash 63
Gregg Klerkx 152

Habitat 30, 96, 109
Happiness 15, 22, 46, 105, 112, 126, 146
Heathrow 28-29
Heating, boiler 87
Heating, central 45, 48, 50
Henry Ford 1, 13, 17
Hilary Clinton 13, 131, 152
Holland 118, 57-58
Holocaust 5, 132
Humanist, humanism 103-104, 132,
   143, 149
Hurricane Katrina 57, 133
Hypermobility 16

Immigrants 33-34

James Lovelock 41-42, 54
Janet Leigh 39
Japan 51, 55, 90, 98
Jared Diamond 5
Jeremy Rifkin 16, 133
John F Kennedy 153
John Gray 9, 54
John McCain 13, 130-131
John Muir 133
Jonathon Porritt
   environment 82, 104, 110, 122, 154
   population 104, 122, 154

Kenya 116, 124
Kyoto 129, 131, 142

Laurie David 16, 18, 85

Live Earth 31, 81, 136
Local Agenda 21, 84

Maglev 92
Mali 116
ManTowNHuman 72
Mao 93, 96, 105
Margaret Thatcher 20, 38
Merton Rule 59
Michael R Bloomberg 8
Michael Shellenberger 4, 105, 145, 147
Mozambique 117-118

Nappies 79
National Curriculum 43, 79
New Economics Foundation 5, 112,
   122, 123
New Orleans 56-58
New Urbanism 57
New York
   Manhattan 26, 45, 61-62
   Statue of Liberty 141
Nicholas Stern 28, 40
Nihilism 10, 52, 143
Norman Mailer 3
Nuclear 43, 50-51, 88-82

Oil 26, 41-43, 50, 80, 122, 130, 152, 156

Palestine 119
Pester power 85-86
Population: Malthus, Malthusian 54,
   103-105
Prince Charles 27-28, 41, 53, 55, 65, 69
Prison 35, 147
Protest
   airports 24
   China 101-102
   energy 43, 138
   general 27, 31, 100, 106, 118-119
   roads 10
Public transport: underground
   (subway) 95

Qualifications and Curriculum
   Authority (QCA) 80, 121

Rag-picking 140
Reith lectures 16, 151
Religion
   Baptist 24
   Islam 143-144
   Pope 18-19, 28

2008–2009

# SOCIETAS

essays in political and cultural criticism
imprint-academic.com/societas

# Who Holds the Moral High Ground?

### Colin J Beckley and Elspeth Waters

Meta-ethical attempts to define concepts such as 'goodness', 'right and wrong', 'ought' and 'ought not', have proved largely futile, even over-ambitious. Morality, it is argued, should therefore be directed primarily at the reduction of suffering, principally because the latter is more easily recognisable and accords with an objective view and requirements of the human condition. All traditional and contemporary perspectives are without suitable criteria for evaluating moral dilemmas and without such guidance we face the potent threat of sliding to a destructive moral nihilism. This book presents a possible set of defining characteristics for the foundation of moral evaluations, taking into consideration that the female gender may be better disposed to ethical leadership.

128 pp., £8.95/$17.90, 9781845401030 (pbk.), January 2008, *Societas,* Vol.32

# Froude Today

### John Coleman

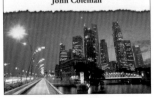

A.L. Rowse called fellow-historian James Anthony Froude the 'last great Victorian awaiting revival'. The question of power is the problem that perplexes every age: in his historical works Froude examined how it applied to the Tudor period, and defended Carlyle against the charge that he held the doctrine that 'Might is Right'.

Froude applied his analysis of power to the political classes of his own time and that is why his writings are just as relevant today. The historian and the prophet look into the inner meaning of events – and that is precisely what Froude did – and so are able to make judgments which apply to ages far beyond their own. The last chapters imagine what Froude would have said had he been here today.

96 pp., £8.95/$17.90, 9781845401047 (pbk.), March 2008, *Societas,* Vol.33

**Imprint Academic, PO Box 200, Exeter EX5 5HY, UK**
Tel: +44(0)1392 851550.   Email: sandra@imprint.co.uk

# The Enemies of Progress
*Austin Williams*

This polemical book examines the concept of sustainability and presents a critical exploration of its all-pervasive influence on society, arguing that sustainability, manifested in several guises, represents a pernicious and corrosive doctrine that has survived primarily because there seems to be no alternative to its canon: in effect, its bi-partisan appeal has depressed critical engagement and neutered politics.

It is a malign philosophy of misanthropy, low aspirations and restraint. This book argues for a destruction of the mantra of sustainability, removing its unthinking status as orthodoxy, and for the reinstatement of the notions of development, progress, experimentation and ambition in its place.

Al Gore insists that the 'debate is over'. Here the auhtor retorts that it is imperative to argue against the moralizing of politics.

Austin Williams tutors at the Royal College of Art and Bartlett **School of Architecture.**

96 pp., £8.95/$17.90, 9781845400989 (pbk.), May 2008, *Societas,* Vol.34

# Forgiveness: How Religion Endangers Morality
*R.A. Sharpe*

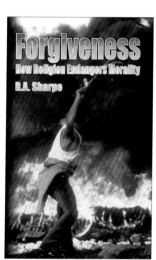

In his book *The Moral Case against Religious Belief* (1997), the author argued that some important virtues cease to be virtues at all when set in a religious context, and that, consequently, a religious life is, in many respects, not a good life to lead. In this sequel, his tone is less generous to believers than hitherto, because 'the intervening decade has brought home to us the terrible results of religious conviction'.

R.A. Sharpe was Professor Emeritus at St David's College, Lampeter. The manuscript of *Forgiveness* was prepared for publication by his widow, the philosopher Lynne Sharpe.

128 pp., £8.95 / $17.90, 9781845400835 (pbk.), July 2008, (*Societas* edition), Vol.35

---

To qualify for the reduced (subscription) price of £5/$10 for current and future volumes (£2.50/$5.00 for back volumes), please use the enclosed direct debit form or order via imprint-academic.com/societas

# Healing, Hype or Harm? Scientists Investigate Complementary or Alternative Medicine

*Edzard Ernst (ed.)*

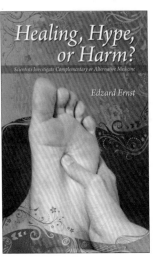

The scientists writing this book are not 'against' complementary or alternative medicine (CAM), but they are very much 'for' evidence-based medicine and single standards. They aim to counter-balance the many uncritical books on CAM and to stimulate intelligent, well-informed public debate.

TOPICS INCLUDE: What is CAM? Why is it so popular? Patient choice; Reclaiming compassion; Teaching CAM at university; Research on CAM; CAM in court; Ethics and CAM; Politics and CAM; Homeopathy in context; Concepts of holism in medicine; Placebo, deceit and CAM; Healing but not curing; CAM and the media.

Edzard Ernst is Professor of Complementary Medicine, Universities of Exeter and Plymouth.

190 pp., £8.95/$17.90, 9781845401184 (pbk.), Sept. 2008, *Societas,* Vol.36

# The Balancing Act: National Identity and Sovereignty for Britain in Europe

*Atsuko Ichijo*

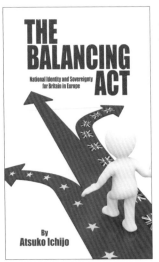

This is a careful examination of the historical formation of Britain and of key moments in its relations with the European powers. The author looks at the governing discourses of politicians, the mass media, and the British people.

The rhetoric of sovereignty among political elites and the population at large is found to conceive of Britain's engagement with Europe as a zero-sum game. A second theme is the power of geographical images – island Britain – in feeding the idea of the British nation as by nature separate and autonomous. It follows that the EU is seen as 'other' and involvement in European decision-making tends to be viewed in terms of threat. This is naive, as nation-states are not autonomous, economically, militarily or politically. Only pooling sovereignty can maximize their national interests.

Atsuko Ichijo is Senior Researcher in European Studies at Kingston University.

150 pp., £8.95/$17.90, 9781845401153 (pbk.), Nov. 2008, *Societas,* Vol.37

# Seeking Meaning and Making Sense

*John Haldane*

Here is an engaging collection of short essays that range across philosophy, politics, general culture, morality, science, religion and art.

The author contributes regularly to *The Scotsman* and a number of radio programmes. Many of these essays began life in this way, and retain their direct fresh style.

The focus is on questions of Meaning, Value and Understanding. Topics include: Making sense of religion, Making sense of society, Making sense of evil, Making sense of art and science, Making sense of nature.

John Haldane is Professor of Philosophy and Director of the Centre for Ethics, Philosophy and Public Affairs in the University of St Andrews.

128 pp., £8.95/$17.90, 9781845401221 (pbk.), Jan. 2009, *Societas,* Vol.38

# Independent: The Rise of the Non-aligned Politician

*Richard Berry*

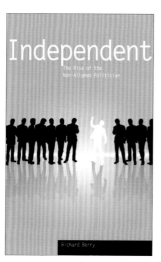

Martin Bell, Ken Livingstone and Richard Taylor (the doctor who became an MP to save his local hospital) are the best known of a growing band of British politicians making their mark outside the traditional party system.

Some (like Livingstone) have emerged from within the old political system that let them down, others (Bell, Taylor) have come into politics from outside in response to a crisis of some kind, often in defence of a perceived threat to their local town or district.

Richard Berry traces this development by case studies and interviews to test the theory that these are not isolated cases, but part of a permanent trend in British politics, a shift away from the party system in favour of independent non-aligned representatives of the people.

Richard Berry is a political and policy researcher and writer.

128 pp., £8.95/$17.90, 9781845401283 (pbk.), March 2009, *Societas,* Vol.39

# Progressive Secular Society and other essays relevant to secularism

*Tom Rubens*

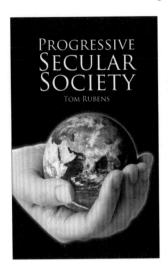

A progressive secular society is one committed to the widening of scientific knowledge and humane feeling. It regards humanity as part of physical nature and opposes any appeal to supernatural agencies or explanations. In particular, human moral perspectives are human creations and the only basis for ethics.

Secular values need re-affirming in the face of the resurgence of aggressive supernatural religious doctrines and practices. This book gives a set of 'secular thoughts for the day' – many only a page or two long – on topics as varied as Shakespeare and Comte, economics, science and social action.

Tom Rubens teaches in the humanities at secondary and tertiary levels.

128 pp., £8.95/$17.90, 9781845401320 (pbk.), May 2009, *Societas,* Vol.40

# Self and Society (enlarged second edition)

*William Irwin Thompson*

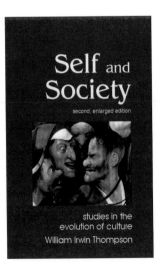

The book contains a series of essays on the evolution of culture, dealing with topics including the city and consciousness, evolution of the afterlife, literary and mathematical archetypes, machine consciousness and the implications of 9/11 and the invasion of Iraq for the development of planetary culture.

This enlarged edition contains an additional new second part, added to include chapters on 'Natural Drift and the Evolution of Culture' and 'The Transition from Nation-State to Noetic Polity' as well as two shorter reflective pieces.

The author is a poet, cultural historian and founder of the Lindisfarne Association. His many books include *Coming into Being: Artifacts and Texts in the Evolution of Consciousness*.

150 pp., £8.95/$17.90, 9781845401337 (pbk.), July 2009, *Societas,* Vol.41

# Universities: The Recovery of an Idea (revised second edition)

## Gordon Graham

RAE, teaching quality assessment, student course evaluation, modularization – these are all names of innovations in modern British universities. How far do they constitute a significant departure from traditional academic concerns? Using themes from J.H.Newman's *The Idea of a University* as a starting point, this book aims to address these questions.

'It is extraordinary how much Graham has managed to say (and so well) in a short book.' **Alasdair MacIntyre**

£8.95/$17.90, 9781845401276 (pbk), *Societas* V.1

# God in Us: A Case for Christian Humanism

## Anthony Freeman

*God In Us* is a radical representation of the Christian faith for the 21st century. Following the example of the Old Testament prophets and the first-century Christians it overturns received ideas about God. God is not an invisible person 'out there' somewhere, but lives in the human heart and mind as 'the sum of all our values and ideals' guiding and inspiring our lives.

The Revd. Anthony Freeman was dismissed from his parish for publishing this book, but remains a priest in the Church of England.

'Brilliantly lucid.' *Philosophy Now*
'A brave and very well-written book' *The Freethinker*

£8.95/$17.90, 9780907845171 (pbk), *Societas* V.2

# The Case Against the Democratic State

## Gordon Graham

This essay contends that the gross imbalance of power in the modern state is in need of justification and that democracy simply masks this need with the illusion of popular sovereignty. The book points out the emptiness of slogans like 'power to the people', as individual votes do not affect the outcome of elections, but concludes that democracy can contribute to civic education.

'Challenges the reigning orthodoxy'. *Mises Review*

'Political philosophy in the best analytic tradition… scholarly, clear, and it does not require a professional philosopher to understand it' *Philosophy Now*

'An excellent candidate for inclusion on an undergraduate syllabus.' *Independent Review*

£8.95/$17.90, 9780907845386 (pbk), *Societas* V.3

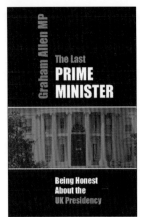

# The Last Prime Minister
## Graham Allen MP

This book shows how Britain has acquired an executive presidency by stealth. It is the first ever attempt to codify the Prime Minister's powers, many hidden in the mysteries of the royal prerogative. This timely second edition takes in new issues, including Parliament's impotence over Iraq.

'Iconoclastic, stimulating and well-argued.' **Vernon Bogdanor**, *Times Higher Education Supplement*

'Well-informed and truly alarming.' **Peter Hennessy**

'Should be read by anybody interested in the constitution.' **Anthony King**

£8.95/$17.90, 9780907845416 (pbk), *Societas* V.4

# The Liberty Option
## Tibor R. Machan

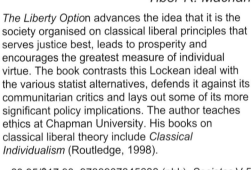

*The Liberty Option* advances the idea that it is the society organised on classical liberal principles that serves justice best, leads to prosperity and encourages the greatest measure of individual virtue. The book contrasts this Lockean ideal with the various statist alternatives, defends it against its communitarian critics and lays out some of its more significant policy implications. The author teaches ethics at Chapman University. His books on classical liberal theory include *Classical Individualism* (Routledge, 1998).

£8.95/$17.90, 9780907845638 (pbk), *Societas* V.5

# Democracy, Fascism & the New World Order
## Ivo Mosley

Growing up as the grandson of Sir Oswald, the 1930s blackshirt leader, made Ivo Mosley consider fascism with a deep and acutely personal interest. Whereas conventional wisdom sets up democracy and fascism as opposites, to ancient political theorists democracy had an innate tendency to lead to extreme populist government, and provided unscrupulous demagogues with the ideal opportunity to seize power. In *Democracy, Fascism and the New World Order* Mosley argues that totalitarian regimes may well be the logical outcome of unfettered mass democracy.

'Brings a passionate reasoning to the analysis'. *Daily Mail*

'Read Mosley's, in many ways, excellent book. But read it critically.' **Edward Ingram**, *Philosophy Now*

£8.95/$17.90, 9780907845645 (pbk), *Societas* V.6

# Off With Their Wigs!
## *Charles Banner and Alexander Deane*

On June 12, 2003, a press release concerning a Cabinet reshuffle declared as a footnote that the ancient office of Lord Chancellor was to be abolished and that a new supreme court would replace the House of Lords as the highest appeal court. This book critically analyses the Government's proposals and looks at the various alternative models for appointing judges and for a new court of final appeal.

'A cogently argued critique.' *Commonwealth Lawyer*

£8.95/$17.90, 9780907845843 (pbk), *Societas* V.7

# The Modernisation Imperative
## *Bruce Charlton & Peter Andras*

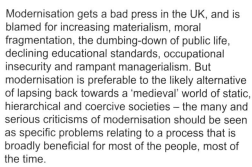

Modernisation gets a bad press in the UK, and is blamed for increasing materialism, moral fragmentation, the dumbing-down of public life, declining educational standards, occupational insecurity and rampant managerialism. But modernisation is preferable to the likely alternative of lapsing back towards a 'medieval' world of static, hierarchical and coercive societies – the many and serious criticisms of modernisation should be seen as specific problems relating to a process that is broadly beneficial for most of the people, most of the time.

'A powerful and new analysis'. **Matt Ridley**

£8.95/$17.90, 9780907845522 (pbk), *Societas* V.8

# Self and Society, *William Irwin Thompson*

£8.95/$17.90, 9780907845829 (pbk), *Societas* V.9
now superceded by Vol.41 (see above, p.S6)

# The Party's Over
## *Keith Sutherland*

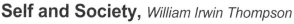
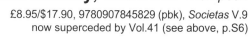

This book questions the role of the party in the post-ideological age and concludes that government ministers should be appointed by headhunters and held to account by a parliament selected by lot.

'Sutherland's model of citizen's juries ought to have much greater appeal to progressive Britain.' *Observer*

'An extremely valuable contribution.' *Tribune*

'A political essay in the best tradition – shrewd, erudite, polemical, partisan, mischievous and highly topical.' *Contemporary Political Theory*

£8.95/$17.90, 9780907845515 (pbk), *Societas* V.10

# Our Last Great Illusion
*Rob Weatherill*

This book aims to refute, primarily through the prism of modern psychoanalysis and postmodern theory, the notion of a return to nature, to holism, or to a pre-Cartesian ideal of harmony and integration. Far from helping people, therapy culture's utopian solutions may be a cynical distraction, creating delusions of hope. Yet solutions proliferate in the free market; this is why therapy is our last great illusion. The author is a psychoanalytic psychotherapist and lecturer, Trinity College, Dublin.

'Challenging, but well worth the engagement.' *Network*

£8.95/$17.90, 9780907845959 (pbk), *Societas* V.11

# The Snake that Swallowed its Tail
*Mark Garnett*

Liberal values are the hallmark of a civilised society, but depend on an optimistic view of the human condition, Stripped of this essential ingredient, liberalism has become a hollow abstraction. Tracing its effects through the media, politics and the public services, the book argues that hollowed-out liberalism has helped to produce our present discontent.

'This arresting account will be read with profit by anyone interested in the role of ideas in politics.'
**John Gray**, *New Statesman*

'A spirited polemic addressing the malaise of British politics.' **Michael Freeden**, *The European Legacy*

£8.95/$17.90, 9780907845881 (pbk), *Societas* V.12

# Why the Mind is Not a Computer
*Raymond Tallis*

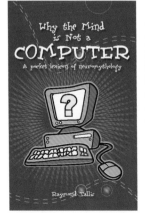

The equation 'Mind = Machine' is false. This pocket lexicon of 'neuromythology' shows why. Taking a series of keywords such as calculation, language, information and memory, Professor Tallis shows how their misuse has a misled a generation. First of all these words were used literally in the description of the human mind. Then computer scientists applied them metaphorically to the workings of machines. And finally the use of the terms was called as evidence of artificial intelligence in machines *and* the computational nature of thought.

'A splendid exception to the helpless specialisation of our age' **Mary Midgley**, *THES*

'A work of radical clarity.' *J. Consciousness Studies*

£8.95/$17.90, 9780907845942 (pbk), *Societas* V.13

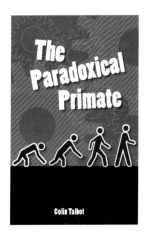

# The Paradoxical Primate
## Colin Talbot

This book seeks to explain how human beings can be so malleable, yet have an inherited set of instincts. When E.O. Wilson's *Consilience* made a plea for greater integration, it was assumed that the traffic would be from physical to human science. Talbot reverses this assumption and reviews some of the most innovative developments in evolutionary psychology, ethology and behavioural genetics.

'Talbot's ambition is admirable…a framework that can simultaneously encompass individualism and concern for collective wellbeing.' *Public* (The Guardian)

£8.95/$17.90, 9780907845850 (pbk), *Societas* V.14

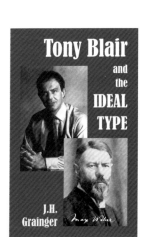

# Tony Blair and the Ideal Type
## J.H. Grainger

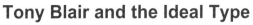

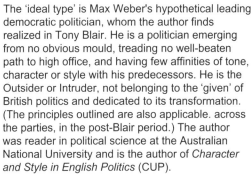

The 'ideal type' is Max Weber's hypothetical leading democratic politician, whom the author finds realized in Tony Blair. He is a politician emerging from no obvious mould, treading no well-beaten path to high office, and having few affinities of tone, character or style with his predecessors. He is the Outsider or Intruder, not belonging to the 'given' of British politics and dedicated to its transformation. (The principles outlined are also applicable. across the parties, in the post-Blair period.) The author was reader in political science at the Australian National University and is the author of *Character and Style in English Politics* (CUP).

'A brilliant essay.' **Simon Jenkins**, *Sunday Times*
'A scintillating case of the higher rudeness.' *Guardian*

£8.95/$17.90, 9781845400248 (pbk), *Societas* V.15

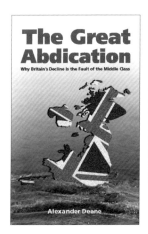

# The Great Abdication
## Alex Deane

According to Deane, Britain's middle class has abstained from its responsibility to uphold societal values, resulting in the collapse of our society's norms and standards. The middle classes must reinstate themselves as arbiters of morality, be unafraid to judge their fellow men, and follow through with the condemnation that follows when individuals sin against common values.

'[Deane] thinks there is still an element in the population which has traditional middle-class values. Well, maybe.' **George Wedd**, *Contemporary Review*

£8.95/$17.90, 9780907845973 (pbk), *Societas* V.16

Neil MacCormick

Who's Afraid of a
European
Constitution?

# Who's Afraid of a European Constitution?
## Neil MacCormick

This book discusses how the EU Constitution was drafted, whether it promised any enhancement of democracy in the EU and whether it implied that the EU is becoming a superstate. The arguments are equally of interest regarding the EU Reform Treaty.

Sir Neil MacCormick is professor of public law at Edinburgh University. He was an MEP and a member of the Convention on the Future of Europe.

£8.95/$17.90, 9781845392 (pbk), *Societas* V.17

# Darwinian Conservatism
## Larry Arnhart

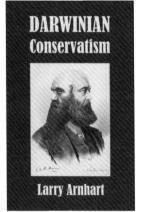

DARWINIAN
Conservatism

Larry Arnhart

The Left has traditionally assumed that human nature is so malleable, so perfectible, that it can be shaped in almost any direction. Conservatives object, arguing that social order arises not from rational planning but from the spontaneous order of instincts and habits. Darwinian biology sustains conservative social thought by showing how the human capacity for spontaneous order arises from social instincts and a moral sense shaped by natural selection. The author is professor of political science at Northern Illinois University.

'Strongly recommended.' *Salisbury Review*
'An excellent book.' **Anthony Flew**, *Right Now!*
'Conservative critics of Darwin ignore Arnhart at their own peril.' *Review of Politics*

96 pp., £8.95/$17.90, 9780907845997 (pbk.), *Societas,* Vol. 18

# Doing Less With Less: Making Britain More Secure
## Paul Robinson

Doing Less with Less
Making Britain More Secure

Paul Robinson

Notwithstanding the rhetoric of the 'war on terror', the world is now a far safer place. However, armed forces designed for the Cold War encourage global interference through pre-emption and other forms of military interventionism. We would be safer with less. The author, an ex-army officer, is assistant director of the Centre for Security Studies at Hull University.

'Robinson's criticisms need to be answered.'
**Tim Garden**, *RUSI Journal*
'The arguments in this thesis should be acknowledged by the MOD.' **Major General Patrick Cordingley DSO**

£8.95/$17.90, 9781845400422 (pbk), *Societas* V.19

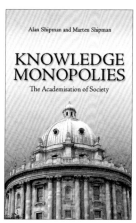

# Knowledge Monopolies
## Alan Shipman & Marten Shipman

Historians and sociologists chart the *consequences* of the expansion of knowledge; philosophers of science examine the *causes*. This book bridges the gap. The focus is on the paradox whereby, as the general public becomes better educated to live and work with knowledge, the 'academy' increases its intellectual distance, so that the nature of reality becomes more rather than less obscure.

'A deep and searching look at the successes and failures of higher education.' *Commonwealth Lawyer*

'A must read.' *Public* (The Guardian)

£8.95/$17.90, 9781845400286 (pbk), *Societas* V.20

# The Referendum Roundabout
## Kieron O'Hara

A lively and sharp critique of the role of the referendum in modern British politics. The 1975 vote on Europe is the lens to focus the subject, and the controversy over the referendum on the European constitution is also in the author's sights.

The author is a senior research fellow at the University of Southampton and author of *Plato and the Internet*, *Trust: From Socrates to Spin* and *After Blair: Conservatism Beyond Thatcher* (2005).

£8.95/$17.90, 9781845400408 (pbk), *Societas* V.21

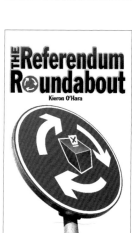

# The Moral Mind
## Henry Haslam

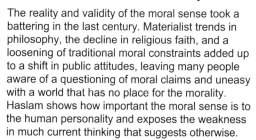

The reality and validity of the moral sense took a battering in the last century. Materialist trends in philosophy, the decline in religious faith, and a loosening of traditional moral constraints added up to a shift in public attitudes, leaving many people aware of a questioning of moral claims and uneasy with a world that has no place for the morality. Haslam shows how important the moral sense is to the human personality and exposes the weakness in much current thinking that suggests otherwise.

'Marking a true advance in the discussion of evolutionary explanations of morality, this book is highly recommended for all collections.'
**David Gordon**, *Library Journal*

'An extremely sensible little book. It says things that are really rather obvious, but which have somehow got forgotten.' **Mary Midgley**

£8.95/$17.90, 9781845400163 (pbk), *Societas* V.22

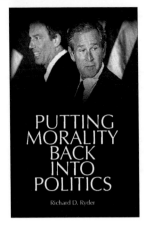

# Putting Morality Back Into Politics   *Richard D. Ryder*

Ryder argues that the time has come for public policies to be seen to be based upon moral objectives. Politicians should be expected routinely to justify their policies with open moral argument. In Part I, Ryder sketches an overview of contemporary political philosophy as it relates to the moral basis for politics, and Part 2 suggests a way of putting morality back into politics, along with a clearer emphasis upon scientific evidence. Trained as a psychologist, the author has also been a political lobbyist, mostly in relation to animal welfare.

£8.95/$17.90, 9781845400477 (pbk), *Societas* V.23

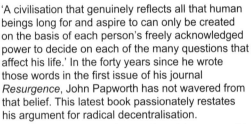

# Village Democracy   *John Papworth*

'A civilisation that genuinely reflects all that human beings long for and aspire to can only be created on the basis of each person's freely acknowledged power to decide on each of the many questions that affect his life.' In the forty years since he wrote those words in the first issue of his journal *Resurgence*, John Papworth has not wavered from that belief. This latest book passionately restates his argument for radical decentralisation.

'If we are to stand any chance of surviving we need to heed Papworth's call for decentralisation.'
**Zac Goldsmith**, *The Ecologist*

£8.95/$17.90, 9781845400644 (pbk), *Societas* V.24

# Debating Humanism   *Dolan Cummings (ed.)*

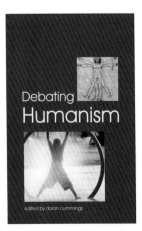

Broadly speaking, the humanist tradition is one in which it is we as human beings who decide for ourselves what is best for us, and are responsible for shaping our own societies. For humanists, then, debate is all the more important, not least at a time when there is discussion about the unexpected return of religion as a political force. This collection of essays follows the Institute of Ideas' inaugural 2005 Battle of Ideas festival. Contributors include Josie Appleton, Simon Blackburn, Robert Brecher, Andrew Copson, Dylan Evans, Revd. Anthony Freeman, Frank Furedi, A.C. Grayling, Dennis Hayes, Elisabeth Lasch-Quinn, Kenan Malik and Daphne Patai.

£8.95/$17.90, 9781845400699 (pbk), *Societas* V.25

## The Right Road to Radical Freedom *Tibor R. Machan*

This work focuses on the topic of free will – do we as individual human beings choose our conduct, at least partly independently, freely? He comes down on the side of libertarians who answer Yes, and scorns the compatibilism of philosophers like Daniel Dennett, who try to rescue some kind of freedom from a physically determined universe. From here he moves on to apply his belief in radical freedom to areas of life such as religion, politics, and morality, tackling subjects as diverse as taxation, private property, justice and the welfare state.

£8.95/$17.90, 9781845400187 (pbk), *Societas* V.26

## Paradoxes of Power: Reflections on the Thatcher Interlude
### *Sir Alfred Sherman*

In her memoirs Lady Thatcher herself pays tribute to her former adviser's 'brilliance', the 'force and clarity of his mind', his 'breadth of reading and his skills as a ruthless polemicist'. She credits him with a central role in her achievements. Born in 1919 in London's East End, until 1948 Sherman was a Communist and fought in the Spanish Civil War. But he ended up a free-market crusader.

'These reflections by Thatcherism's inventor are necessary reading.' **John Hoskyns**, *Salisbury Review*

£8.95/$17.90, 9781845400927 (pbk), *Societas* V.27

## Public Health & Globalisation
### *Iain Brassington*

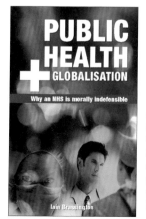

This book claims that the NHS is morally indefensible. There is a good moral case in favour of a *public* health service, but these arguments do not point towards a *national* health service, but to something that looks far more like a *transnational* health service. Drawing on Peter Singer's famous arguments in favour of a duty of rescue, the author argues that the cost of the NHS is unjustifiable. If we accept a duty to save lives when the required sacrifice is small, then we ought also to accept sacrifices in the NHS in favour of foreign aid. This does not imply that the NHS is wrong; just that it is wrong to spend large amounts on one person in Britain when we could save more lives elsewhere.

£8.95/$17.90, 9781845400798 (pbk), *Societas* V.28

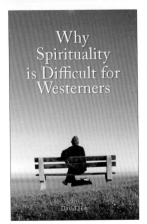

# Why Spirituality is Difficult for Westerners   *David Hay*

Zoologist David Hay holds that religious or spiritual awareness is biologically natural to the human species and has been selected for in organic evolution because it has survival value. Although naturalistic, this hypothesis is not intended to be reductionist. Indeed, it implies that all people have a spiritual life. This book describes the historical and economic context of European secularism, and considers recent developments in neurophysiology of the brain as it relates to religious experience.

£8.95/$17.90, 9781845400484 (pbk), *Societas* V.29

# Earthy Realism: The Meaning of GAIA
## *Mary Midgley (ed.)*

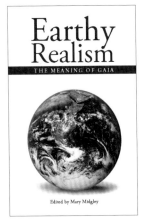

GAIA, named after the ancient Greek mother-goddess, is the notion that the Earth and the life on it form an active, self-maintaining whole. It has a *scientific* side, as shown by the new university departments of earth science which bring biology and geology together to study the continuity of the cycle. It also has a visionary or *spiritual* aspect. What the contributors to this book believe is needed is to bring these two angles together. With global warming now an accepted fact, the lessons of GAIA have never been more relevant and urgent. Foreword by James Lovelock.

£8.95/$17.90, 9781845400804 (pbk), *Societas* V.30

# Joseph Conrad Today
## *Kieron O'Hara*

This book argues that the novelist Joseph Conrad's work speaks directly to us in a way that none of his contemporaries can. Conrad's scepticism, pessimism, emphasis on the importance and fragility of community, and the difficulties of escaping our history are important tools for understanding the political world in which we live. He is prepared to face a future where progress is not inevitable, where actions have unintended consequences, and where we cannot know the contexts in which we act. The result can hardly be called a political programme, but Conrad's work is clearly suggestive of a sceptical conservatism of the sort described by the author in his 2005 book *After Blair: Conservatism Beyond Thatcher*.

£8.95/$17.90, 9781845400668 (pbk.), *Societas* V.31